T0320879

Mediated Business Interactions

Mediated Business Interactions

Intercultural Communication Between Speakers of Spanish

ROSINA MÁRQUEZ REITER

EDINBURGH UNIVERSITY PRESS

© Rosina Márquez Reiter, 2011

Edinburgh University Press Ltd
22 George Square, Edinburgh

www.euppublishing.com

Typeset in 10/12 Times New Roman MT
by Servis Filmsetting Ltd, Stockport, Cheshire, and
printed and bound in Great Britain by
CPI Antony Rowe, Chippenham and Eastbourne

A CIP record for this book is available from the British Library

ISBN 978 0 7486 3720 1 (hardback)

The right of Rosina Márquez Reiter
to be identified as author of this work
has been asserted in accordance with
the Copyright, Designs and Patents Act 1988.

Contents

Acknowledgements

As is usually the case with most major projects, of which this is one, many people deserve my thanks for helping me at various stages of this book and in their various capacities.

The road to the book's completion has been, at times, hazardous and extremely difficult, given my own emotional and professional trajectory. At a professional level, I have found my incursion into the world of conversation analysis fascinating. Although I have merely sketched an outline and remain very much at its periphery I have, through this journey, met some wonderfully generous academics, who for no credits or merits have kindly read and commented on the chapters which comprise the book. I would, thus, like to express my sincere gratitude to Ilkka Arminen, Ann Weatherall, Harrie Mazeland and Fabienne Chevalier for their thorough comments on earlier drafts of the chapters. I would also like to thank Alessandra Fassulo, Jörg Zinken and Eva Ogiermann for their insights during a data session to which I was kindly invited. Other colleagues who deserve my heartfelt thanks are Luisa Martín Rojo, Francesca Bargiela and Kristine Fitch for their help at the initial and final stages of this project. Thus, many of the ideas contained in this book are based on the incisive comments made by colleagues on earlier drafts of the chapters. It goes without saying that any errors in analysis or interpretation are mine.

I would like to acknowledge the help received from the University of Surrey with regard to this project and express my gratitude to 'Holidays to Remember' and to its most cooperative staff. I would also like to record a special thanks to Maura and Isobel for assisting me in my quest for cultural comparability.

Last but not least, I would like to thank my husband, Malcolm, and my wonderful daughter, Stephanie, for their encouragement and puzzling questions.

Figures

1 Introduction

1.1 Mediated business (inter)action

In this book I explore the activities that human beings, in their roles of service providers and customers, engage in to supply and demand a service over the phone. I look at the way in which language, understood as a cultural tool, mediates action and how this, in turn, reflects socio-cultural practices.

Wertsch (1991) argued that '[H]uman action typically employs "mediational means" such as tools and language, and that these means shape the action in essential ways' (p. 12). Thus, for Wertsch, all human actions are mediated. Drawing on this idea, Scollon (1998) proposed that '[M]ediated action is the site in which social and discursive practice are instantiated as actions of humans; at the same time it is the site in which individual humans act upon society and its discursive practices' (p. 10). Traditional mediational means, such as texts and conversations, are seen as cultural tools with which humans mediate action, in as much as they become 'the means by which socio-cultural practice is interpolated into human action' Scollon (1998: 15).

In face-to-face conversations, the action is mediated by the ways of speaking of the participants (Gumperz and Hymes 1972) as well as by other cultural tools, such as the space in which the encounter takes place – in a restaurant, for instance – and the way in which the participants are dressed for the occasion. Although telephone conversations, too, are mediated social interactions, they are differentiated from face-to-face encounters by the technological medium that enables them: the telephone. In such interactions, the telephone represents one of the cultural tools called upon by the participants to mediate their actions, and the choice of the medium affects the type of interaction that is possible.

The telephone is a form of pervasive and remote synchronous communication. Unlike other forms of mediated communication, such as videoconferencing, the telephone transmits purely linguistic information. It supports synchronous bidirectional communication; participants provide feedback to each other, and, in doing so, they contribute to, negotiate and modify the content of what is said (Whittaker 2003). Communication over the phone is normally ephemeral, unless, as is the case of the calls examined in this book, it is recorded.

Mallard (2004) observed that, '[T]he telephone is one of the most mundane and powerful means to combine absence and presence, and to push back the boundaries of space' (p. 117). The general availability of telephones, together with their low cost, at least in some cultures, has transformed this communication means into a pervasive communication mode. The telephone enables participants to exchange information and carry out transactions at a distance. The capability of the medium to remove distance in interaction has contributed to decreasing transaction costs in the search for information.

This is particularly salient in the economic sphere, where the telephone has become one of the tools *par excellence* for connecting supply and demand. Support for this can be found in the creation and proliferation of call centres around the globe as they enable people from different corners of the world to supply and demand services to and from one another over the phone in real time twenty-four hours a day, seven days a week.

It is precisely mediated business (inter)actions between suppliers and demanders which constitute my focus in this book. More specifically, I examine the interactions to and from the Latin American call centre operation of a multinational company specialising in time shares. Clients of the company have bought the use of a property, typically a holiday resort unit, for an allotted period of time, generally one to two weeks, from a hospitality brand or an independent developer and have become members of the company, which I shall refer to as 'Holidays to Remember'. 'Holidays to Remember' is an exchange agency. It offers its clients the possibility of exchanging their resort unit for an equivalent at one of the various worldwide resorts that the company is affiliated to. 'Holidays to Remember' provides its services over the telephone. Consequently, both agents and clients telephone one another to request and offer specific services. The conversational participants of these calls are native speakers of Spanish who come from different cultural backgrounds and, in most cases, have had little contact with one another's culture but who share roughly the same basic language. The type of calls examined can thus be described as intercultural, mediated service calls.

One of my goals for this book is to pursue a general line of research, investigating the various activities that telephone conversationalists engage in to supply and demand a service over the phone through the mediational means of Spanish. With this in mind, this book seeks to shed light on the following questions:

1. Do speakers of Spanish display similar communicative practices to those observed in other languages when the speakers are requesting or being offered a service over the phone?

2. Do specifically located activities, such as the call openings and closings, display similar coordination and ritualisation to that observed in other languages?
3. Does the language, the means by which socio-cultural practice is inter-polated into action, reflect a different orientation towards such activities?
4. What role does intercultural communication play in the construction of these practices?

1.2 Service encounters over the phone

The calls I analyse constitute mediated service encounters. Service encounters represent everyday social activities characterised by socially shared regular patternings (Ventola 1987). They thus provide us with a window into socio-cultural practices. They unfold in stages, and in so doing, achieve a certain purpose, such as imparting information and carrying out transactions. Given their ubiquity and routine nature, they also provide us with a 'uniform' start-ing point for intercultural comparisons. Through their study, patterns emerge and this, in turn, will help us to uncover either the pragmatic commonalities or differences, or both, between varieties of Spanish, and to consider possible sources of miscommunication between speakers who have in common the same basic language but come from different backgrounds.

Nowadays people spend a considerable amount of time on telephone inter-actions where they are requesting or are being offered a service. The modern pervasive nature of negotiating services through faceless interactions, via either the telephone or the internet, is commonplace in both developed and developing capitalist economies. This is evidenced, among other things, by the relatively recent trend in developed economies to relocate and outsource their call centres to developing economies, such as India and the Philippines, where more economically sustainable business platforms are offered. It is also evident in the recent tendency of (privatised) public utilities in some developed and developing economies to deal with their customers via a call centre in order to maximise existing human resources and 'improve' customer services. Mediated service encounters from a call centre were, therefore, chosen as the focus of analysis for this book, given the key role they play in modern consumer behaviour in respect of the exchange of goods and serv-ices. Further, the multinational nature of the call centre represents a unique opportunity for contact between speakers of different varieties of Spanish who may, otherwise, come in contact with one another only through the media, the internet, tourism and immigration.

The services are given on the basis of information provided directly by the caller and the call-taker, over the phone, and through the medium of speech. They represent a type of institutional talk, that is, service talk which occurs within the parameters of the medium: the telephone. Thus, participants in this type of synchronous and real-time encounters do not have access to paralinguistic features such as body language, gestures or facial expressions.

Theoretically speaking, communication through this medium is ephemeral; accordingly, participants have to remember what was said in previous business encounters. In spite of the fact that a large proportion of the calls made to, and received from, the call centre are recorded for monitoring purposes (see Chapter 2), participants rarely recur to the actual recordings in cases of potential misunderstanding or conflict, or both. The recording of calls is primarily seen as a managerial tool to ensure the company's transparency and accountability, rather than as a customer support tool.

Mediated service encounters of this type involve a certain degree of planning. When telephoning a (prospective) client, telephone agents have to relate to the preparation of presence from the situation of absence. In the light of the absence of visible support to help determine whether the called[1] will be receptive to an unexpected call, the telephone agents have to schedule their calls strategically, placing them when they know the called are likely to be present and receptive to conversation. Thus, calls to the (prospective) clients' homes need some preliminary planning even in those cases where a call is arranged. At the call centre researched in this book, this planning is typically based on client information, which is available on the agents' computer screens and includes client contact details – for example, address, home, mobile and work numbers – and each client's history, as illustrated by past holiday accommodation exchanges, payment record and availability of offers based on membership type. Additionally, agents are aware of more general information such as working hours in the clients' respective countries and information on different time zones. Calls to clients' places of work also require planning. Although the workplace is usually conceived as a public space, calling clients at certain times, such as during lunch breaks or first thing in the morning, might prove counterproductive. Similarly, before placing their calls, clients also tend to plan their calls on the basis of their holiday agenda and their knowledge of the services offered by the company.

Unlike more traditional service encounters, such as those carried out over the counter or at open markets, telephone mediated services appear to produce an unusual individualisation of the link between participants. The telephone agents become mediators, whose job is to ensure and guarantee access to the holiday accommodation exchange being sold (Liccope 2001). The telephone thus plays an important role in facilitating specific mediations in the establishment of the relationship between the supplier and the consumer (Liccope 2001). As we will see in the analysis, the agents at times fulfil the role of salesperson and, at others, that of counsellor, given that, in order to achieve a sale, they engage in the giving of advice to enhance the chances of achieving their conversational goal. The encounter between the consumer and 'the goods' is for the most part a conversational achievement. The interaction is not simply an encounter between offer and demand but an encounter in 'selling space' through the medium of the telephone. When placing outbound calls, agents interrupt the domestic or work activities of (prospective) clients to engage in business talk.

1.3 Call centres and intercultural communication

The way in which language enables the new practices emerging from a globalised marketplace, in particular the work of call centre interactions, has received attention from discourse analysts (see, for example, Cameron 2000, 2008 for one of the first studies of call centre communication), sociologists of language and multilingualism (Duchêne 2009) and critical sociolinguists (see, for example, Budach et al. 2003); these studies are concerned with elucidating how the management and marketing of language practices are ideologically and contextually conditioned in the new economy. Scholars interested in the intercultural communication issues that emerge from the contact between native speakers of different languages who employ a lingua franca to communicate with one another have also examined call centre interactions. Prime examples of this line of research can be found in the work of applied linguists on interactions at outsourced call centres where clients whose native language is English interact with service providers who speak English as a second language (see, for example, Forey and Lockwood 2007; Hood and Forey 2008; Friginal 2009; Lockwood et al. 2009). With the exception of a small number of studies (see, for example, Márquez Reiter 2009, 2010), however, intercultural communication between speakers who share the same basic language, but come from different cultural backgrounds and have had little contact with one another, has not received much attention. The dearth of research in this area may reside in the economic trajectory of call centres and in the traditional remit of intercultural communication studies, which have typically examined communication between native speakers of different languages.

Call centres were introduced in North America and Western Europe in the 1980s. They were pioneered by the financial service sector to centralise dispersed customer service and sales operations in order to minimise costs and maximise profits. The creation of call centres was made possible by, amongst other things, the modern 'global borderless economy' (Ohmae 1995), in which we now live, and by the integration of computer and telephone technologies, in particular by the creation of the Automatic Call Distribution system. Other facilitating factors included the availability of low-cost property, regional development policy, tax incentives and skilled labour supplies.

In their early days, call centres were located onshore with national and transnational operations within the major regions of developed economies, albeit generally in regions with relatively high unemployment, such as Glasgow in the UK or Quebec in Canada, and with comparatively cheap labour. It is only relatively recently that call centres have become a truly globalised phenomenon owing to the technological advances which provide customers with services at a distance, in real time, twenty-four hours a day, seven days a week. 'Call centres exemplify Castells' informationalism (2000), which, in the context of a networked, globalized economy, replaces the "space of places" with the "space of flows",[2] and represents the "death of distance" (Cairncross 1997)' (Taylor and Bain 2005: 262). The very financial sector which pioneered the migration of call centres to the developing world is, however, beginning to question the extent to which this 'death of distance' exists now that the benefits of offshoring and relocating call centres to developing economies are being challenged under the goal of 'understanding customers' needs'.[3] Several banks and insurance companies have been assessing which types of work could be successfully offshored and which should be provided onshore, taking into account that certain services, such as opening new accounts, as opposed to more routine services, such as requesting a statement, entail better-trained staff with home language skills and a high level of cultural similarity.[4] Added to this, salary costs in developing market economies like India are rising, with the result that some of the financial advantages of offshore call centres are diminishing. Further, lack of cultural similarities and communication difficulties reported in providing non-routine services can lead to calls taking twice as long as in onshore operations,[5] resulting, thus, in lower profitability.

The labour requirements of this new economy have created the need for a new type of telephone agent: one that is highly qualified in terms of both lingua-cultural knowledge and communication skills; in other words, university graduates (NASSCOM-McKinsey 2005). The choice of university graduates over more traditional customer service representatives, who principally had to deal with customers in intra-cultural face-to-face interactions, has brought about changes in service provision and in the way customers and service representatives interact with one another. This, in turn, helps, to some extent, to explain the commonly reported differing expectations between customers and agents at these modern mediated communication spaces. In other words, connecting to remote places in the world can bring to the fore the cultural distance and not just the physical distance between customers and those who serve them. The cultural distance I am referring to here is nothing more, and nothing less, than the intercultural communication (Gudykunst 1998) issues which result from the mediated contact between, for example, a native speaker of English (a British customer) and a speaker of English as a second or foreign language (an Indian telephone agent), or, in the case that concerns us here, the contact between native speakers of the same basic language, Spanish, who come from different backgrounds, namely, diverse Latin American countries.

Call centres were introduced in Latin America at the beginning of the millennium. Since then, a number of multinational companies with onshore call centres in given Latin American countries have been migrating their 'home-based' call centres; for example, a call centre based in Mexico servicing the needs of Mexican customers might be transferred to one of several other Latin American regions which offer state-of-the-art infrastructure and office layouts, better financial incentives, such as relatively low salaries and tax inducements, and a more skilled workforce. Several multinational companies have likewise set up their headquarters for the Spanish-speaking world in Latin American countries which offer these benefits. The case that interests us is the Spanish-speaking operation of a multinational company specialising in offering high-standard holiday exchange accommodation for their various Latin American clients. Communication between the agents and the clients at this call centre is monolingual and intercultural. Although, broadly speaking, the conversational participants share a language, in this case Spanish, they come from different cultural backgrounds and speak different varieties of that language. Importantly, the multinational nature of the call centre represents an ideal opportunity for contact between speakers of different varieties of Latin American Spanish, who, as mentioned earlier, may otherwise only come in contact with one another through the media, the internet, tourism or immigration.

Until now, research that has (in)directly focused on intercultural communication in Spanish has principally examined languages in contact. Thus, rather than study contact between native speakers of Spanish from different backgrounds, scholars in this area of inquiry (see, for example, Zimmerman and de Granda 2004) have investigated the intercultural patterns that emerge when Spanish is in contact with other languages. Most studies of intercultural communication have mainly focused on bridging the cultural differences (see, for example, Gudykunst 1998) that result from differing 'mental programmes' (Hofstede 2001). Given that the cultural groups examined have derived from different linguistic and cultural origins and have not shared similar communicative norms, the underlying assumption is that many of the communication problems reported in intercultural encounters stem from the lack of a shared native language experience. In this study, however, the participants are all native speakers of the same basic language; nevertheless, interactional misfires occur. In terms of this book, and in line with Scollon and Scollon (1981), therefore, intercultural communication is understood as an instance of interpersonal communication between participants who are culturally different but share the same basic language. They are culturally different in terms of their ethnic composition, in the varieties of Spanish they speak, in religion, music and dance, in membership of trading blocks, in access to education, in socioeconomic performance indicators including the poverty index, and so on.

Communication between the agents and the (prospective) clients in this research is, therefore, monolingual and intercultural. It is monolingual in that it is carried out in the participants' native language, Spanish, and intercultural in that the participants come from different backgrounds and speak different varieties of the same basic language. Thus, they do not necessarily share the same assumptions and perspectives; nor can it be presumed that they are sensitised to cultural differences. Communication between the participants is institutional and primarily transactional.

1.4 On the ordinary–institutional continuum

Unlike ordinary talk, which is not confined to specialised settings or related to the execution of particular tasks, institutional talk tends to occur in more restricted environments. In these more 'controlled' speech settings:

1. The goals of the participants are more limited and institution-specific, as shown by the design of their interactional behaviour, which is geared to meet various institutional tasks tied to their institutionally relevant identities.
2. There are restrictions on the nature of contributions, as evidenced, for example, by what can be done in certain settings, such as a court of law.
3. There are inferential frameworks which are specific to both the institution and the activity; that is, particular forms of reasoning or inference making are in place. (adapted from Drew and Heritage 1992: 22–5)

For conversation analysts, therefore, ordinary talk is the predominant medium of interaction in the social world. Institutional talk involves the systematic restriction and variation of activities and their design relative to ordinary conversation (Drew and Heritage 1992). This is because 'the institution of mundane talk exists, and is experienced prior to institutional interaction both in the life of the individual and the life of the society' (Heritage 2005: 109). Also, in ordinary talk, participants design their interactional behaviour according to an array of rules and practices, and use various inferential frameworks, in order to meet an infinite number of social goals. In contrast, institutional interaction involves a reduction in the range of practices employed by participants and some specialisation and re-specification of the interactional relevance of these practices (Drew and Heritage 1992). Thus, in institutional interactions, ordinary conversation practices are adapted and put to the service of more specialised and restricted speech settings (Schegloff 1999).

The boundaries between ordinary and institutional interaction are, however, not clear cut in as much as the mechanisms of talk-in-interaction permeate all institutional practices (Drew and Heritage 1992: 21). Thus, even if formal features of talk are deployed to distinguish between ordinary and institutional interaction, formality in itself does not make the interaction institutional. What makes the interaction institutional is the way in which this formality is used to perform a given institutional job according to a work-task-related identity, or the extent to which it demonstrates a specific institutional inferential framework, or both. Put differently, institutional talk is not confined to a specific physical setting, such as the place where one works. It can occur in any physical setting; for example, on a train journey during which one discusses work-related matters with a work colleague. In the same vein, ordinary talk, like the kind of gossip one engages in with colleagues at work, can occur in any institutional setting. In other words, not all settings that involve specialised turn-taking systems generate institutional interaction that is formal. Institutional interaction can also be quasi-formal and informal:

> [F]ormal institutional interactions are constitutively different from everyday talk so that the institutional event is created via the parties' orientations to pattern their interaction in a manner specific to the event, and to that event only. This allows us to study the ways in which the formal pattern of interaction is maintained and departures sanctioned. Informal institutional interactions may also differ from the regulative patterns of ordinary conversation, but the parties are allowed to depart from the institutional interactional format and resort to ordinary conversational forms. (Arminen 2005a: 20)

Early research into institutional talk concentrated on settings, such as courtrooms, characterised by a specialised turn-taking system and a certain degree of formality (see, for example, Atkinson and Drew 1979), on class-rooms (see, for example, McHoul 1978) and on news interviews (see, for example, Greatbatch 1988), possibly in an effort to demonstrate clearly the differences between institutional and ordinary talk. In addition, over a time-span of fifteen years, Zimmerman and collaborators set out to examine the overall structural organisation of talk in the context of institutional telephone conversations, in particular calls to emergency services. They noticed that, besides a specialised turn-taking system, exemplified, among other things, by the presence of an interrogative series of questions, these calls display specifi-cally located activities, such as reduced and specialised openings and closings.

1.5 Why openings and closings?

However interactionally vacuous and routine-like telephone openings may sound, Schegloff's (1979, 1986) pioneering work on the subject has adum-brated the social practices through which they are constituted. It has dem-onstrated that, on opening a telephone conversation, participants engage in distinctive, coordinated and ritualised interactional activities. 'T]he opening is a place where the type of conversation being opened can be proffered, displayed, accepted, rejected, modified – in short, incipiently constituted by the parties to it' (Schegloff 1979: 25).

The interactional activities that telephone conversationalists engage in may be seen as communicative jobs and, in the case of openings, they essentially entail three tasks. First, participants have to open up the channel of communication. Unlike face-to-face communication, where visual clues allow participants to judge whether the channel is open and where participants may, to a greater or lesser extent, be certain that they can hear each other, the lack of visual clues in this form of mediated communication explains the conversationalists' need to ascertain that the channel of communication is open and that the recipient's interactional availability is guaranteed. Second, participants (re)construct the relationship between them. Once this has been achieved, they establish what they will talk about.

In ordinary calls, these main tasks, or communicative jobs, are realised in four sequences: (1) the summons/answer sequence, where the telephone ring represents the 'summons' and the 'answer' the first thing said by the person who picked up the telephone; (2) the identification/recognition sequence, in which the identities of the participants as caller and call-taker are established through self-identification or recognition displays; (3) a greeting sequence, where greeting tokens are exchanged; and (4) an initial enquiry/response sequence where 'how-are-yous' are exchanged. Although these sequences may not all occur in a given call, when present, they normally appear in this order. The ordering of these sequences is what is referred to as the 'canonical opening' (Hopper 1992) in everyday telephone conversations.

The sequences are distinct and logically independent of one other although they may sometimes overlap. For instance, in English and in many varieties of Spanish, a telephone summons is usually answered by uttering 'hello' (see Chapter 3, Section 3.3.2). Although 'hello' is generally recognised as a greeting, its sequential placement tells us that its main function is to open the channel of communication and convey interactional availability. The answer to the summons also serves to provide a first token of the recipient's voice sample, through which the caller may recognise him or her. Thus, it also functions as an identification display. Schegloff (1986) has shown that there is a preference for identification by recognition over self-identification in his corpus of American English mundane calls, as shown at lines 3 and 4 in Excerpt 1.

Excerpt 1 [# 1. (HG) – from Schegloff 1986: 114]

```
        ((ring))                01
Nancy:  H'll:?                  02
Hyla:   Hi:,                    03
Nancy:  ^Hi::.                  04
Hyla:   Hwaryuhh=               05
Nancy:  =Fi:ne how'r you,       06
```

```
Hyla:   Okay: y,            07
Nancy:        Goo:d,         08
         (0.4)               09
Hyla:   Mkhh hhh             10
Nancy:        What's doin,   11
```

A similar pattern was observed by Márquez Reiter (2006) in a corpus of Montevidean Spanish mundane calls. After the summons/answer sequence, conversationalists proceeded to establish their identities by other recognition rather than self-identification, as illustrated at lines 2–5 in Excerpt 2.[6]

Excerpt 2 [adapted from Márquez Reiter 2006: 16–17; C = caller, CT = call-taker]

```
0       ((ring))
1   CT: Hola::
         Hello::
2   C:  Hola, Rosana?
         Hello Rosana?
3   CT: Sí↑
         Yes↑
4   C:  Pero ya no me conocés la voz?
         So you no longer recognise my voice?
5   CT: Qué decís Julio?
         What's up Julio?
6   C:  Todo bien y vos?
         Everything's fine and you?
7   CT: Muy bien por su:erte
         Very well fortunately
8   C:  Che, está tu hermana por ahí?
         Hey, is your sister around?
```

Unlike face-to-face communication, where the identities of the participants can be established prior to the talk, telephone conversationalists normally want to know whom they are speaking to. As Hutchby (2001) pointed out, while it is not uncommon to have accidental face-to-face encounters, the notion of a fortuitous call is strange, given that someone needs to have dialled the number in the first place. With this in mind, there is always a reason for a telephone call and this is shown, among other things, by the fact that the offering of the reason for the call generally occurs immediately after the participants have ratified their identities. These communicative jobs are patterns of behaviour that have evolved around the development of the telephone as a key technology of the nineteenth century (see, for example, Hutchby 2001) and as the then new form of mediated social (inter)action (Wertsch 1991; Scollon 1998).[7]

Similarly, in closings, conversationalists engage in distinctive, coordinated and ritualised activities in order to bring conversations to a close collaboratively.

The way in which conversations are brought to a close was first identified by Sacks (1992) and later systematised by Schegloff and Sacks (1973). The authors noted that the initiation of the closing activity allows conversationalists to depart from each other's presence without the expectation that a turn at talk is still to come. By embarking upon a closing routine, one of the conversationalists offers the other the opportunity to contribute a turn at talk, which will eventually allow for post-turn silence without the implication of fault (Antaki 2002). Schegloff and Sacks (1973) observed that the closing sequence may be started with tokens such as 'well' and 'okay' – what they termed 'possible pre-closings' – and concluded with a 'terminal exchange', whereby each participant contributes one of such pre-closings pairs and a final 'bye-bye'. Button (1987) called the two pairs of closings first and second close components and first and second terminal components, respectively.

Closings thus normally extend over four turns at talk, namely a first and second close component and a terminal exchange, as shown in Excerpt 3.

Excerpt 3 Button (1987: 102) [NB:III:5:10]

```
    Guy:    I'll be down there, oh en you'll-you'll be aroun'
            then when I (come in)
    Emma:   Yeah.
1   Guy:    Okay.
2   Emma:   Okay dear,
3   Guy:    Buh bye,
4   Emma:   Bye bye,
            . . . end of call . . .
```

Turns 2 and 3 (my numbering) contain what Schegloff and Sacks (1973) termed pre-closing tokens and Button called elements bereft of topic implicativeness. This, in turn, allows the other participant to return to topical talk or to move towards terminating the encounter. Essentially, they propose a warrant for closure and provide the other participant with the opportunity to retopicalise a previous point, or topicalise a new one. When reciprocated, the warrant for closing is accepted and this, in turn, allows for the terminal exchange (turns 3 and 4). The first two closing turns are known as first and second close components, respectively, and the third and fourth as the terminal exchange, which, in the example above, is realised by an exchange of goodbyes. The terminal exchange is a prototypical device for lifting transition relevance (Maynard and Schaeffer 2002).

Schegloff and Sacks (1973) suggested that there could be further optional close components to this canonical four-turn sequence. Subsequently, Button (1987) identified seven sequence types that are used to move towards, and out of, closure: arrangements, back-references, topic initial elicitators, in-conversation objects, solicitudes, reasons-for-calls and appreciations. These sequences normally occur between the pre-closing and the terminal exchange.

The initiation and cessation of interactional contact between participants reflects the way in which their relationship is (re)constructed and the socio-cultural norms that underlie the performance of these activities, and these are reflected in their ritualisation. Openings and closings thus represent socio-interactional phenomena, where a potential for misunderstanding between participants who speak different varieties of the same basic language may surface. Speakers of Spanishes (different varieties of Spanish) may not necessarily share the same ritualised practices or the same formulae to index such practices. Before examining the ways in which the calls were initiated and brought to a close, in Chapters 3 and 5, respectively, I provide a review of the lessons learnt from extant research into these activities.

1.6 Previous research on openings and closings in institutional calls

Zimmerman (1984, 1992), Whalen and Zimmerman (1987) and Wakin and Zimmerman (1999) have shown that emergency calls display both specialisation and reduction of the sequential machinery of ordinary telephone openings (Schegloff 1986). Wakin and Zimmerman (1999) proposed that these calls are specialised in that they regularly make 'use of specific utterance types in particular sequential locations' and that they are reduced as displayed by 'the omission of elements of some standard sequence' (p. 411). The structural pattern observed in these calls has been shown to be relatively constant for emergency calls and, as we will see, applicable to other types of service calls. The structural organisation of these calls is illustrated in Excerpt (4).

Excerpt 4 [MCE/21–9/12/simplified – from Whalen and Zimmerman 1987: 174; D= dispatcher, C = caller]

```
01  D:  Mid-City Emergency        Answer/Identification  ⎤
02  C:  Um yeah (.) somebody      Acknowledgement/       ⎥
        jus' vandalized my        Reason for Call        ⎥ Opening
        car,                      (request for help)     ⎦
03  D:  What's your address.      ⎤
04  C:  Thirty three twenty       ⎥
        two: Elm                  ⎥
05  D:  Is this uh house or an    ⎥
        apartment                 ⎥  Contingency
06  C:  Ih tst uh house           ⎥  questions
07  D:  Uh-your las' name.        ⎥
08  C:  Minsky,                   ⎥
09  D:  How do you spell it.      ⎥
10  C:  M.I.N.S.K.Y.              ⎦
```

```
11  D:  Wull sen' somebody out              Response
        to see you
12  C:  Than' you
13  D:  Umhm bye.     ⎤
                      ⎥                      Closing
14  C:  Bye.          ⎦
```

The structure of the call is based on activities which involve the pursuit of a specific sub-goal. These activities are co-constructed by the participants as constituent tasks of the call; hence, they occur in a given order. First, there is an opening in which identification and recognition are displayed (lines 1–2). Second, a request for service is made. In the case of the above call, this is formulated as a description of the problem (line 2). Third, the call-taker initiates an interrogative series of questions to elicit the necessary information for the service to be delivered (lines 3–10). Fourth, a response to the caller's request for service is given (line 11). Finally, the participants bring the conversation to a close (lines 13–14).

With regard to the opening (lines 1–2), the call-taker, in this case the radio-dispatcher, responds to the summons (telephone ring) by providing categorical identification (Schegloff 1986) or organisational identification, that is, by offering the name of the institution ('The Mid-City Emergency') the caller has got through to. Whalen and Zimmerman (1987) pointed out that the selection of an answer type, such as organisational identification, 'turns on the status of the anticipated callers of that number' and 'the status of the number itself' (p. 180) as institutional. The proffering of organisational identification thus appears to be a business convention in the Western world and, as we will see in the analysis of outbound calls, in Latin America too, albeit followed there by a greeting (see Chapter 3, section 3.3.2).[8]

The caller displays recognition by uttering the acknowledgement token 'yeah' (line 2). In so doing, the caller shows that he or she has got through to the right number and proceeds to the main goal: the reason for the call. Unlike in ordinary telephone calls, reciprocal greetings and identifications are either partial or omitted and the exchange of how-are-yous is absent. Additionally, the reason for the call ('somebody jus' vandalized my car') is offered at the first available opportunity, that is, once it has been ascertained that the caller has got through to the right place and the recipient's communicative ability has been established; this is evidenced by the uttering of 'yeah' at line 2. The absence, or partial presence, of greetings and identifications signals that the accountable action, the reason for the call, is the only motive for the participants' contacting each other. In other words, institutional reasons replace everyday reasons for the social exchange, and the interaction is thus framed from the start as institutional rather than ordinary.

The caller's description of the problem, that is, the main business of the call, is treated as the first pair part of a request–response adjacency pair. The caller makes the request for service at the start of the call and the call-taker provides the required response at the end of the call, as shown at lines 2 and 11, respectively. After a series of inserted question–answer sequences (lines 3–10), the call-taker grants the request (line 11) and is thanked by the caller (line 12), and the closing is thereafter enacted.

Subsequent studies of call openings in a variety of institutional settings and languages have shown the extent to which the patterns of talk observed in these studies depart from Schegloff's (1986) canonical model for ordinary calls and from Zimmerman's (1984, 1992) account of the openings of emergency calls.[9] Prominent examples include the research carried out by Frankel (1989), Meehan (1989), Tracy (1997), Tracy and Anderson (1999), Tracy and Agne (2002), Landqvist (2005) and Raymond and Zimmerman (2007) on calls to various emergency services. These studies have (in)directly dealt with the openings and have reported a reduction of Schegloff's (1986) four-slot sequential model for ordinary calls. In so doing, they have also provided further support for Zimmerman's (1984) structural account of an emergency call. Concretely, the studies concur in reporting that the greeting sequence is either partial or, what is more likely, omitted, and that how-are-you exchanges are absent. When the latter are present, it has been suggested they signal that 'what the caller is about to say is not [police] business as usual' (Tracy and Agne 2002: 81). This should not come as a surprise, given the general urgency or immediacy of the reason for the call and the fact that the provision of service usually means the dispatch of a particular service, for example an ambulance or a police officer (Edwards 2007).

On the other hand, Danby et al. (2005) and Emmison and Danby (2007) reported the presence of greeting exchanges and the occurrence of how-are-yous in several calls to an Australian children's help line. Despite the high incidence of how-are-yous, these researchers do not claim that these are essential sequential elements or that their presence signals that the call is not business as usual. In view of this, I would like, briefly, to consider their results. It is interesting to note that the answer to the summons is informal: 'Hi there Kids Help Line' and 'Hi Kids Help Line'. It can, thus, be argued that the presence of an informal lexical greeting ('Hi') in the answer to the summons would make the greeting return conditionally relevant on the occurrence of a first pair part by the call-taker. Also noteworthy is the presumably institutional choice of 'kids' over 'children' as one of the elements of organisational identification. This adds a further element of informality to the talk and conveys friendliness. The cumulative informality of the answer to the summons, as in 'hi there' and 'kids', combined with the age of the population which makes use of the service (5–18-year-old children) may help to explain the instantiation of a conversational footing (Goffman 1979), such as 'how are you', by both the call-takers and the callers. Emmison and Danby (2007) also reported the lack of offers of assistance, such as 'how can I help you?', in the openings, attributing this absence to the counsellors' efforts to give callers more choice as to how to enter into the talk. These researchers claim that the presence of an offer of assistance would imply that the caller wants help. It should be noted, however, that the work-task-related identity of help-giver is, nonetheless, instantiated in the choice of organisational identification: Help Line.

Offers of assistance have, however, been reported in the openings of calls to a software help line. Baker et al. (2001) observed that call-takers open with an offer of assistance, such as 'what seems to be the problem?', 'what can I do for you this morning?', and so on. After an in-breath ('.hh') or an acknowledgement token ('ok'), the caller starts to explain the reason for the call. This is then followed by contingency questions before a diagnosis of the problem is offered. Thus, in keeping with the results of the studies undertaken into the openings of emergency calls, in these calls for technical help, the kind of conversational footings (Goffman 1979) usually found in ordinary calls, that is, greetings and how-are-yous, are also absent and callers proceed to the reason for the call at the first available opportunity.

Telephone service centres set up to offer an additional platform to support customer services, besides the more traditional face-to-face services offered over the counter, have also received some attention. Márquez Reiter (2005, 2006) examined the openings of calls to a Montevidean-based carer-provider company and to a service repair company. Although offers of assistance were absent in both studies, greeting exchanges were reported as recurrent. The author explained that, following organisational identification, call-takers produce the first pair part of a greeting and this, in turn, triggers the production of a second pair part by the caller. She argued that the occurrence of greetings in service calls between strangers who are unlikely to be in touch with each other again displays an orientation to interpersonal connectedness (Fitch 1991) and is seen as a sign of politeness. Likewise, Gabbiani (2006) investigated the openings of calls to a Uruguayan public utility company, and her findings coincide with those made earlier by Márquez Reiter (2005, 2006). More recently, a pragma-linguistic analysis of the sequences which comprise call openings in similar institutional settings has been undertaken by Palotti and Varcasia (2008). The authors examined calls to bookstores, travel agencies, hairdressers, libraries, student halls and university departments in English, French, German, Italian and Spanish. With the exception of those calls conducted in English, the examples provided from the data show the presence of greetings in all the excerpts. Some of the English openings contain a greeting token in the call-taker's first turn but no greeting return by the caller. Interestingly, the Italian and Spanish excerpts show that the answer to the summons does not always consist of organisational identification or an offer of assistance, or both, which, as we have seen, helps to signal right from the start the institutional character of the call. Instead, some of the calls in Italian and Spanish were answered in the same way as ordinary calls, that is, by uttering *pronto* and *diga(me)*, respectively.

Inter-organisational call openings – calls between two organisations or two institutional representatives – have been examined by Firth (1995) and Amthor Yotskura (2002). The latter explores, from a broad discursive perspective, the rhetorical strategies displayed in calls to a Japanese shipping company. She reported the mandatory nature of mutual identification by the conversationalists, followed by an obligatory exchange of business salutations. She claimed that greeting exchanges and requests for identification are optional elements and that they occur between the obligatory phases of mutual identification and business salutations. Once these are achieved, participants proceed to discuss the business transaction, that is, the reason for the call. Similarly, though in the previous decade and from a conversation analytic perspective, Firth (1995) observed a modified core sequence almost analogous to the openings of ordinary calls in a corpus of intercultural business calls, conducted in English as a lingua franca. In the case of these calls, the parties were, to some extent, acquainted with each other as the calls had been triggered by a letter from one of the parties to another. Thus, Firth found that the reason for the call, that is the actual business to be negotiated, was proffered after greetings and how-are-yous had been achieved; in other words, after the relationship had been re-established.

More recently, telephone conversations where English is used as a lingua franca have received some attention from applied linguists. For instance, Forey and Lockwood (2007)[10] have concentrated on inbound call centres where American customers telephone in for services and their calls are answered by non-native speakers of English; in this case, Philippine calltakers. As part of the examination of the generic structure (Halliday and Hasan 1976) of the calls, these researchers focused on the obligatory and optional phases of the openings. The results show a similar pattern to that observed by Whalen and Zimmerman (1987) and Wakin and Zimmerman (1999), despite differences in research objectives, in theoretical and methodological frameworks, and in institutional settings. Specifically, the answer to the summons comprises organisational identification, followed by an offer of assistance. The caller then offers the reason for the call and the call-taker initiates an interrogative series of questions before a response is offered. In keeping with most of the results reported so far into institutional call openings in English, in these calls there is also an absence of greetings and how-are-you exchanges. The results discussed so far seem to indicate that, in English, conversational footings (Goffman 1979) of the kind observed in institutional calls conducted in Spanish may only be deemed appropriate in those cases where the participants feel that their relationship needs to be (re-) established before they can get down to business or when the reason for the call is not business as usual (Tracy and Agne 2002).

Despite differences in analytic perspectives, institutional settings and languages examined, Zimmerman's (1984, 1992), Whalen and Zimmerman's (1987) and Wakin and Zimmerman's (1999) account of emergency call openings has triggered a wealth of studies into institutional telephone conversations and, particularly, into their openings. As I have attempted to show, subsequent studies have found Zimmerman's model helpful in their efforts to account for: the general unfolding of an array of institutional telephone openings; the constraints and contingencies of seeking a given service in a particular environment (public v. private); the way in which different languages construct their openings; and the potential for miscommunication in calls where the participants do not share the same first language. In doing so, these studies have provided further support for Zimmerman's (1984, 1992) model and demonstrated its general applicability to calls for service, irrespective of the service offered and of the setting and the language examined.

The closings of telephone conversations, in particular the closings of institutional calls, have received little attention relative to the research carried out into the openings. This is perhaps a reflection of the fact that bringing a conversation to a close can be a delicate matter. According to Kendon:

> [T]o close a conversation, one party does not simply turn off his receivers, but an elaborate process of forewarning of closure is gone through, prior agreement to close is sought and entered into, and the closing ceremony itself is hedged about with expressions that mutually assure the participants that the severing of the communications channels that is about to take place does not imply that neither will be willing to reopen them in the future, should circumstances permit. (1986: 34, quoted in Sigman 1991: 113)

This, in my opinion, could apply just as much to the current encounter as to any future interaction.

To the best of my knowledge, there have been, until now, only two studies that have explicitly analysed the tasks that participants engage in to bring institutional telephone conversations to a close. Davidson (1978) examined a call made by a private citizen, during a hurricane, to Civil Defence, a public service organisation. The study focused on a negotiation sequence between an institutional agent (the call-taker) and a private citizen (the caller) during the activity of closing. In this telephone conversation, the call-taker proposes that the caller telephone her relatives to ascertain whether or not they have been adversely affected by the hurricane, and the caller displays some resistance until the former persuades the latter to do so. Drawing on Schegloff and Sacks' (1973) notion of a monotopical call, Davidson cogently argued that, in essence, the closing down of a topic in a call of the kind examined – that is, a service call – triggers a possible close-down of the call. She analysed the sequences for closing down a topic (Schegloff and Sacks 1973), with particular attention to the occurrences of 'okay?', 'alright', 'yeah' and minimal responses, such as 'mm hm', which were functioning as potential closing devices and as components in an extended negotiation sequence. She noted that, while these tokens typically operate to invite agreement with some prior utterance and are also followed by agreement tokens ('okay' and 'alright'), according to their sequential placement and the contingences of the talk, they may also signal ambiguity with respect to stance. Davidson's (1978) study thus provides further support for the activities that Schegloff and Sacks (1973) identified in the closings of telephone conversations and for one of the key notions in conversation analysis (CA), namely that understanding is not achieved on the basis of pre-established shared meanings but is procedurally and contextually accomplished (Garfinkel 1967).

Maynard and Schaeffer (2002a, 2002b) investigated the practices for opening and closing telephone interviews in a corpus of calls in which interviewers solicited participation in a survey and call recipients granted or declined the request. Basing their work on Schegloff and Sacks (1973) and on Button's (1987) subsequent taxonomy for bringing telephone conversations to a close, the authors observed that polite declinations created a closing-relevant environment after which the calls were systematically closed. Polite declinations comprised telephone conversations in which the recipients expressed that the timing of the call was inopportune or that they were not interested in participating in the survey. The authors' incisive analysis demonstrates that polite declinations sequentially comprise the declining action as dispreferred (Pomerantz 1984) and 'observe the propriety of opening up closings or systematically terminating the call' (Schegloff and Sacks 1973, cited in Maynard and Schaeffer 2002a: 188). Specifically, polite declinations were constructed in a dispreferred mode and this, in turn, triggered the participants' move towards closing and terminating the encounter. The authors thus maintained that polite declinations offer conversationalists an opportunity to discontinue the conversation collaboratively and represent a solution to the question of how to lift turn-transition relevance mutually without the implication of fault or abruptness. Additionally, the authors observed that bad timing declinations are more effective than not-interested declinations in effecting closure and termination and that this, in turn, explains the fact that they were deployed 'independently of their actual involvements in activities (making dinner, going out of the door) or states (not feeling well, for example) that compete with participation in the interview' (Maynard and Schaeffer 2002a: 200). The authors further noted that bad timing declinations triggered mutual or unilateral arrangements for a call back, while not-interested declinations generated cycles of appeals before an initial declination was finalised and the participants closed and terminated the encounter.

The closings of institutional telephone conversations have also received some attention from applied linguists working primarily from a systemic-linguistics perspective. As mentioned earlier, Forey and Lockwood (2007) examined the mandatory phases in inbound calls to a Philippines-based call centre servicing American clients. Although they adopted a different theoretical and analytic perspective and had a different research objective in mind, the authors reported that the summarising and reiteration of conversational topics is a non-mandatory phase in the activity of closings. On the other hand, they noted that the expression of thanks is a mandatory phase, at least from the perspective of the call centre agent.

I have now presented a rationale for examining the construction of mediated service encounters in Spanishes at a pervasive and modern mediated communication setting. I have discussed the importance of exploring the way in which specifically located activities, that is, openings and closings, are enacted and have also explained that these activities, as well as the conversational manoeuvres employed by the participants to pursue a sale and to obtain the best value for money, are worthy of examination. In the next chapter, I outline the research perspective adopted and describe the ways in which the data for this study were collected. In Chapter 3, I present the analysis of the openings of the calls; in Chapter 4, I examine the strategies deployed by the participants to pursue their (sometimes difficult) conversational goals; this is followed, in Chapter 5, by an examination of the closings. Finally, in Chapter 6, I offer some reflections in the light of the main findings obtained and with reference to the research questions outlined in Section 1.1 of this chapter with a view to informing intercultural communication across Spanishes.

Notes

1. Sacks (1992) observed that not everyone who is in the proximity of a telephone when it is ringing may be a potential answerer, as they may not answer it, and that the person who picks up the telephone to answer the call may not necessarily be the person whom the caller intended to talk to, that is, the called.
2. Castells' 'space of flows' refers to the material and immaterial components of the global information networks through which more and more of the economy is coordinated in real time across distances.
3. Support for this can be found in the number of television adverts which proudly advertise the 'come back' of national call centres (see, for example, NatWest bank adverts in the UK and the number of offshore call centres servicing US customers which have recently relocated to the USA).
4. 'Offshore call centre benefits challenged'. Retrieved on 21 December 2007 from www.ft.com.
5. 'National news: Barclaycard call centre jobs blow'. Retrieved on 21 December 2007 from www.ft.com.
6. Studies conducted into the linguistic realisation of mundane telephone openings in Spanish have also reported a preference for recognition over self-identification (see, for example, Placencia 1997 for Ecuadorian

Spanish, Santamaría García 1996 and Ávila Muñoz 1998 for Peninsular Spanish, and Coronel-Molina 1998 for calls between Hispanic family and friends from Chile, Cuba, Mexico, Panama, Peru and Puerto Rico).

7. For a discussion of new ways of answering calls as a result of the affordances brought about by mobile telephones, see, for example, Arminen and Leinonen (2006). For a discussion of how mobile telephone openings have retained, rather than changed, many of the features of landline openings, see, for example, Hutchby and Barnett (2005).

8. Firth (1995) reports the omission of organisational identification in favour of a 'hello' token as the answer to the summons by Middle Eastern companies that deal with international clients and shows how this, in turn, triggers a 'candidate recognition' of the organisation called by the caller.

9. For an overview of the array of studies that have examined openings in a variety of institutional settings and languages, see, for example, Márquez Reiter and Luke (2010).

10. See also Friginal (2009) for a corpus-based analysis of cross-cultural interaction (American–Philippine dyads) conducted in English as a lingua franca at an outsourced call centre.

2 Methodology

2.1 Background to the research

The data for this book come from the Latin American call centre operation of a multinational holiday exchange company, which is run along similar lines to time shares organisations worldwide. Clients of the company own or have the right to use a property, typically a holiday resort unit overseas or at a resort in their country of abode, for an allotted period of time, generally one to two weeks and almost always at the same time every year.

Membership of the company entails a yearly fee. In return for this, clients deposit their allotted period of time at their holiday resort unit in order to have the possibility of exchanging it for one of the various other resorts that the company has worldwide. Normally, clients have to pay a handling fee once an exchange has been found for them. An exchange can only be found once the client's allotted time has been deposited and maintenance of the holiday unit paid for.

The company used to offer their services in the home country of the clients; for example, a Venezuelan-based call centre, typically staffed with Venezuelan telephone agents, was in place to deal with the Venezuelan clientele. In line with the worldwide trends of the new economy, however, the company centralised its various operations for the Latin American clientele into one call centre, which was set up in a Latin American financial hub.

The call centre is located in a business and technology park that offers state-of-the-art office layouts and infrastructure; these include fibre optic connections with key business capitals, and an exclusive teleport for satellite communication and for toll-free 800 numbers from the USA. Unlike other call centres, this centre deals with both inbound and outbound calls. Inbound calls are those made by (prospective) clients to the call centre, and outbound calls are those made by the telephone agents to (prospective) clients. The data for this study consist, thus, of both inbound and outbound calls, providing a more encompassing picture of the activities the participants engage in when supplying and requesting a service over the phone.

The call centre has eight departments: Finance, Human Resources, Information Technology, Marketing, Operations, Outsourcing Services, Customer Care and Planning. The Operations department will be the primary focus of attention, given that its sole purpose is to deal with the company's various Latin American clients. The department is divided into five sections according to business purpose: Acquisitions, Contract Renewals, Customer Care, Deposits and Memberships. Operations representatives make and receive calls to and from clients. With the exception of Customer Care, which makes and receives calls to and from any of the Latin American clients of the company, each section has a team of telephone operators who work with clients from specific Latin American countries: Argentina, Bolivia, Brazil, Chile, Colombia, Ecuador, Mexico, Peru, Uruguay and Venezuela. The vast majority of the clients and calls are to and from: Argentina, Colombia, Mexico and Venezuela. In view of this, calls to and from these four countries will be the main focus of attention. Owing to the nature of the product offered by the company and to the socio-economic situation of the countries where the client pool comes from, these clients, generally speaking, belong to the (upper) middle-class stratum within their respective countries of origin;[1] hence, they can afford not only these holiday facilities but other luxuries such as housekeepers.

The call centre has more than 300 agents, all of whom are native speakers of Spanish, with the vast majority being speakers of what is known as River Plate Spanish. This is the variety spoken in the Argentine cities of Buenos Aires, La Plata and Rosario, and in Montevideo, the capital of Uruguay. Like all varieties of Spanish, River Plate Spanish has some identifiable features: a generally ascending melodic curve; *yeísmo*, where the sounds represented by 'll' (the palatal lateral /ʎ/) and 'y' (historically the palatal approximant /j/) have merged into a post-alveolar fricative, either voiced [ʒ] or voiceless [ʃ]) (Lipski 1994); *voseo*, that is, the use of the second person singular instead of *tú*; and a reported tendency towards relative informality in interaction (see, for example, Márquez Reiter 2009).[2]

The telephone agents have completed secondary school and more than a third of them have university degrees or equivalent qualifications.[3] The environment chosen by the company to set up its centralised operation for Latin America thus meets the financial prerogatives of the new economy: a modern infrastructure with tax incentives, matched with a relatively cheap workforce, which is suitably qualified in terms of lingua-cultural knowledge and educational background. Theoretically speaking, these characteristics are believed to be part and parcel of the good communication skills required of the telephone agents (see Chapter 1, Section 1.3).

Each agent is allocated a cubicle with a console. There are 18 agent cubicles per call centre 'island'. Each island deals with a different aspect of the services provided by the different sections of the Operations department. Thus, there is an island devoted to membership renewals, one to deposits, another to acquisitions, and so on. Additionally, the islands are further classified into the geographical regions where the clientele come from and according to the nature of the calls handled; that is, inbound or outbound calls and, in the case of the latter, first-attempt, call-back and follow-up outbound calls (see Chapter 3, Section 3.3.1). For instance, there is a renewal island that deals with inbound and outbound calls from the southern regional countries of Chile, Argentina and Uruguay, a renewal island to service clients from the northern regions of Colombia and Venezuela, and another to service Mexican clients. It should be noted that inbound calls from a country which does not form part of an island's geographical remit may also be received, mainly thanks to the automatic re-routing service which is in place to decrease waiting times.

At the front of every island sits a supervisor, a senior telephone agent, typically from one of the countries within the island's geographical remit, with his or her own headset. The cords of the headsets are long enough for agents to stand up and walk a few steps from their cubicles; this enables them to talk to other agents who are not necessarily seated in an adjacent cubicle. Talking to a supervisor is possible if the agent's and supervisor's cubicles are adjacent and if the agent manages to attract the supervisor's attention from a distance. The supervisor is the first port of call should problems arise in the communication between agents and clients. Given that there is usually a physical distance between the agents and the supervisor, when problems do arise, agents normally stand up and wave their hands in order to get the supervisor's attention. In those cases where the supervisor is attending to another call and the agent is unable to attract his or her attention, an MSN is sent to the supervisor or to the Customer Care department in charge of dealing with quality assurance.

Island supervisors, together with team leaders and other staff, typically from the Human Resources department, are meant to monitor procedures. However, given that supervisors are normally on the phone themselves, monitoring is not very rigorous or systematic. Nevertheless, the activity of telephone agents is measured and publicly displayed by computerised boards showing calls in progress, calls held in a queue, average handling time of calls, average waiting time and so on. These display boards appear to have at least two functions: to remind the telephone agents of the backlog of calls building up so that they can work more efficiently; to keep them informed of the island's ongoing activities; and, in some cases, to show the agent within an island who meets the set targets in the shortest period of time or even surpasses them. This statistical information is collated and disseminated among call centre employees in order to encourage collective animation. The basis of this collective animation resides in the possibility of winning, among other prizes, holidays; inevitably, these consist of free accommodation, together with free airline tickets, for a stay at one of the company's various luxurious resorts.

In between and during calls, agents read or talk to each other. During their breaks, the majority of agents gather in the refectory area, where there is a television set and complementary tea and coffee. It is also very common for agents to meet at each other's homes and go out together on their days off. Social contact between the agents also takes place during cigarette breaks and in the company transportation which takes the agents to and from their homes.

Call centre agents are required to attend a two-week training course before they start working in the call centre. During the training period, the agents are given information about the company's products and operations across the world, in particular about the Latin American operation. They are also given training in managing calls. Specifically, they are told to follow a script, one for taking inbound and the other for placing outbound calls, as illustrated in Figures 2.1 and 2.2.

As observed in the scripts, placing and receiving calls involves a certain degree of planning. This is particularly evident in the case of outbound calls, where the script indicates that previous planning is the preliminary step in making a call. Drawing on the information available on their computer screens, the agents need to revise the deposits made by the clients, check their confirmations and financial balances and, on the basis of each client's history, figure out their eligibility for special offers and other products. Thus, in the planning stage of the call, that is prior to placing the call, the agents should be in a position where they have relevant information on the clients. Owing to the nature of inbound calls, the corresponding script does not contain a planning stage as such. Nonetheless, planning is subsumed under the stage of 'learning', where the agents have to build a profile of the clients before giving them advice. In practice, the 'learning' stage is realised by the set of sub-questions outlined in the script, together with the client's 'history', which is available on each agent's screen.

2.2 Data and ethics

For this study, I conducted fieldwork at the call centre for about one month in 2006. During this period, I gained access to recorded conversations from the various sections of the Operations department; conducted non-participant observations of the agents at work; and carried out interviews with agents and supervisors. I collected: policy documents, such as the scripts used for guiding call management; promotional materials; and configuration plans of the call centre. I was also given access to human resources information about the telephone agents, such as date and place of birth, place of abode, education and so on, and to the general profile of the clients. I was, however, unable to conduct video recordings as it was deemed that this would be a further distraction from the employees' daily working routines. Before

I. Opening

1. Answer. Greet the caller and identify yourself as an agent of the company (name and surname):
   Gracias por llamar a Vacaciones Inolvidables Latinoamérica, mi nombre es (Nombre y Apellido)
   'Thank you for calling Holidays to Remember Latin America, my name is (First Name and Surname)'
2. Offer your help:
   ¿Cómo le puedo ayudar el día de hoy?
   'How can I help you[U] today?'
3. Listen:
   • Do not interrupt the client
   • Listen and take notes of what the client says
   • Pay attention to non-verbal communication (the environment where the client is)
4. Personalise the call:
   • Confirm your understanding:
     Entiendo su situación . . . Comprendo cual es su inconveniente . . .
     'I understand your[U] situation . . . I understand your[U] predicament . . .'
   • Offer help:
     Déjeme ayudarle . . . Voy a hacer todo lo posible por resolverlo. . .
     'Allow[U] me to help . . . I'm going to do my upmost to resolve it . . .'

II. Learn

1. Ask questions to: profile the client; develop objectives; find out criteria for holiday choice; and to understand the client's habits
   • Open questions:
     ¿Por qué eligió ese destino? ¿Cuál es su plan de vacaciones?
     'Why did you[U] choose this resort? What are your[U] holiday plans?'
   • Closed questions:
     ¿Cuántas personas viajan? ¿Le gusta la playa?
     'How many people will be travelling? Do you[U] like going to the beach?'
2. Verify
   • Summarise
   • Request confirmation:
     Entonces quiere viajar a Colombia. ¿Cierto? ¿Es verdad? ¿Es correcto?
     'So you want to travel to Colombia. Right? Don't you? Is this correct?'

III. Advise

1. Explain your recommendation:
   Sr. (Apellido), la mejor opción disponible en este momento es . . .
   'Mr (Surname), the best available option at the moment is . . .'
2. Explain why the offer is convenient.
   No vendas características, vende beneficios, la forma en cómo estos cubren las necesidades del socio
   'Do not sell[T] characteristics, sell[T] benefits, the way in which these cover the client's needs'

Figure 2.1 In-house rules for inbound calls

Características	Beneficios
Characteristics	Benefits
Grande	*Confort*
'Large'	'Comfort'
Blanco	*Limpieza*
'White'	'Cleanliness'
Distinción	*Lujo*
'Difference'	'Luxury'

IV. Agree

1. Ask the client to establish a commitment:
   ¿Entonces le confirmo este espacio en este momento Sr. (Apellido)?
   'So can I now book this for you Mr (Surname)?'
2. Ask the client to perform an action:
   Confirm, deposit, renew, give credit card details
3. Ask if you can be of further assistance:
   ¿Hay algo más que pueda hacer por usted Sr. (Apellido), algo más en que le pueda ayudar . . . ?
   'Is there anything else I can do for you[U] Mr (Surname), is there anything else I can help you[U] with . . . ?'
4. Say goodbye and thank you:
   Muchas gracias por su atención, le recuerdo que mi nombre es (Nombre y Apellido) y estamos para ayudarle, que tenga un hermoso día
   'Thank you very much for your time, let me remind you that my name is (First Name and Surname) and that we are here to help you[U], have a wonderful day'

Figure 2.1 (continued)

describing the data collection procedures, I would like to discuss the ways in which ethical issues were addressed.

Ethical issues are extremely important to this study as personal information on the participants, including clients' credit card details, were gathered during the recording of the calls. Furthermore, I acquired knowledge of the various operations of the company, and some strategies for dealing with the competition emerged from this. Permission was obtained from the legal department of the call centre and from the Latin American administrative headquarters to use the recorded calls, interviews, policy documents and notes from observations, provided that an appropriate system for the safe custody of confidential information was in place. To this end, a legally binding, mutual non-disclosure agreement was signed between the company and the University of Surrey for a period of three years. In spite of the fact that the agreement is no longer in effect, confidential information, such as credit card details, will remain undisclosed and every effort will be made for the company not to be identified as the source of data associated with this study. Thus, throughout the book, pseudonyms will be used instead of the

I. Prior planning

1. Revise the client's details:
   - Deposits made
   - Confirmations made
   - Payments made
   - Special offers
   - Account balance
2. Decide what you want the client to do:
   - Renew for five years
   - Deposit his or her allotted week for 2011
   - Confirm two weeks in Puerto Vallarta during low season, and so on . . .

II. Opening

1. Greet the (potential) client and provide organisational identification:
   Buen día, mi nombre es (Nombre y Apellido), y le estoy llamando de Vacaciones Inolvidables Latinoamérica, su empresa de Intercambio Vacacional
   'Good morning, my name is (First Name and Surname) and I am calling you[U] from Holidays to Remember Latin America, your holiday exchange company'
2. Explain the reason for the call:
   Le estoy llamando porque tenemos una promoción especialmente para usted . . .
   'I am calling you[U] because we have a special offer just for you[U] . . .'
3. Establish the client's interest:
   Es interesante ¿cierto?, suena atractivo ¿verdad?
   'It is interesting, isn't it?', 'it sounds enticing, doesn't it?'
4. Request permission to continue

III. Learn

1. Ask questions in order to: find out what the client is like, develop objectives and establish criteria to select the holiday destination and understand the client's habits:
   - Open questions:
     ¿Por qué eligió ese destino?
     'Why did you choose[U] this holiday destination?'
     ¿Cuál es su plan de vacaciones?
     'What is your[U] holiday plan?'
   - Closed questions:
     ¿Cuántas personas viajan?
     'How many people will be travelling?'
     ¿Le gusta la playa?
     'Do you[U] like going to the beach?'
2. Verify:
   - Summarise
   - Ask confirmation question:
     Entonces quiere viajar a Londres ¿Cierto? ¿Verdad? ¿Es correcto?
     'So you want[U] to travel to London. Right? Don't you? Is this correct?'

Figure 2.2 In-house rules for outbound calls

IV. Advise

1. Explain your recommendation:
    Sr. (Apellido), la mejor opción disponible en este momento es . . .
    'Mr (Surname), the best available option at the moment is . . .'
2. Explain why the offer is convenient:
    No vendas características, vende beneficios, la forma en cómo estos cubren las necesidades del socio
    'Do not sell[T] characteristics, sell[T] benefits, the way in which these cover the client's needs'

Características	*Beneficios*
Characteristics	Benefits
Grande	*Confort*
'Large'	'Comfort'
Blanco	*Limpieza*
'White'	'Cleanliness'
Distinción	*Lujo*
'Difference'	'Luxury'

V. Agree

1. Ask the client to establish a commitment:
    ¿Entonces le confirmo este espacio en este momento Sr. (Apellido)?
    'So can I book this for you now Mr (Surname)?'
2. Ask the client to perform an action:
    Confirm, deposit, renew, give credit card details
3. Ask if you can be of further assistance:
    ¿Hay algo más que pueda hacer por usted Sr. (Apellido), algo más en que le pueda ayudar . . . ?
    'Is there anything else I can do for you[U] Mr (Surname), is there anything else I can help you[U] with . . . ?'
4. Say goodbye and thank you
    Muchas gracias por su atención, le recuerdo que mi nombre es (Nombre y Apellido) y estamos para ayudarle, que tenga un hermoso día
    'Thank you very much for your time, may I remind you that my name is (First Name and Surname) and that we are here to help you[U], have a wonderful day'

Figure 2.2 (continued)

real names of the participants and the Latin American financial hub where it is based. Furthermore, any information that might help to identify the participants, such as telephone numbers and addresses, will either be deleted or, if procedurally relevant to the unfolding of the calls, strategically altered.

Although the company records the calls between the agents and (prospective) clients, and the latter are informed of this via an automated disclaimer which announces that their call may be recorded for quality assurance purposes, the Human Resources department still deemed it important to email the call centre employees to inform them that I would be collecting data *in situ* for the purposes of examining communication in Spanish. The email explained that participation, though welcome, was not obligatory and that following my research visit, the company would receive a report outlining the ways in which communication might be improved.[4] Notwithstanding the approach to the research outlined above, some telephone agents could not resist asking me, when I was conducting the non-participant observation, for my thoughts on their working procedures. Given their interest, and the general interest provoked by the email announcing the visit of a researcher from a British university who speaks River Plate Spanish, I conducted, informally, debriefing sessions with the telephone agents during their breaks. Some of these debriefing sessions took the form of interviews in which the telephone agents adopted the role of interviewers and I that of interviewee.

Permission was consistently sought to conduct interviews either with the centre employees or with the clients (only a few in the case of the latter). At the beginning of every interview, I also made a point of reiterating the company's assurances of confidentiality and anonymity of data handling. All the data were transferred to electronic form and filed securely. Telephone calls and interview data were anonymised after they had been transcribed. Most of the transcription was initially carried out by a research assistant. Owing to the nature of the confidentiality agreement, a further legally binding, mutual non-disclosure agreement along the lines of the agreement with the company was signed between the research assistant and the researcher.

2.3 Document analysis

In order to understand the duties of the telephone agents and the ways in which the call centre organises its work, I collected certain policy documents; in this case, the scripts for receiving and placing calls, promotional materials in which the company's services are explained, and Human Resources documents. The Human Resources documents consist primarily, though not exclusively, of the configurations of the islands, including the ID of the agents in each island, the shifts of the agents and their background information.

Promotional materials, which were gathered, for the most part, prior to conducting the fieldwork, helped me familiarise myself with the company's services and to make the most of my time with members of the Human Resources and Outsourcing departments, who kindly explained their operations in one-to-one sessions with me at the start of my research visit.

Information on the various island configurations, including the agents who formed part of those islands, was essential in order to establish the agents' variety of Spanish. Similarly, it was important to know the place of abode of the (prospective) clients to whom the agents were talking on the phone so as to obtain further clues as their variety of Spanish.

The script for managing calls was collected as this forms an integral part of the telephone agents' training and adherence to it is, in theory, monitored. Given that the regulation of talk is demonstrable, at least on paper, it was essential to have a written record of the script of the telephone calls in order to examine the extent to which such regulation affects the ways in which the participants constructed their interactions (see Chapter 3, Section 3.2.1).

2.4 Non-participant observation

I conducted non-participant observation in order to understand how the call centre organises its work and how the agents and other members of the call centre, such as supervisors and managers, go about their daily work routines. When watching the employees of the call centre, I paid particular attention, with their knowledge, to the telephone agents but did not take an active part in the practices under scrutiny.

The kind of non-participant observation I conducted is best described as initially unstructured, at least during the first few days of the fieldwork, when my main purpose was to understand the ways in which the call centre manages its workload. During these initial observations, I took notes, focusing mainly on the activities of the telephone agents. These included observations of their working conditions, such as where and for how long they were seated in an island; whether or not they talked to other agents seated adjacently to them; and what they did to speak to the island supervisor, in the event of potential interactional difficulties. Once I had a general idea of the work of the call centre and, in particular, of the agents' work, I carried out more specific observations; thus, I sat next to several agents in different islands and took notes; for instance, on the information on the client which is available on their screens, and on the basis of which offers were made; and on the ways in which MSN is deployed during calls.

As important as the above-mentioned information is to understand activity coordination in call handling and the skilled ways in which agents ensure the transition between calls (see, for example, Mondada 2008, 2010), observation would have been greatly enhanced with the use of video recording, but this, unfortunately, was not possible. The company considered it an additional intrusion on the work of the agents. Furthermore, the question of video recording had not been raised when designing the mutual non-disclosure agreement, which was approved and signed prior to the fieldwork. Even if permission had been granted to video record the various bits of information that need to be taken into account in the coordination of the activities in which these agents engage, the logistics of such a study would have entailed the recording of a much smaller sample of calls. The research would, therefore, have followed a different objective. Furthermore, as topical a concern as multimodality is, particularly in the field of CA, the relationship between talk and action remains rather elusive (see Goodwin 2010 for an exemplary exception) and at times (implicitly) contested. For example, Goodwin (2010) examines the role of talk-in-interaction in the larger picture of the semiotic resources which are available to participants to build human action, and Schegloff (2009) discusses the lack of technical attention to the ongoing talk in some of these studies.

What emerged from these observations is, therefore, field notes on call handling. They describe the ways in which the information on their screens is accessed while the agents are on the phone to clients; however, the interactions on which they are based were not recorded. In view of this, and bearing in mind the main purpose of this book, the analysis of the calls will be principally based on the actual talk between the participants and supplemented, where necessary, with ethnographic data, that is, with field notes, document analysis and interviews.

As mentioned earlier, when problems in the communication with (prospective) clients arise and the agents cannot get hold of the supervisor, an MSN is sent to the respective supervisor. Supervisors typically respond immediately through the same channel, forwarding the MSN to the Customer Care department when they believe that the issue in hand is one of quality assurance. Given the importance of this arrangement, and in the light of the fact that I did not have access to the relevant recordings, I spent two days observing the work of the Customer Care team.

Unlike the parallel islands of the various other sections within the Operations department, Customer Care is placed at the front of the call centre floor on a mezzanine overlooking the islands; thus, it is easily visible from most islands. I sat next to the supervisor and to the other four members of the team, all of whom were telephone agents. During these two days, the team members, including the supervisor, kindly explained the nature of their work and allowed me to carry out what is known as 'silent or monitoring listening'. This is the practice, followed by call centre managers or senior agents such as supervisors, of listening to the interaction between a (prospective) client and an agent when the latter often does not necessarily know that the call is being monitored while in progress. In this case, however, Customer Care agents knew that I was listening to their calls and could see me doing so. Once the calls I had 'silently' listened to were completed, the agents took the time to justify their communicative behaviour on the basis of the company's policies. Most of the calls I monitored at Customer Care were forwarded by the telephone agents. Prior to forwarding the call, the agents typically sent an MSN to Customer Care, alerting them to potential trouble and explaining the reason for it. Customer Care agents responded via the same medium, generally requesting to speak to the client in question, after which the call was transferred to them. Given that most of the calls received by this department are complaint calls and that many of those are preceded by an inter-organisational MSN or by a previous form of communication between the client and the company, typically a fax where clients complain about the service received, I collected photocopies of the corresponding documents. This was done with a view to obtaining the call recordings and to conducting another study into cross-media communication and its effect on the unfolding of complaints. To my disillusionment, the recordings were beyond my reach. This is not surprising, given that the content of some of the calls, at least the ones I listened to, may have put the company in a bad light. Nonetheless, my experience of 'silent listening' at Customer Care helped me to fine tune my ear for my next task: 'silent listening' to calls to and from the Operations Department.

In order to carry out 'silent listening', I was allocated a desk with a telephone unit outside the call centre floor. With the help of a member of the IT department, I was able to key in the IDs of the telephone agents whose calls I wished to listen to without their knowledge. I was, however, unable to see the agents when I listened; the notes I took during 'silent listening' were, therefore, based only on the actual talk and did not include any other kind of communicative behaviour, such as paralinguistic features. Nonetheless, the notes helped me to make sense of the activities conversationalists engage in during the calls and to add a further perspective to the information I gathered from the interviews.

2.5 Interviews

The 52 interviews I carried out resulted in about 10 hours of recordings, which were transcribed by the research assistant and later anonymised. The main purpose of the interviews was to gather the agents' perceptions of the various Latin American cultures they have had experience of working with. The interviews were carried out during the agents' breaks, that is, in the refectory area during the lunch break or outside the call centre when the agents had a cigarette break. I also interviewed the agents in the transportation that takes them to and from their homes.

The interviews were informal and unstructured as I did not have a preplanned schedule. They were thus more like a conversation. They took place after my initial non-participant observations, in which, as mentioned earlier, agents took the opportunity to quiz me on my views of their work and to discuss my interest in communication in Spanish. Thus, before embarking upon the interviews, I had developed some rapport and trust with my interviewees and was able to converse 'freely' with them. In fact, many of the agents volunteered to be interviewed and a couple of agents had complained to me about not being interviewed, as, in their own words, they 'had interesting stories to tell'; in such cases I naturally agreed to interview them.

I began by seeking permission to record the interview and by explaining to the interviewees that their identity would be treated anonymously; I also

informed them that, in the event that any information which emerged from
the interviews could jeopardise their employment in any way, it would be
treated confidentially and not passed on to Management. Interestingly, a
couple of interviews turned out to be complaints about Management in the
hope that I, as a researcher approved by the company's Latin American
administrative headquarters, would pass this information to higher authori-
ties. Similarly, Management seemed interested to find out if any 'sensitive'
human resources issues had emerged from this activity or from any of the
other activities I had engaged in. Thus, both the interviewees who had complaints about Management and the Management staff themselves attempted
– unsuccessfully – to add a surveillance duty to my research agenda.

Once permission to record was granted by the interviewees, I would continue the interview with general questions; for example, about which island
they worked in, what kind of clients they normally dealt with, and how much
experience they had of dealing with such clients. Using this general information, I then proceeded to ask more specific questions, such as why they
preferred to work with clients from one country as opposed to another, or
others, and whether they could recall any memorable experiences they had
had with clients. As initially anticipated, the interviews brought to the fore
the agents' perceptions of the differences between Latin American cultures.
Although interview data cannot tell us how people actually behave, the meta-
communicative comments yielded through this exercise were in line with
deep-rooted stereotypes about certain Latin American cultures.

Despite the fact that the researcher might influence the respondents'
answers and that these may be 'socially expected', the interviewees were
decisively confident in expressing their negative perceptions of certain Latin
American cultures, even when they knew that I was allegedly a member of
one of those negatively viewed cultures. Thus, some Venezuelan agents commented on how boring social life was in the River Plate relative to that in
their home country; a couple of Colombian and Mexican agents remarked on
the 'outrageous' lack of respect and good manners of people from the River
Plate. According to them, this is evidenced in the informality with which
River Plate people treat others, irrespective of hierarchy or age. Examples
included the River Plate custom of kissing people when they meet them for
the first time and of sitting very close to people and touching their arms or
hands when they want to attract their attention. Interestingly, some perceptions of the various Latin American cultures and their communicative style
generated by the interviews are evidenced in the actual calls, although clearly
this is not the case with the tactile.

As mentioned earlier, I was able to conduct a handful of interviews with
clients immediately after a call to or from them had been completed. In
this sense, these interviews are retrospective and mainly address the clients'
perception of service. In line with the interviews with the agents, I sought
the clients' permission before conducting the interview and explained my

research interest. On learning about the aim of my research, the clients, rather surprisingly, volunteered their perceptions of the communicative style – more specifically, the lack of politeness – of some Latin American cultures. The clients did not grant permission for the interviews to be recorded; consequently, only notes were taken.

2.6 Telephone conversations

The company records the calls between agents and (prospective) clients for monitoring and quality assurance purposes and both conversational participants are aware of this. However, in practice, not all the telephone conversations are recorded as this is seen as time-consuming and cost-ineffective, since a member of the IT department would need to be devoted to this sole task. Instead, the company records randomly the calls from the various sections of the Operations department, as it does also with some calls made to and received from the Customer Care department. As mentioned earlier, the calls to the latter department were not made available. It should be noted that if the telephone agents are underperforming, individualised surveillance is sometimes explicitly put into practice; this involves, among other measures, the recording of all their telephone interactions during their work shifts.

The IT department provided me with a set of wav files of randomly recorded calls between agents and (prospective) clients. Upon looking through the files, it emerged that some of the islands which comprise the Operations department had not been recorded and that consequently, I lacked data from some of the countries which constitute the bulk of the company's clientele. The IT department remedied this situation by recording conversations from the missing countries during my research visit. All in all, I was equipped with about 80 hours of recorded conversations.

The call database is not a representative sample of the call centre operations. The recording of the conversations followed the principles of purposive sampling. The conversations were recorded using judgement and knowledge of the call centre interface between the agents and (prospective) clients to allow Management to identify 'the quality' of a certain percentage of the population in a given island or the overall performance of a given island.

Thanks to the financial support of the University of Surrey, 15 of the 80 hours of recorded telephone conversations have been transcribed. Funding was not available, however, for more than 15 hours. The transcriptions were initially made by a research assistant and follow, as closely as possible, the transcription conventions of CA. The choice of which calls to transcribe also followed the principles of purposive sampling.

When conducting the fieldwork, my initial goal was to examine intercultural communication between speakers of different varieties of Spanish. With this in mind, I instructed the research assistant to select a comparable number of interactions from the bulk of the clientele, that is, from Argentinean, Colombian, Mexican and Venezuelan (prospective) clients. However, in practice this was not possible. First, specific islands deal with specific geographical areas and may, thus, make and receive more calls from a given country than from others within their geographic remit. Second, without access to the Human Resources documentation where the ID of the agents, their working shift and their remit within their islands is outlined, it was difficult for the research assistant, a native speaker of River Plate Spanish, to distinguish between clients from Colombia, Mexico and Venezuela. As a result, the original transcriptions did not generate enough calls from the bulk of the clientele. Thereafter, having obtained the relevant Human Resources documentation and drawing on my training in sociolinguistics, I transcribed the remainder of the calls in order to obtain comparable numbers of conversations from the above-mentioned countries.

In essence, the 15 hours of telephone conversations largely consist of calls with Argentinean, Colombian and Venezuelan clients and, to a lesser though not insignificant extent, of interactions with Chileans, Mexicans and Uruguayans, as well as a few calls with Ecuadorian and Peruvian clients. The 15 hours of recorded calls have translated into a total of 131 calls: 36 inbound calls received by 12 agents and 95 outbound calls made by 34 agents. In view of this, the communicative patterns observed in the analysis cannot be attributed to the particular communicative style of any of the participants. As the analysis will show, a small proportion of the recordings obtained are representative of the interaction sequence between given telephone agents and clients in that they contain the first call and the follow-up (that is, a call in which the transaction was finalised). Although the database contains only a very small number of these cases, thus making it difficult to establish recurrent patterns, close examination shows how the openings and closings of first and follow-up calls are achieved differently in the light of prior and potential future contact between the participants.

2.7 Analytic perspective

Given that the main goal of this study is to examine the various activities that the telephone conversationalists engage in to supply and demand a service over the phone through the medium of Spanish, the primary source of data is the recorded telephone conversations.

Field notes from non-participant observation, call centre documents and interviews will be used to supplement the analyses as the calls alone may prove insufficient to account for aspects of the talk, one such example being the way in which participants enter into the talk. Bearing in mind that the study also aims to shed light on intercultural communication between speakers of Spanish and on how this, in turn, may affect the construction of talk, perceptions of cultural difference, as yielded by the interviews, will primarily be used to this end. These will aid the examination of the conversational manoeuvres deployed by participants from different Spanish-speaking cultures and will shed light on the possible sources of interactional misfires.

The analytical stance I adopt, in line with my recent work on institutional telephone conversations in Spanish (Márquez Reiter 2005, 2006, 2009, 2010), is integrative. I draw on some Conversational Analysis techniques to examine the structure of the calls, in particular how the opening and closing sequence, as well as other sequences, are locally managed and sequentially organised; I also use elements of sociolinguistics and pragmatics, such as politeness orientations and codification of the rules of interaction, to account fully for interactional (a)symmetries in intercultural communication. One, albeit not the only, reason why my analysis draws on CA is the type of talk I examine. The topic of telephone conversations 'is virtually a creation of CA' (Schegloff 2009: 399), and there is now a rich body of knowledge on the activities human beings engage in while on the phone. This can be used to inspect the extent to which the participants of these calls engage in similar practices.

My approach is comparative in that it is based on the belief that institutional talk, of which the calls I examine represent a type, involves the systematic restriction and variation of activities and of their design relative to ordinary conversation (Drew and Heritage 1992). In this sense, these calls deviate from the canonical pattern of ordinary telephone calls. However, the patterns of ordinary telephone conversations in Spanish remain largely unknown. This, in effect, would weaken the everyday v. institutional point of comparative departure. Comparability, as I hope to demonstrate in this book, is nonetheless achievable by the recurrent actions observed in the inbound v. outbound calls, as well as in the recurrent moves observed in the various calls made to, or received by, participants who speak different varieties of Spanish; for example, calls made by Venezuelans v. calls made by Argentineans. Furthermore, a small number of calls are intra-cultural, that is, calls between participants who speak the same variety of Spanish. With this in mind, the actions observed across intercultural calls can be compared with those observed in intra-cultural calls in order to shed further light on the significance of the patterns observed.

I do not assume that there will be misunderstandings or significant differences, or both, in the way the calls are constructed by virtue of the fact that most of the participants come from different backgrounds and speak different varieties of Spanish. I do, however, allow for the possibility that participants from different backgrounds may show a preference for certain actions over others. Similarly, some routine expressions in one variety of Spanish may not necessarily be shared in another and this, in turn, may lead to misunderstandings. However, that certain expressions may not be shared, or may be shared but have different interactional meaning attributed in different varieties of Spanish, does not necessarily mean that this will be consequential for the ensuing talk. Rather than hypothesise on the basis of introspection, I draw on my experience of communicating with participants who speak the varieties of Spanish represented in the calls I examine and on knowledge gained from the examination of speech (not talk) in dialectology and sociolinguistics; thus I contend that if differences in the linguistic packaging of the turns matter, the participants themselves will orient to them and, as such, they will become relevant.

The patterns observed in the analysis may well apply to other (mediated) business interactions and to other segments of the population. However, this cannot be established on the basis of this study. Put differently, the conversational patterns I observe here describe the interactional behaviour of the participants in the calls examined and contribute to the knowledge of the differences and similarities in the ways in which speakers of Spanish go about the business of supplying and demanding services over the phone.

Notes

1. This information was gathered from the Human Resources department. Perceptions of the clientele's socio-economic stratum were confirmed in the interviews conducted with call centre employees and reflected in the content of the telephone conversations; for example, in their choices of resort, number of holiday exchanges per annum, and so on.
2. It should be noted that some of these features are not unique to this variety of Spanish or may in fact always be displayed in the participants' talk.
3. This information was gathered from the Human Resources department.
4. The report was duly submitted and well received.

3 Openings

3.1 Introduction

In this chapter, I provide an analysis of the sequences found in the openings of the inbound and outbound calls, using Zimmerman's (1984, 1992) model as a point of departure. It will be recalled that the calls in question are non-emergency calls, that is, they are calls in which a telephone agent aims to sell a specific commodity, in this case a holiday unit, to a (prospective) client. Given the more negotiable nature of the institutional setting examined and the fact that, in most cases, there is, or has been, an existing relationship between the client and the company, the participants' orientation to pattern the interaction as quasi-formal or informal should not come as a surprise. The chapter is divided into two main parts. In the first, I present the analysis of the inbound calls (see Section 3.2) and, in the second that of the outbound calls (see Section 3.3). In both cases, I provide a discussion of the in-house rules for receiving and placing calls before offering the structural account of the calls themselves. I conclude the chapter with a summary of the findings (see Section 3.4).

3.2 Inbound calls

In this section, I begin by offering a discussion, based primarily on documentary evidence, of the in-house rules for opening an incoming call. The analysis is supplemented by an interview with an agent and notes from non-participant observation. I then provide an examination of the sequences found in the openings of the inbound calls of the corpus.

3.2.1 In-house rules for opening inbound calls

The telephone agents are required to attend a two-week training course before they start their work in the call centre (see Chapter 2, Section 2.1). During training, they are given information about the company's products and operations across the world, in particular about the Latin American

Stage 1
Answer the telephone. Greet the person and identify yourself as a representative of the company (First Name and Surname):
Gracias por llamar a Vacaciones Inolvidables Latinoamérica, mi nombre es (Nombre y Apellido)
'Thank you for calling Holidays to Remember Latin America, my name is (First Name and Surname)'

Stage 2
Offer help:
¿Cómo le puedo ayudar el día de hoy?
'How can I help you today?'

Stage 3
Listen
Do not interrupt the client
Listen and take notes of what the client says
Pay attention to non-verbal communication (background noise where the call is being made)

Stage 4
Personalise the call
Confirm your[U] understanding:
Entiendo su situación . . . Comprendo cual es el inconveniente . . .
'I understand your situation . . . I understand what the problem is . . .'

Offer help:
Déjeme ayudarle . . . Voy a hacer todo lo posible por resolverlo
'Let[U] me help you[U] . . . I will do my utmost to find a solution. . .'

Note: The name of the company is fictitious.

Figure 3.1 In-house rules for the opening of inbound calls

operation. They are also given training in managing calls. Specifically, they are told to follow a script for receiving and placing calls. The recommended opening for answering an incoming call is illustrated in Figure 3.1.

As illustrated in Figure 3.1, the phases of the recommended 'opening' do not coincide with the activities that conversationalists have been shown to engage in during the initial stages of an institutional call (see Chapter 1, Section 1.6, Excerpt 4) or, as we will see later on, with those performed by the participants of the calls examined here. Significantly, the call-taker is expected to provide a preliminary response to the caller's first turn, the reason for the call, irrespective of what this might be or who the caller might be (*Entiendo su situación*: 'I understand your situation'). The suggested inter-actional routines assume that the caller is reporting some sort of a problem that needs to be resolved and that the institutional representative's main job is to help (prospective) clients out, rather than pursue the institution's interests (*Comprendo cual es el inconveniente. Voy a hacer todo por resolverlo*: 'I understand what the problem is. I will do my utmost to find a solution'). It is also suggested that notes should be taken and that call-takers should try to capture details of the physical environment from where the caller is telephoning (see Stage 3 in Figure 3.1). Although this is a sound piece of advice, it is not always possible to carry it out and is not a practice I observed while carrying out non-participant observation.

There are about 300 agents working at this call centre. They are distributed over call centre islands with 18 agent cubicles per island. The agents are constantly on the phone so this makes for palpable general background noise. Although all agents are allocated individual cubicles and given a set of headsets, they do not always stay in the cubicles: the headset cords are long enough for the agents to stand up and walk a few steps. This enables them to talk to an agent who is seated in an adjacent cubicle or simply manage part of their calls while standing next to another telephone agent. This, in turn, adds to the general noise level and, in some cases, makes the task of picking up details of the caller's physical environment too difficult. The agents are further challenged by the need to access their computers in order to find out information about the (prospective) client, that is, the caller, as well as the characteristics and general availability of the product or service that is being requested. They need, moreover, to do so as fast as possible, given that the time they spend handling calls is regularly monitored by the island team leader and occasionally by the call centre senior management team. The last, although by no means the least, source of pressure is that agents are given incentives for speed and effectiveness, that is, for the number of sales secured within a given time; accordingly, the number of calls handled per island and the time taken to handle them are regularly displayed in the call centre. In the light of the exigencies outlined above, agents rarely take notes as it is seen as counterproductive. In the words of one agent:

> *Tomar nota de lo que quiere el cliente es casi imposible, no hay tiempo para ello. Encima tenemos que estar al tanto de la información que nos sale en el computador y todo está allí. Si uno se pone a hacer todo lo que dice el reglamento eso pues se pasa una vida en las llamadas.*

> Taking notes of what the client wants is almost impossible, there is no time for that. Besides, we have to be alert to the information that comes up in the computer and everything is there. If one starts doing everything the rules say, well one can spend one's life on the calls.

Interactionally, call centre agents are expected to offer organisational identification by thanking the (prospective) client for calling the company, proffer self-identification by giving their full name and offer assistance in their first turn of the call. Additionally, they are expected to address the caller with *usted*, the respectful second-person singular, as evidenced by the examples provided in the house-style rules. Call centre agents are thus told to be polite, that is, to express gratitude for the call and treat the caller respectfully and to treat all calls to that number and the number itself as institutional (cf. Whalen and Zimmerman 1987) right from the start.

The recommended answer to the summons is in line with the Western business convention of providing some sort of organisational identification when answering the phone and reflects a somewhat North American business convention, namely, the presence of expressions of gratitude ('thank you for calling', 'thank you for visiting, shopping') before a sale and even when a sale is not achieved. In the case of these calls, the convention comprises the name of the company, followed by its geographical location, 'Latin America'. The presence of location identification reflects the multinational nature of the company and the centralisation of the company's different Latin American 'home-based' operations; for instance, a Mexican-based call centre serving the needs of Mexican customers. The uttering of the words 'Latin America' implies remoteness of location in the sense that, if the service were offered nationally, it would be unnecessary to stipulate so, and the caller would be more likely to speak to an institutional agent with a local accent. It also reflects concentration of function as it implies that the number to which the caller has got through deals with various Latin American clients and not just those from the caller's home country. Thus, the inclusion of location identification as part of the organisational identification highlights the company's global v. local operations while allowing for the 'local' in the all-encompassing identity-laden meaning of 'Latin America'. It is also possible that the callers may have known this before making the call, because they may have known that the company's various Latin American operations had been merged into one. In short, the inclusion of location identification signals to the callers, at least to those who are call centre acculturated, or are informed as to the rapid growth of the business outsourcing industry, that they have connected to a call centre.

Openings, and in particular the first turn of the calls, are thus regulated by the company. Put differently, the company (un)successfully imposes the standard performance of common interactional routines. These regulated opening routines are oriented to both the callers and the company itself. As far as the callers are concerned, the opening turn is sufficiently informative in the sense that confirmation of the destination reached is given before they have to say anything. This is inadvertently supplemented with information about the company's infrastructural operation. The insertion of 'Latin America' after the company's name implies that the service is no longer offered locally but regionally. In the context of these calls, 'Latin America' is generic enough to encompass geographic (Central, North and South America) and cultural (Latin American v. American) belonging. The opening turn also meets the politeness requirements for the occasion. The distance between the participants is respectfully signalled by the use of *usted*. This choice is made in the light of the facts that, prior to the call, there has been very little, or no, contact between the participants although there could have been previous contact between the client and the institution, and that calls to the number are treated as primarily transactional. From the company's perspective, the codification of the opening is aimed at maximising effectiveness in terms of speed, time spent answering the summons and the company's global face, that is, the company's desired business image, which should, ideally, be invariant across the company's various operations. A friendly, though respectful, image is further conveyed by the recommended elements that follow organisational identification: self-identification and an offer of assistance. Both units are aimed at personalising the interaction with the client. While the former enables callers to visualise institutional agents in faceless encounters, the latter reassures callers that agents are there to help.

That the regulation of talk is demonstrable on paper, that is, in the in-house rules, sits rather uncomfortably with the basic tenet of CA that talk is jointly accomplished by the participants. Put differently, if codification of the kind of language used by the agents is in place, then it can be argued that this might, to a greater or lesser extent, influence the way in which the interaction is co-constructed. Additionally, and for the purposes of unpacking this idea, let us remind ourselves of the conditional relevance rule which states that '[T]he relevance of some turn type which can be a second pair part is conditional on the occurrence of a first pair part from the same pair type' (Schegloff 2007: 20). It then follows that the presence of a recognition display, such as an acknowledgement token, followed by a first name, as in, *Sí Patricia* ('Yes Patricia'), in the caller's first turn is conditional on the call-taker's having provided her first name in the first turn of the call. Had the agent answered the summons with a simple 'Hello', the caller might have chosen to confirm that the channel of communication was open by simply uttering *Sí* ('Yes'), unless of course he or she had recognised the call-taker's voice or knew in advance that Patricia would pick up the phone.

In view of this, the regulation of talk has an effect not only on the way the agents engage with the (prospective) clients but also on the way the latter enter into the talk and continue to co-construct it throughout the interaction. Despite the potential soundness of this argument, its empirical demonstration is not fully achievable, at least not at the interactional level, unless the regulation of talk is explicitly lexicalised as propositional content by the participants and unless it is consequential for the ensuing talk; this is illustrated in Excerpt 1 from a call between a Uruguayan agent and an Argentinean client.[1]

Excerpt 1 [9:3]

```
9    C:    Ay por favor, no me tratés de usted(.)me hacés
10         sentir muy vieja::,
```

```
           Ah please, don't ᵛ address me by usted(.)you makeᵛ me
           feel very old::,
11   A:    Bue::no señora(.) ja: es que así nos pi:den viste,
           O::K ma'am (.) ha: they a:sk us to do so you seeᵀ/ⱽ,
```

Thus, with the aid of document analysis, in this case the analysis of the call centre's in-house rules for answering inbound calls (see Figure 3.1 above), it is easy to observe the influence of the institution's regulation on the agent's talk in the initial turns of the conversation. However, the point at which a particular stretch of talk or interactional move can be attributed to the agents' observance of the in-house rules, to their own style or simply to following what they hear other agents doing, or to all three factors, is impossible to establish. Consequently, I will not advocate the general superiority of the context-endogenous conversation analytic position or the context-exogenous sociolinguistic and pragmatic position. Rather, I see theoretical and methodological value in embracing an integrative approach as both these stances make potentially unique contributions to an overall understanding of the intercultural calls examined in this book. From a sociolinguistics perspective, regulation has consequences for the type of Spanish that is prescribed by the institution. Whose language and whose norms of Spanish does it represent? For what reasons has this variety of the language been chosen over others? The answers to these questions cannot be found merely at the micro interactional level, they also require a macro interactional perspective: one where context-exogenous factors are taken into account as in, for example, the role of language standardisation, the influence of English in Latin American business practices, covert and overt prestige, among others; issues that are beyond the remit of this book.

3.2.2 Opening sequences of inbound calls

The number of inbound calls which form the database of this study is smaller than that of outbound calls. The calls were randomly recorded by the company as part of quality assurance procedures and transcribed in a conversation analytic format (see Appendix for transcription conventions). They amount to about 4 hours of inbound telephone conversations. This has translated into 36 perfectly audible calls. The median call length is 20 minutes. The calls were made by clients from Argentina, Colombia, Mexico and Venezuela and answered by 12 call centre agents. The agents came from Colombia, Mexico and Uruguay. Given the combination of participants, the patterns observed cannot necessarily be attributed to the clients' or the call-takers' personal style.

The summons answer: channel confirmation and identification
In all 36 telephone conversations, agents responded to the summons (telephone ring) with a routinised answer, which closely resembles the one

recommended in the in-house rules for answering calls (see Figure 3.1 above). The summons answer comprised two-turn constructional units (Sacks et al. 1974). Although these units consist of lexical and grammatical components which constitute different recognisable actions in context, they were phonetically realised as one 'package' (Schegloff 2007).

Specifically, the first turn-construction unit in all the summons answers consisted of the proffering of organisational identification, as shown at line 1, in all the excerpts of inbound calls. In the majority of calls (25 out of the 36), organisational identification was accompanied by a greeting, as illustrated at line 1 in Excerpts 2 and 3 (see also Excerpts 6, 7 and 9 on pp. 49, 50 and 51).

Excerpt 2 [2:4]

```
1   A:   Vacaciones Inolvidables buenas tardes (.) mi
2        nombre es Liliana²>en qué lo puedo ayudar<,
         Holidays to Remember good afternoon (.) my name is
         Liliana >how can I help youᵛ,<
3   C:   Sí: mirá buenas tardes.(.)e::mm yo quería hacerte
4        la siguiente consulta.=
         Yes: lookᵀ/ᵛ good afternoon (.) u:m I would like to ask
         youᵀ/ᵛ the following question.=
```

Excerpt 3 [13:10]

```
1   A:   Vacaciones Inolvidables buenas tardes,(.)habla
2        Diego Ruiz,
         Holidays to Remember good afternoon,(.) Diego Ruiz
         speaking,
         (0.3)
3   C:   Buenos días Diego.
         Good morning Diego.
         (0.3)
4   A:   Buenos días
         Good morning
5   C:   Carlos Alvarez de Venezuela.
         Carlos Alvarez from Venezuela.
6   A:   Sí señor.
         Yes Mr Alvarez.
```

Although, in the majority of calls, the first turn-constructional unit of the summons answer comprises two different lexical items, namely organisational identification, *Vacaciones Inolvidables (Latinoamérica)* ('Holidays to Remember [Latin America]'), and a greeting, *buenas tardes* ('good afternoon'), the latter was realised immediately after the former without a hearable pause. This absence of a hearable pause was established only after the assistant who transcribed the calls in the first instance and I had listened repeatedly to the calls. Organisational identification and greetings were thus uttered as if they were part and parcel of the same phrase, after which a micro-pause is observed before the production of the second turn-construction unit. The presence of a micro-pause potentially implicates a response and makes the production of the second turn-construction unit contingent on lack of caller uptake. The observed micro-pause after the first turn-construction unit suggests that the issue at stake, at least from the agents' perspective, is move-ment to the reason for the call. Thus, while the call-takers show that they are ready to engage in the next communicative task – the reason for the call – the callers clearly are not. This is evidenced by the fact that the callers do not take the floor until after the second turn-construction unit has been uttered, or they overlap before or during the uttering of this unit. This reflects the non-urgency of the calls. It underlies the role of the callers as clients who, in this sense, are less pressed for time to inquire about possibilities for forthcoming holiday plans. It also illustrates the role of the call-taker as a service provider whose main job is to handle hundreds of calls per day and who would thus welcome an early reason for the call.

In 33 of the 36 calls, the second turn-constructional unit of the summons-answer sequence contains two components: self-identification, *mi nombre es Liliana* ('my name is Liliana'), and an offer of assistance, *en qué lo puedo ayudar?* ('how can I help you°?').When an offer of assistance was proffered after the call-taker had self-identified, it was done without a detectable pause, as can be observed in all the excerpts of the inbound calls. Additionally, either one, or both, of these components was rushed, as shown at lines 1 in Excerpts 2 above and 4 below.

Excerpt 4 [10:6]

```
1    A:    Gracias por comunicarse con Vacaciones
2          Inolvidables Latinoamérica(.)
           >mi nombre es Jimena en qué le puedo ayudar<?
           Thank you for calling Holidays to Remember Latin
           America(.)
           >my name is Jimena how can I help you°<?
3    C:    Sí:: buenas tardes,(.) mire e:::h la molesto:mmm:
4          el tema es el siguiente.
           Yes:: good afternoon, (.) look° um sorry to bother you°
           mmm: the thing is . . ..
5    A:    Sí.
           Yes.
```

This, I argue, is indicative of the volume of calls agents have to handle and of the speed with which they are meant to deal with them. It also underlies the routinised nature of the answer to the summons and suggests that the issue of recognition or self-identification of the particular agent who took the call is irrelevant here. It is irrelevant for both conversational parties in the sense that, in most cases, what the callers recognise is having connected to the right institution and made contact with a representative of that institution. From experience of working at the call centre, the agents, for their part, know that the chances of a particular client speaking to them again are negligible. Pragmatically speaking, the offer of assistance is redundant as the implicature of an institutional answer to a summons is that someone is there to offer some sort of assistance. That it is generally proffered is possibly the result of the in-house rules and reflects the non-emergency nature of the calls.

In all the calls, the telephone agents responded to the summons by first providing organisational identification. This was done by merely offering the name of the organisation to which the caller had connected, *Vacaciones Inolvidables* ('Holidays to Remember'), as shown in Excerpts 2 and 3 above, or by proffering a formulaic expression of gratitude in which the name of the organisation and its location is included, *Gracias por llamar a Vacaciones Inolvidables* ('Thank you for calling Holidays to Remember'), as illustrated in Excerpts 4 above and 5 below. It was also formulated by uttering a combination of these.

Excerpt 5 [12:11]

```
1   A:   Gracias por llamar a Vacaciones Inolvidables(.)soy
2        Laura en qué puedo ayudar?
         Thank you for calling Holidays to Remember (.)I'm
         Laura how can I help you?
3   C:   H-o::la Laura.sabés qué,(.)e::h yo necesito e::h:
4        tomar una semana en (sitio) con (nombre de la
5        empresa), te doy el número de socio?
         H-e::llo Laura you knowʳ/ᵛ what,(.) um I need u:m: to take
         a week in (place) with (company's name),
         shall I giveʳ/ᵛ you the membership number?
6   T:   Sí.
         Yes.
```

The presence of organisational identification in the summons answer, irrespective of its pragma-linguistic formulation, confirms to the caller that he or she has reached the right number and projects, from the start, the institutional rather than the ordinary character of the call.[3] Immediately after the organisational identification, and as part of the same turn-construction unit, most calls (25 out of the 36) contained a greeting, *buenos días/tardes* ('good morning/afternoon'), in spite of the fact that they are not prescribed by the institution (see Figure 3.1 above for the in-house rules). The presence of a neutral-respectful greeting (compare *buenos días/tardes* ['good morning/afternoon'] with *hola* ['hello/hi']) in the opening turn also helps to construct the institutional character of the call, given that greetings of this kind are not likely to occur in the first turn of ordinary calls, at least not in the varieties of Spanish that have been examined so far (see Chapter 1, Section 1.5).

After a micro-pause, the second turn-construction unit was formulated by means of self-identification and, in the vast majority of the calls (33 out of 36), it was followed by an offer of assistance. The presence of self-identification by the telephone agent reinforces the institutional character of the call as self-identification is uncommon in ordinary calls, where a preference for recognition over self-identification has been reported (see Chapter 1, Section 1.5 and Section 3.3.2 of this chapter).[4] Agents gave either their first names or their full names, that is, first, middle and family name. Interestingly, both in the inbound calls and in the outbound calls (see Section 3.3 below), most agents provided their first names only and, in doing so, distanced themselves from the actual utterance. Specifically, in uttering *mi nombre es* ('my name is') and *le habla* ('This is X speaking') instead of *soy Laura* ('I'm Laura'), they use the third rather than first person, thus distancing themselves from their own private persona while adopting an institutional one (see Excerpts 5 and 6). Thus, they bring to the fore their role as telephone agents and emphasise the non-mundane nature of the call. The inclusion of self-identification serves to signal incipient recipiency in the sense that the telephone agents convey that they are ready to serve the caller. From the callers' perspective, it also serves, literally speaking, to put a name to a faceless interaction. Although the callers may be aware of the fact that they have telephoned a call centre and that the call could, therefore, have been answered by one of hundreds of agents, they are, nonetheless, talking to a human being with a name; a human being who volunteers his or her identity. In doing so, the agents personalise what might otherwise be interpreted as a standard business opening (see Section 3.2.2). While the offering of a personal name might somehow empower the client, in the sense that it makes the agent accountable, it does not guarantee that the caller will be able to speak to that particular agent again. First, there are hundreds of telephone agents working at the call centre and many of them have the same first name; thus, unless the agents provide their last names, this accountability might be diminished. Second, and as the senior management team explained to me, telephone agents are not permanently assigned to a specific team, campaign or department but tend to be rotated as part of further training. Third, it is company policy that the agent who takes the call has to deal with the (prospective) client's request even when the latter formulates a switchboard request, in the first topic slot, to speak to a given agent. The reason for this procedure is that clients' details, including notes on their preferences as well as on previous conversations, are entered into the system. Thus, agents who answer a (follow-up) call by (prospective) clients can access the original telephone agent's notes on the call, as well as general information on the client. They are, therefore, at least in theory, fully equipped to deal with the caller's query or request.

Further evidence of the institutional footing (Goffman 1979) adopted by the call-takers is the inclusion of an offer of assistance which underlies their role as service providers and positions the callers as service seekers. With the exception of Excerpts 3 above and 6 below, where an offer of assistance is not provided immediately after the proffering of self-identification, in the other extracts provided so far the agents proffered an offer of assistance immediately after self-identifying and without a detectable micro-pause. Offers of assistance were observed in 33 out of 36 openings.

Excerpt 6 [13:6]
```
1    A:    Vacaciones Inolvidables buenas tardes(.)habla Juan
2          Pablo Robles,
           Holidays to Remember good afternoon(.) Juan Pablo Robles
           speaking,
           (0.3)
3    C:    Mira: es que eh: para averiguar una cosa,
           Lookᵀ: the thing is: I need to ask about something ,
```

Despite the semantic difference between self-identification and an offer of assistance, these two components are realised together phonetically, as if to say, this is who I am and I am telling you this as a way of assisting you with your request for service. Offers of assistance are the last element of the agents' first turn. Their presence reiterates the institutional character of the call and of the number and emphasises the telephone agents' incipient recipiency. Offers of assistance also signal that it is assumed that those who telephone the number are not doing so for conversational purposes but are in search of help, the kind of help that is related to the business already announced by the offering of organisational identification. They help to underline the telephone agents' role as service provider rather than mere gatekeeper (Goffman 1974).

In short, with the summons answer, the telephone agents perform various communicative tasks. They convey that the channel of communication is open, inform the callers of the institution that has been reached, identify themselves as institutional agents and express incipient recipiency. The principal difference observed in the construction of the agents' routinised summons answer is the presence, or absence, of a lexical greeting and, to a lesser extent, the absence of an offer of assistance. It will be recalled that while offers of assistance are recommended by the company, greetings are not.

Recognition and the reason for the call
The reason for the call was usually presented in the first topic slot, that is, in the callers' first turn (second turn of the call) after the summons answer and identification. However, in many calls, a greeting sequence followed the summons-answer and identification sequences and preceded the reason for the call. In these telephone conversations, the reason for the call was offered in the callers' second turn, that is, the third turn of the call. Thus, the main difference observed in the sequential placement of the proffering of the reason

for the call by the (prospective) clients was the presence, or absence, of a greeting exchange beforehand.

In the majority of the calls, (prospective) clients responded to the agents' first turns by providing a greeting. Specifically, the clients' first turns were constructed in three ways: by launching into the reason for the call immediately after having displayed recognition that they had connected to the right number and reciprocated the agents' greeting (15 out of 36); by initiating a greeting exchange after displaying recognition and before announcing the reason for the call (13 out of 36); and by announcing the reason for the call after displaying recognition (8 out of 36).

In most calls, 28 out of 36, (prospective) clients conveyed recognition of having reached the right organisation by means of speech particles such as *sí* ('yes') or discourse markers such as *mirá* ('look$^{T/V}$') and by including a lexical greeting before proceeding to the reason for the call, as illustrated at line 3 in both Excerpts 7 and 8. These were given above as Excerpts 2 and 4 and are reproduced here as 7 and 8 respectively.

Excerpt 7 [2:4]

```
1    A:    Vacaciones Inolvidables buenas tardes(.) mi
2          nombre es Liliana >en qué lo puedo ayudar<,
           Holidays to Remember good afternoon (.) my name is
           Liliana >how can I help youᵛ<,
3    C:    Sí: mirá buenas tardes(.) e::mm yo quería hacerte
4          la siguiente consulta,=
           Yes: lookᵀ/ᵛ good afternoon(.) u:m I wanted to ask youᵀ/ᵛ
           the following question,=
```

Excerpt 8 [10:6]

```
1    A:    Gracias por comunicarse con Vacaciones
2          Inolvidables Latinoamérica (.)
           mi nombre es Jimena >en qué le puedo ayudar<?
           Thank you for calling Holidays to Remember Latin
           America(.)>my name is Jimena how can I help youᵛ<?
3    C:    Sí:: buenas tardes, (.) mire e:::h la molesto:
4          mmm: el tema es el siguiente.
           Yes:: good afternoon, (.) lookᵛ sorry to bother you:ᵛ
           mmm: the thing is.
5    A:    Sí.
           Yes.
```

Out of 36 second turns, 8 did not contain a lexical greeting as part of the recognition display. Instead, after displaying recognition, callers launched into the reason for the call, as illustrated at line 3 in Excerpt 9 (given above as Excerpt 6, and repeated below).

Excerpt 9 [13:6]

```
1   A:   Vacaciones Inolvidables buenas tardes (.)habla
2        Juan Pablo Robles,
         Holidays to Remember good afternoon (.) Juan Pablo
         Robles speaking,
         (0.3)
3   C:   Mira: es que eh: para averiguar una cosa,
         Look^{T/V}: the thing is is: I need to ask about something ,
```

The data show that (prospective) clients display recognition that they are connected to the right institution by uttering:

1. speech particles such as *ah sí* ('oh yes'), *sí* ('yes');
2. conversational tokens which are normally associated with the answer to a telephone summons such as *aló* ('hello'), *hola* ('hello/hi'), *buenos días/tardes* ('good morning/afternoon');
3. titles such as *señorita* ('Miss') and *Don/ña* (respectful 'Mr/Mrs') often followed by the first name of the agent, *Don Juan Carlos* ('Mr Juan Carlos'), or simply the first name of the agent, *Patricia* (Patricia);
4. any combination of (1), (2) and (3), as in, *Sí Patricia* ('Yes Patricia)*, Hola Juana* ('Hello Juana').

In initial position, the above serve to acknowledge that the caller has connected to the right institution. They also help to confirm that there are no problems with the channel of communication, that is, that the callers can hear the call-takers, and signal an ensuing turn. The uttering of titles, such as *señorita* ('Miss'), *Don/ña* (respectful 'Mr/Mrs') or the agent's first name, as (one of) the first things that the callers says, signals that they are connected to the right organisation in as much as they have identified the call-takers as agents of that organisation.

As far as greetings are concerned, Excerpts 2–5 illustrate their occurrence as among the first words uttered by clients. However, a closer look at these examples indicates that not all of them necessarily trigger a second pair part. In Excerpt 2, the presence of the first pair part of a greeting as part of the agent's answer to the summons may have prompted the inclusion of *buenas tardes* ('good afternoon') after the recognition display formulated by affirmative particle *sí* ('yes') and the attention getter *mirá* ('look^v'). In this example, the caller produces a micro-pause after the greeting. In doing so, he or she indicates the completion of the turn-constructional unit in progress. This, then, offers the participants the following conversational possibilities. Given that the production of a micro-pause signals potential transition to the next speaker, at this juncture, the agent can now offer another greeting token, confirm that she is still on line, or interpret the micro-pause as signalling an ensuing turn by the caller and thus say nothing. I argue that she does the last of these, given that the second pair part of the greeting is preceded by a discourse marker, *mirá* ('look^v'), which creates in the agent the expectation of something more to come, and the micro-pause is hearable but not interpreted as silence owing to its brevity – less than 0.2 seconds – among other things.

Lexical greetings, such as, *hola, buenas días/tardes* ('hello/hi', 'good morning/afternoon'), also appear in initial position in calls in which the agents had not offered a greeting in their first turns or a response in their second turns (third turn of the calls); see, respectively, Excerpts 4 and 5 above. In Excerpt 4, reproduced below as 10, recognition is conveyed through the affirmative particle *sí* ('yes'), followed by a neutral/respectful greeting *buenas tardes* ('good afternoon').

Excerpt 10 [10:6]

```
1    A:   Gracias por comunicarse con Vacaciones
2         Inolvidables Latinoamérica (.)
          mi nombre es Jimena >en qué le puedo ayudar<?
          Thank you for calling Holidays to Remember Latin America
          (.)
          >my name is Jimena how can I help you^v<?
3    C:   Sí:: buenas tardes, (.) mire e:::h la molesto:mmm:
4         el tema es el siguiente.
          Yes:: good afternoon, (.) look^v um sorry to bother you :
          the thing is.
5    A:   Sí.
          Yes.
```

In Excerpt 5, reproduced below as 11, the caller displays recognition by uttering *hola* ('hello'), followed by the agent's first name and the discourse marker *sabés que* ('you know$^{T/V}$ what'), after which a micro-pause is produced.

Excerpt 11 [12:11]

```
1    A:   Gracias por llamar a Vacaciones Inolvidables (.)
2         soy Laura en qué puedo ayudar,
          Thank you for calling Holidays to Remember (.) I'm
          Laura how can I help you,
3    C:   H-o::la Laura.sabés qué,(.) e::h yo necesito e::h:
4         tomar una semana en (sitio) con (nombre de la
5         empresa),te doy el número de socio?
          H-e::llo Laura you know^{T/V} what,(.) um I need u:m: to take
          a week in (place) with (company's name),
          shall I give^{T/V} you the membership number?
6    A:   Sí.
          Yes.
```

The initial positioning of *hola* ('hello'), the semantic meaning of the discourse marker *sabés que* ('you know^{T/V} what') and the micro-pause which follows immediately all combine to indicate that the caller will hold the floor and, in line with other calls, announce the reason for the call. In this environment, therefore, there is no place for the agent to return the greeting, as *hola* ('hello') serves mainly to display recognition of having connected to the right organisation. Furthermore, the fact that it was followed by the agent's name reinforces the display of organisational recognition by bringing to the fore the recognition of the call-taker as an agent of that particular institution.

The greetings volunteered by the callers in Excerpts 4 and 5, reproduced as 10 and 11 respectively, occurred as part of the recognition display in turns which were initiated by speech particles and discourse markers followed by a micro-pause, thus creating in the recipient the expectation that there is more to come. The agents may, therefore, have interpreted these greetings as a sign that the caller might have more to say. I argue that, in those cases where the telephone agents did not offer a greeting in their first turns but were, nonetheless, greeted by the clients, they did not reciprocate the greetings because they interpreted them as serving mainly to display recognition and as signalling that the caller was about to explain the reason for the call. In sum, where greetings were part of the recognition display in turns initiated with particles or markers which index further talk, agents did not offer a second pair part.

On the other hand, in 13 out of the 36 calls, agents returned the greeting. In these calls, a greeting was offered by the callers after they displayed recognition and either produced a pause (see line 4 in Excerpt 12) or triggered a greeting return through self-correction, as illustrated at line 2 in Excerpt 13. In these calls, greetings were not followed by discourse markers, such as *sabés que* ('you know what') and *mirá* ('look'), which may indicate that the caller has something else to say. They were, however, followed by a pause (Excerpt 12) and by self-correction (Excerpt 13), thus making a response relevant.

Excerpt 12 [10:1]

```
1    A:    Gracias por comunicarse con Vacaciones
2          Inolvidables (.) mi nombre es Juana en qué lo
3          puedo ayudar,
           Thank you for calling Holidays to Remember (.) my name
           is Juana how can I help you",
4    C:    Sí:::buenos días.
           Yes::: good morning.
           (0.3)
5    A:    Buenos días.
           Good morning.
6    C:    E::h: ustedes en lo que es alojamiento, tienen
7          algo en Asia?
```

U::m: in terms of accommodation, do you have anything in Asia?

Excerpt 13 [9:5]

```
1    A:   >Vacaciones Inolvidables Latinoamérica buen
2         día<(.)>habla Juan Carlos Peña en qué le puedo
3         colaborar<,
          >Holidays to Remember Latin America good morning<  (.)
          >Juan Carlos Peña speaking,<
4    C:   Aló. buenas tardes,=buenos días,
          Hello. good afternoon,= good morning,
5    A:   Buen día,
          Good morning,
6    C:   E::h: mire disculpe (.) yo lo estoy llamando por
7         lo siguiente. Yo tengo una semana programada,
          U::m: look⁰ sorry to bother you⁰ (.) I'm calling you⁰
          about the following. I have booked a week,
```

In sum, greeting exchanges are present in the openings of these calls when greeting tokens, *hola, buenas, buenos días/tardes,* are produced by callers in their first turns, which are the second turns of the calls, and are heard as primarily functioning as greetings rather than primarily serving other functions, such as displaying recognition or indexing an ensuing action or doing both. Although all the openings contain at least one first pair part of a greeting exchange, the agents returned greetings when the first pair part was formulated after a potential transitional place, regardless of which conversational participant proffered it. The transitional places in these calls were marked by the presence of a pause or by the repetition of the lexical greeting after which a micro-pause was produced. In these cases, rather than wait for the caller to offer the reason for the call (pre-request for service), the telephone agents returned the greeting, and only then was the first topic slot achieved. That the presence of first pair part greetings does not always trigger a second pair part by the callers or the call-takers suggests that they are not, strictly speaking, essential elements for the opening to be achieved. In spite of this, greeting exchanges occur in both calls where a first pair part was not offered by the call-taker and in those where a greeting was proffered.

In the light of the above, we should ask ourselves what motivates the agents to reiterate a greeting. A possible answer could reside in the fact that the first greeting token forms part of the answer to the summons. It is thus formulated in 'automated' mode in the same standard way in which other calls may be answered. On the other hand, the agent's second greeting token responds to the contingencies of the call in question, to the marking of a transition relevance place in the client's first turn after the recognition display. This being the case, the client proffers what counts as the first pair part of a greeting, and a lack of response would make the agent's reaction accountable and normatively sanctionable, at least as far as politeness is considered.

While the above discussion has sufficed to account for the presence and absence of greeting exchanges, it has not explained the presence of greeting tokens in the agents' first turns; although it has been noted that they are not, strictly speaking, essential for the opening to unfold. The presence of greeting tokens and greeting sequences, even though they are not institutionally prescribed, responds to the exigencies of the social institution of Spanish v. English business talk. The analysis of the outbound calls placed at (prospective) clients' places of work shows that the standard business practice in Latin America, at least in the various organisations which received calls from *Vacaciones Inolvidables* ('Holidays to Remember'), is to respond to the telephone summons by offering organisational identification, followed by a neutral-respectful greeting, *buenos días/tardes* ('good morning/afternoon').

Divergent cases

Three of the openings exhibited a how-are-you sequence, initiated by the callers, before they launched into the reason for the call, as illustrated at line 4 in Excerpt 14.

Excerpt 14 [10:5]

```
1    A:    Gracias por comunicarse con Vacaciones
2          Inolvidables (.)mi nombre es Juana >en qué le
3          puedo ayudar<,
           Thank you for calling Holidays to Remember (.)my name is
           Juana >how can I help youᵛ<,
4    C:    E::h : qué tal Juana?
           Um: how are you Juana?
5    A:    Sí.
           Yes.
6    C:    buenos días.=buenas tardes.
           Good morning.=good afternoon.
7    A:    buenas tardes=
           Good afternoon=
8    C:    =Mirá yo te llamo::,(.) mi nombre es Rosa
9          Rodríguez mi esposo es Juan Rodríguez,
           =Lookᵀ/ᵛ I am calling you::ᵀ/ᵛ,(.) my name is Rosa
           Rodríguez mi husband is Juan Rodríguez ,=
10   A:    =Sí.
           =Yes.
11   C:    nosotros ahora estamos en este mo[mento::]
           we are at the mo                 [ment]
12   A:                                      [Sí]
                                             [Yes]
```

```
13   C:   en un condomino en Villa Pre[ciosa],
          in a condo in Villa Pre      [ciosa],
14   A:                                [Sí.]
                                       [Yes.]
15   C:   que ustedes me vendieron a mí po:- por teléfono,
16        yo lo acepté y todo lo de[más],
          that you sold me ov:-: over the phone, I
          accepted and everything el[se]
17   A:                               [Sí.]
                                      [Yes.]
18   C:   e:::h bueno yo: no estoy conforme con este
19        condominio. quisiera saber cuál es el criterio por
20        el cual nos adjudicaro::n la unidad que tenemos y
21        de[más],
          u::m well I: am not happy with the condo. I want to know
          what the criterion is, for allocating the unit we've got
          and [so on ],
22   A:       [bien.]
              [okay.]
```

The organisation of the call in Excerpt 14 accounts for three calls in which a how-are-you sequence was observed, prior to the proffering of the first topic slot by the caller. At the organisational level, the first three components of the agent's first turn are the same as those identified in the rest of the calls (organisational identification, self-identification and an offer of assistance), and the first component of the client's first turn, in line with the calls examined so far, also serves to display recognition. However, in this call, after the uttering of the speech particle *Eh* ('Um'), through which the caller displays recognition and signals that something else is to come, she offers the first pair part of a how-are-you followed by the agent's name, as in, *qué tal Juana* ('how are you Juana'). The agent takes this up; however, instead of offering a second pair part of a 'how-are-you' exchange which would help to co-construct the call as (temporarily) conversational, she repositions the call as institutional by uttering the affirmative particle *sí* ('yes'). In doing so, she makes way for the client to offer the reason for the call, and thus tries to reconstruct the anchor position. The client, nevertheless, proffers the first pair part of a greeting, followed by immediate self-correction and emphasis on its second compound (line 6). This, in turn, triggers a second pair part of a greeting by the agent (line 7). The three calls in the inbound database where how-are-yous were observed were all complaints. The presence of this sequence, thus, suggests that the reason why the client is calling is not for normal business purposes, as noted by Tracy and Agne (2002) in calls to the police. Rather, its presence is in line with the results of studies into non-emergency service calls in Montevidean Spanish (Márquez Reiter 2005, 2006), where the sequence was found to be non-canonical and its deployment indicative of synthetic person-alisation (Fairclough 1989) in order to obtain a better service. I will return to this when examining the incidence of 'how-are-yous' in the outbound calls.

In 5 out of the 15 calls in which callers displayed recognition and recipro-cated the agent's greeting, clients self-identified as members of the organisa-tion before they launched into the reason for the call. Three out of the five calls where client self-identification was observed were complaint calls. In these three telephone conversations, the clients self-identified after a failed attempt to obtain a second pair part of a how-are-you exchange and before offering the reason for the call, as illustrated at lines 8–9 in Excerpt 14 above. The other two calls where clients self-identified show that the client has a clear understanding of how the system works. Specifically, experi-enced clients know that the telephone agents cannot give them an informed response or a full service unless they know the kind of membership the clients have got, as shown in Excerpts 14 above and 15 below, where the client is seeking accommodation at a specific hotel, which he knows is part of the *Vacaciones Inolvidables* ('Holidays to Remember') portfolio.

Excerpt 15 [13:4]
```
1   A:    Gracias por llamar a Vacaciones Inolvidables
2         Latinoamérica (.)
3         habla Luisa >en qué le puedo ayudar<,
          Thank you for calling Holidays to Remember
          Latin America (.)
          Luisa speaking >how can I help youᵛ,<
4   C:    Doña Luisa buena::s.= Buenos días.(.) le habla:
5         Diego Pérez (.) yo soy:: e::h cliente de ustedes.
6         (.) soy socio de ustedes.(.) necesitamos una
7         reservación para el Hotel Villa Bonita,
          Doña Luisa morning.= good morning. (.) This is Diego Pérez
          speaking:ᵛ (.) I am um a client of yours.(.) I am a member.
          (.) we need a reservation at the Villa Bonita Hotel,
```

In sum, the analysis presented so far indicates that the only essential sequences in these openings are the summons answer and identification–recognition and that, as one would expect in business calls, these naturally precede the first topic slot. The task of identification and recognition was principally realised by the offering of organisational identification, and of confirmation by the callers that they had reached the right destination. In spite of the fact that greetings are not part of the house-style rules, they usually followed organisational identification, after which a micro-pause was observed, thus indicating a potential relevance place and making the next turn-constructional unit contingent upon caller uptake. Greeting exchanges have been shown to be contingent upon the intricacies of the specific calls. It is in this sense that I argue that organisational identification and its recognition are, strictly speaking, the only essential elements needed for the opening to be achieved structurally. The predominance, observed in the corpus, of greetings after the proffering of organisational identification without a detectable micro-pause, and without any cases of overlap, may find a potential explanation in the politeness norms observed by non-Western businesses. As we will see in the analysis of the outbound calls made to (prospective) clients at work, the summons in these calls, in contrast to those made to clients' home numbers, comprises a neutral-formal greeting, *buenos días/ buenas tardes* ('good morning/good afternoon').

The high incidence of offers of assistance immediately after the proffering of self-identification might possibly be explained by the fact that they are part of the house-style rules, as they indicate institutionality and incipient recipiency. The offering of a personal name by the agent is not intended to elicit some sort of personal recognition by the answerer but is to be seen, together with the proffering of an offer of assistance, as organisational identification and a greeting, as 'part of a stream of talk providing who it is that is calling in a nevertheless institutional or organisational capacity' (Maynard and Schaeffer 1997: 47).

3.3 Outbound calls

In line with the examination of the openings of inbound calls, I start this section with a discussion of the in-house rules for placing calls. This is supplemented with information gathered from the interviews conducted with the telephone agents and with my notes from the non-participant observation. After this, I provide an analysis of the elements found in the openings of these calls.

3.3.1 In-house rules for opening outbound calls

Prior to making a call, telephone agents are told to check the system for any information that may be stored about the (prospective) client. This information will typically consist of previous holidays booked with the company, reactions to the company's special offers, account balance and so on. The agents are also told to think about what they want to achieve from the call before placing it. They are asked to reflect upon the main purpose of the call. For example, do they want the clients to: renew their membership; confirm a two-week holiday in Florida; exchange their one-week holiday in Florida for one week in Brazil; or do all three? If it is the last option, how do these objectives rank in terms of benefits to the company?

The strategic nature of the calls is thus made evident in the advice given to the agents before they place their calls. They are told to follow their sales agenda virtually irrespectively of whether or not the (prospective) client is interested in any of the company's products. This is especially true in first-attempt and follow-up calls. Broadly speaking, there are three types of outbound calls: first-attempt calls, call-backs and follow-up calls (see also Chapter 4, Section 4.3). First-attempt calls, as indicated by their name, are those calls in which an existing client, or a client whose membership has lapsed (for a long time), are contacted for the first time with regard to the selling of a particular holiday product, including membership renewal. Call-backs are ring-back calls which generally take place immediately after a first-attempt call has been made. In call-backs, the agents telephone (prospective) clients again to provide further information on a particular product, to enquire about what decision has been taken after the (prospective) client has had a chance to talk it over with (a member of) the family and so on. Thus, call-backs are generally made by the same agent who placed the first call and typically take place within the same day or week. Follow-up calls, on the other hand, are not always made by the agent who placed the first call. In these calls, an arrangement, typically during the closing sequence of the calls, had been made between the parties for the agent to ring back at a particular time, at which point a decision should have been reached. The date when the (prospective) client has to be telephoned again is entered into the system so that it falls to the agent whose shift coincides with the scheduled telephone call to telephone the (prospective) client to follow up the sale.

With the exception of call-backs and those follow-up calls in which the (prospective) client has genuinely requested to be called again at a specific time, arrangements are initiated by the agent to agree a next encounter (see Chapter 5, Section 5.3.1). Outbound calls share a number of features with telesales calls. First, they are unsolicited. As such, the agents have to face up to the fact that the (prospective) clients may not wish to talk to them. This may not necessarily be because the call was made at an inopportune time for the called[5] but, in some cases, because the called may not wish to talk to the agent at all. Had they been interested in talking to the company, they would have telephoned the company directly. It is thus not surprising to encounter some resistance from the (prospective) clients. There is, however, an important difference between these calls and the (random) telesales calls one might receive from companies which offer services or products one has never used. In the case of the calls I examine here, at some point in the past, a business relationship, no matter how temporary, had existed between the caller (the institution on whose behalf the call is being made) and the called (an existing client or a client who is no longer affiliated to the institution). This, in turn, might help to explain the reason why the corpus does not contain any calls in which the call-takers, who could be either mere answerers or the called themselves, hang up on the caller. It follows, therefore, that, first-attempt calls and many of the follow-up calls, although unsolicited, are not necessarily unwarranted or

Stage 1
Greet the person and identify yourself as an agent of *Vacaciones Inolvidables* (First Name and Surname):
Buen día, mi nombre es (Nombre y Apellido), y le estoy llamando de Vacaciones Inolvidables Latinoamérica, su empresa vacacional
'Good morning, my name is (First Name and Surname), and I am calling you[U] from Holidays to Remember Latin America, your holiday company'

Stage 2
Explain the reason for your call:
Le estoy llamando porque tenemos una promoción especialmente para usted...
'I am calling you[U] because we have a special offer which is just right for you[U] ...'

Stage 3
Verify the client's interest:
Es interesante ¿cierto?, suena atractivo ¿verdad?
'It is interesting, isn't it?, it sounds attractive, doesn't it?

Stage 4
Ask permission to continue

Figure 3.2 In-house rules for the opening of outbound calls

totally unexpected, as the called have previously volunteered their personal details and preferences to the institution. Figure 3.2 illustrates the recommended initial steps that the telephone agents need to follow when placing an outbound call.

Despite the fact that the in-house rules for the opening of outbound calls clearly stipulate that the agents should greet the answerer and provide both self- and organisational identification at the beginning of the calls, the agents deploy particular manoeuvres to delay the provision of identification in the pursuit of their own agendas. One of these is to flout the recommended script by omitting any form of identification until it is absolutely necessary. Instead, the agents' first efforts are aimed at identifying the answerer and thus at establishing early on in the conversation whether or not they are the right person to talk to before starting the sales pitch. Another possible reason behind this particular strategy is to minimise the chances of an early declination (see Maynard and Schaeffer 1997).

That this is not an everyday call can be inferred as soon as the respectful greeting *Buenos días* ('Good morning') is heard. People we are familiar with do not tend to offer such greetings to confirm that the channel of communication is open and that they can hear us. Furthermore, as soon as the answerers, who may or may not be the called (Sacks 1992), hear the caller self-identifying or providing organisational identification, they will know that the call is not mundane and are likely to infer that the caller wants to sell them something. Provided that the answerers are the called and in the event that they are not interested in buying anything or in engaging in the call, they can, at this juncture, offer an early declination.

The company's script stipulates that the reason for the call should be given immediately after greeting the (prospective) clients and offering identification; presumably, although this is not specifically stated, this should occur after the call-taker has provided an answer to the summons. In this sense, the greeting is primarily intended to provide confirmation that the channel of communication is open. As we will see in the analysis of the calls, this is also flouted by the agents, who tend to engage in talk reminiscent of everyday interaction before launching into the reason for the call. It is interesting to note that the sales nature of the call is clearly encapsulated in the recommended formulation of the reason for the call: the company has a special offer tailored specifically to the (prospective) client's needs. Besides the potential financial enticement of the *promoción* ('special offer') and personalisation of the offer *especialmente para usted* ('just right for you[U]'), the implication of such a formulation means that the agent, as a representative of the institution, not only knows but also bears in mind the (prospective) client's interests. Added to this, the agents are told to check that the (prospective) client is in fact interested in the special offer before proceeding with the call. They are specifically told to request permission to continue with the call. Such institutional thoughtfulness stands in stark contrast to what happens in practice and, for that matter, to the advice given to the agents prior to making calls. That these rules are strategically ignored also confirms, albeit implicitly, the difficulties in demonstrating, at the interactional level, that the regulation of talk affects its construction. In the words of an agent:

> *Los pasos a seguir no los puedes pues seguir. Primero porque no hay tiempo y segundo porque¿ a quién se le ocurre mostrar todas las cartas en el primer juego?*

> The steps to be followed cannot be followed. First because there is no time and second because who would ever dream of showing his hand at start of play?

And in the words of another:

> *Con un poco de simpatía y picardía los mantienes un rato en línea cosa de que les sea difícil cortarte*

> With a bit of friendliness and craftiness you keep them on the line for a while so that it is more difficult for them to hang up on you.

The recommended steps for opening an outbound call are typically ignored by agents in as much as adherence to the rules would imply 'losing the round

or the whole game' and this, in turn, might result in poor employee performance and the risk of job losses. It would seem that the conversational footings (Goffman 1979) commonly found prior to the reason for the call, as in
everyday enquiries, may also be a manoeuvre to keep the client on the line
by showing *simpatía* ('friendliness') and *picardía* ('cunning or craftiness'). An
expression of *simpatía* is the presence of initial, everyday enquiries initiated
by the agent, and *picardía* is observed in the agent's knowledge of public holidays and other relevant cultural information related to the client's country
(see Márquez Reiter 2010). This type of information allows the agents to telephone the clients at a time when they are likely to be at home; this, then, max-
imises their chances of talking to the right person. *Picardía* is also observed
in the way agents formulate their requests to speak to the (prospective) client
(see Section 3.3.2 below).[4]

On the one hand, it might be less problematic to talk about the regulation
of talk as applied to the first turns of inbound calls, and about how this, in
turn, shapes the answerer's response and possibly subsequent streams of talk.
On the other, however, it would seem that the interactions displayed in the
outbound calls so far are, right from the start, subject to the independent
actions of both agents and clients.

3.3.2 Opening sequences in outbound calls

The database consists of 95 outbound calls, and these generated about 11
hours of recorded telephone conversations made to the (prospective) clients.
The median call length is 25 minutes, 5 minutes longer than that of inbound
calls. The calls were randomly recorded by the company and transcribed in
the same way as the inbound calls. The calls were made by 34 telephone
agents to (prospective) Argentinean, Chilean, Colombian, Mexican and
Venezuelan clients. The agents recorded in these calls are not the same as
those who answered the inbound calls examined above. They came from
Argentina, Colombia and Uruguay. Given the number of calls and the fact
that they were made and answered by a variety of conversational participants, the patterns observed cannot necessarily be attributed to the personal
style of any of the participants.

Before I start the sequential analysis of these calls, it is apposite to mention
that, despite clients' repeated expressions of their lack of interest in the
product being offered, the database does not contain any calls in which
the (prospective) clients put the telephone down on the agents. In the same
vein, the database does not contain any calls in which the agents offer some
sort of identification, either organisational or personal, or, for that matter,
announce the reason for the call before they ensure that they are talking to
the right person. Likewise, there are no instances of requests for permission
to continue with the calls, as recommended in the house-style rules. Instead,
the agents' first efforts are directed at guaranteeing that they are talking to the

right person or that they will be connected to that person as soon as possible. The reason for this resides in the fact that, from the company's perspective, the client is the account holder and the only one who has authority over the account. They consider this to be the case even when, in practice, it is another member of the family who decides the family's holiday fortunes or even when the service is paid for by the account holder but used by someone else. Given the pressure that call centre agents are under to answer, or make, as many calls as possible in the shortest time possible, it makes sense for them to ensure early connection with the (prospective) client, that is, with the (prospective) account holder.

The summons answer
All the calls, regardless of whether they are first-attempt calls, call-backs or follow-up calls, start with an answer to the summons by the person who picks up the telephone and a confirmation by the caller, in this case the agent, that the channel of communication is open. In Mexican and in Peninsular Spanish *bueno* ('well') and *diga(me)* ('tell^U'/'tell^U me') respectively are normally used to answer mundane telephone summons; in Colombian and to a lesser extent in Venezuelan Spanish, as the conversational excerpts of this section demonstrate, *aló* ('*alo*' from French) is usually deployed. Given that none of these verbal tokens is recognisable as a greeting, they serve only to provide an answer to the summons. Put differently, these varieties of Spanish have a summons-specific formulation which prevents potential sequence interlocking at this stage of the conversation. However, in other varieties of Spanish, such as Argentinean and Uruguayan Spanish, the answer to the summons is formulated by the immediately recognisable everyday greeting *hola*. Excerpt 16, a conversation between a Montevidean couple,[6] illustrates the potential for interlocking that *hola* can have.

Excerpt 16 (C = caller, R= call recipient, landline call)

```
1    R:    Hola
           Hello
2    C:    Juan?
           Juan?
3    R:    Sí. qué pasa,
           Yes. What's up,
4          (0.3)
5    C:    Veo que te agarré en un mal momento porque ni
6          saludás
           I see that I caught you^T/v at a bad time because you^T/v
           don't even greet me
7    R:    Y al atender qué hice?
           And what did I do when I picked up the phone?
8          (0.2)
```

```
 9   C:    Quería saber si vamos a llevar algo para el
10         postre, (.) o si te parece mejor hacer unas
11         ensaladas, para el asado.
```
I wanted to know if we are going to take something for
dessert, (.) or if you$^{T/V}$ think it's better to make some
salads, to go with the meat

After the call recipient had confirmed his identity and recognised the
caller by her voice (*Sí*, 'Yes'), instead of proffering a greeting or engaging in
a how-are-you sequence by offering a first pair part, he asked for the reason
for the call (*qué pasa*, 'what's up'). The expectation of a greeting or a how-
are-you at this stage of the call was made relevant by the caller's dispreferred
response (*veo que te agarré en un mal momento porque ni saludás*, 'I see that I
caught you$^{T/V}$ at a bad time because you$^{T/V}$ don't even greet me') following a
0.3-second pause. The caller explicitly verbalises her expectations: to receive
a greeting after being recognised, or a greeting as a form of recognition (line
5). The call recipient, however, claimed that he had done so when answering
the telephone with yet another meta-pragmatic comment (line 7). In uttering
y al atender qué hice? ('and what did I do when I picked up the phone?'), he
spells out one of the potential communicative functions of *hola* ('hello/hi') in
the first turn. Although competent native speakers of the language will know
that *hola* ('hello/hi') at line 1 is, mainly because of its sequential placement,
not a greeting but the answer to the summons, its semantic meaning allows
the call recipient to get away with not providing a greeting and asserting that
he did in fact greet the caller. Thus, in producing *hola* ('hello/hi'), he could
have potentially executed simultaneously an answer to the summons and the
first pair part of the next sequence; in this case, a greeting or a 'how-are-you',
given that they serve both as recognition of the call recipient and as ratified
participation (Goffman 1967).

In those cases where agents telephone the (prospective) clients at work,
the answer to the summons is formulated by the proffering of organisational
identification, followed by a neutral/respectful greeting (see Excerpts 20 and
21 on p. 70, and Excerpt 24 on pp. 74–5). Out of the 95 outbound calls, 36
were made to clients' work numbers. These included calls to Argentinean,
Chilean, Colombian, Mexican and Venezuelan companies. That organisational identification and a greeting were offered indicates that incoming
calls to that number and the actual telephone number are both treated as
institutional. The presence of greetings provides further evidence of the
importance attached to them in Spanish. Additionally, the data show that
institutional answers to summons do not normally contain some of the
turn-construction units, such as self-identification and an offer of assistance,
deployed in English non-mundane calls or recommended by the company
to personalise the call right from the start. Instead, these answers comprise
organisational identification and a neutral-respectful greeting.[7] This, in

turn, provides support for the claim that at least the first turn of inbound calls examined here is a result of the regulation of talk. Immediately after the answer to the summons, participants confirm whether or not the channel is open.

Confirmation that the channel is open and that the caller can hear the answerer is expressed with devices similar to those deployed to display recognition in the inbound calls. Specifically, callers show that the communication channel is fully open through the affirmative particle *sí* (line 2 in Excerpt 19 on p. 69), through conversational tokens normally associated with the answer to a telephone summons, such as *hola, aló* (line 2 in Excerpt 18 on p. 67 and in Excerpt 20 on p. 70), *buenos días/buenas tardes* (line 2 in Excerpt 21 on pp. 70–1), or a combination of these (line 4 in Excerpt 18 below). Once it has been established that the channel is open, the agents, without fail in all 95 calls, either request to speak to the (prospective) account holder or client, or attempt to establish whether the answerer is in fact the (prospective) client or account holder, that is, the called.

At this juncture, it is important to point out that the meta-data on the calls include, among other things, their duration and the agent's call centre identification number. However, it does not specify whether the agent called the client's landline number (home or work) or the client's mobile telephone. In the case of landline calls, whether the agent telephoned the client at work or at home becomes immediately clear by the way in which the answerer constructs the first turn, that is, whether the summons answers are constructed as ordinary or as institutional, and by the fact that the call is usually answered by someone else, such as a receptionist or a secretary. Calls to mobile telephones are revealed as such only when the type of technology being used becomes obvious in the talk, as shown at line 16 in Excerpt 17.

Excerpt 17 [10:3] *Call-back* (T = telephone agent, A = answerer, C = called – mobile phone)

1	A:	Ho͟la.
		Hello
2	T:	Ho::::la. sí: señor Germán?
		He:::llo yes: Mr Germán?
3	C:	Él habla.
		Speaking
4	T:	Juana López de Vacaciones Inolvidables. cómo le
5		va? [hablamos-?]
		Juana López from Holidays to Remember: how are
		you[u]? [we spoke-?]
6	C:	[Juana.]
		[Juana.]
7	T:	Hablamos hoy en la tarde. Recu:erda?
		We spoke this afternoon. Reme:mber[u]?

8   C: Sí Juana. Te escucho.
           Yes Juana. I'm listening[T/V]
9   T: Bien. Le comento lo siguiente, usted tiene la mem-
10   la membresía vencida desde el mes de <u>septiembre</u>.
11   y usted hizo una confirmación para::: e:::h
12   noviembre. para fines de noviembre. Sí?
           OK. Let me put you in the picture. , Your[V] *mem- the*
           membership expired in the month of <u>September</u>. *And you*[V]
           made a booking for::: eh:: November. For the end of
           November. Right?
13   T: Perfecto.
14   Yo lo que necesito es que usted me pase. si no le
15   molesta. el número de tarjeta?
           Perfect.
           What I need is for you to give me. If youu don't mind.
           the credit card number?
16   C: Bueno. Estoy manejando, a ver si puedo hacerlo.
17   Esperá.
           Ok. I'm driving, Let's see if I can do it now. Hold on a
           minute.[T/V]

The database contains only three calls where it becomes evident, from the content of the talk, that the clients had been contacted on their mobile telephones. Consequently, any claims for the possible effects of the medium on the structure of the calls would be highly speculative. Given the lack of studies into mobile phone conversations in Spanish, however, it is interesting to note that, in all three calls, the answer to the summons was formulated in the same way as the answers found in calls to the clients' home numbers. They were not oriented to a personalised summons that conveys information about the person who is calling (see Arminen 2005b; Hutchby 2005; Hutchby and Barnett 2005; Arminen and Leinonen 2006). This, however, should not come as a surprise, given that calls from the company are displayed as private or unknown numbers, a technological advantage which is also shared by modern landline telephones. It is important to note that, after confirming that the channel of communication is open (*hola*, 'hello', in line 2), the agent proceeds to establish whether the answerer is indeed the called; once this is done, she offers identification.

Identification–recognition
In spite of the fact that the request to speak to the account holder is formulated by the agents at the earliest available opportunity, that is, immediately after confirming that the channel of communication is open, in only 25 out of the 95 calls was caller identification requested by the answerers before they (dis)confirmed their identity as the called. Of the 25 calls where the

caller's identification was requested before confirmation of the answerer's
identity was inferred, or given, 16 were answered by a third party, who then
either transferred the call to the called (Sacks 1992) or took a message. In
most cases, the answerers, whether they were the called or not, requested the
caller's identification after (dis)confirming their own telephone identity. The
data show that, in most telephone conversations where the answerer is the
called, self-identification is confirmed before checking the caller's identity, as
illustrated in Excerpt 18 below and in 19 on p. 69. Thus, unlike in the results
of studies conducted into similar types of calls (see Maynard and Schaeffer
1997 on telephone interviews), call recipients tend not to inspect the caller's
identity before allowing the call to proceed even in those calls which represent
first-attempt calls and are, thus, totally unexpected.

Excerpt 18 [5:6] *Call-back* (T = telephone agent, A = answerer, C = called)

```
1    A:    (  )
2    T:    Ho::la:
           He:llo:
3    A:    Sí.quién e:s?
           Yes who's speaking?
4    T:    Sí::? buenos días, con María Pretzi::?
           Yes::? good morning, with María Pretzi:?
5    C:    Sí sí. María Pre-María Gloria Pretzelli quié::n-
6          quién ha:bla?
           Yes yes. María Pre-María Gloria Pretzelli Wh::o-
           who is speaking?
7    T:    María le habla Silvia enton[ces de Vacaciones
8          Inolvidables.cómo está,]
           María Silvia speaking th       [en from Holidays to
           Remember. how are youᵛ,]
9    C:                                    [A::h, qué ta:l?]
                                           [Ah::, how are you?]
10   T:    Muy bien y[ uste::d María?]
           Very well and [youᵛ María?]
11   C:    Sí sí:. [Bien bien]Escuchemé, encontró algo de
12         Brasil?=
           Yes yes:. [fine fine] so tell me, did youᵛ find anything
           in Brasil?
```

Excerpt 18 is a call-back made four days after the first call had been placed,
as articulated later on in the conversation by the participants. At line 3, the
answerer requests the caller's identity, probably because she did not recognise
the caller on the basis of such a short voice sample or because her landline
displays the caller's number as undisclosed. Given the everyday nature of the
channel confirmation (line 2), it is possible that the answerer interpreted the

call, at least at this juncture, as mundane rather than institutional. She, thus, (re)confirms that the channel of communication is open via the uttering of *sí* ('yes') with a final intonation contour at line 3 and, having been unable to recognise the caller, requests the caller's identity. The agent then responds with the affirmative particle *sí* ('yes'), followed by a neutral or respectful greeting. In doing so, she acknowledges the answerer as a human being, as opposed to an answering machine, and constructs the call as institutional, as evidenced in the choice of greeting proffered. Contrary to the answerer's wishes and to the company's rules, however, instead of offering identification as explicitly requested by the answerer, the agent utters a request, which, at this stage of the conversation, may serve as a switchboard request to speak to the account holder or as a recognition attempt: *con María Pretzi::?* ('with María Pretzi?'). Its formulation – the client's first name followed by her surname – further sets the institutional tone of the encounter.

The request is elliptically constructed, with the verb being omitted. As a result, the request can mean either *¿Podría hablar con María Pretzi?* ('Could I speak to María Pretzi?') or *¿Hablo con María Pretzi?* ('I am speaking to María Pretzi?'). This type of elliptical formulation is a recurrent feature of the outbound calls, occurring in 81 out of the 95. For this reason, I shall devote some attention to it in the next few paragraphs.

The elliptical form of this request is revelatory of the working routine of the agents and is one of the manoeuvres they put in place to ensure communication with the right person. The form illustrates the routinised nature of the action it performs. It is also reminiscent of face-to-face service encounters in which the speaker has a high entitlement to the service requested; for instance, a parallel would be ordering a coffee at a coffee shop. It portrays the caller in her institutional role as a telephone agent, whose job is to speak to the (prospective) account holder in order to sell one of the company's products. The everyday nature of this duty, the frequency with which it is enacted, as in the volume of calls handled daily, and the fact that, at some point in the past, the (prospective) client gave the relevant personal details to the company all give the agent a certain entitlement, at least from the agent's perspective, to place the calls even when they are unsolicited. This is evidenced by the fact that the agents do not tend to modify the request to speak to the (prospective) client; for example, they do not use modality markers, such as *podría* ('could'), *quisiera* ('would'), which enquire about the answerer's ability or willingness to comply with the request. Nor do they, as we have seen above, include a verb to indicate the action intended. The elliptical formulation of their requests reflects the low contingency of the request being turned down (Curl and Drew 2008), at least at this juncture, where neither identification nor the reason for the call has been given.

Owing to its sequential placement, the elliptical form functions as a recognition attempt or a switchboard request. In those cases where gender reveals that the answerer cannot be the called, it serves as a switchboard request and, in those calls where the voice sample coincides with the gender of the account holder and the call is made to the account holder's home number or mobile phone, it may also function as a recognition attempt. The determinacy of one function over the other depends on the contingencies surrounding the call. Essentially, it depends on whether the answerer is the called or not. If the answerers are the called, they may or may not wish to confirm their identity before the callers discloses their identities. In those cases where the answerer is not the called but the called is in the immediate physical environment, the answerer may want to establish the extent to which the call may be of interest to the called; and whether or not the called may want to take the call. Thus, the resources of Spanish, in this case grammar and phonology, coupled with the contingencies of the talk itself, allow agents to hook their prey as quickly as possible. This, in turn, enables them to start the sales pitch promptly. The inclusion of *por favor* ('please') at the end of the request, as shown in Excerpt 19 , disambiguates its illocutionary force, reducing its potential meanings to just one: a switchboard request.

Excerpt 19 [1:7 *Call-back* (T = telephone agent, A = answerer, C = called)

1	A:	Aló.
		Hello.
2	T:	Sí:con el señor Ramiro Rodríguez, por favo:r?
		Yes: with Mr Ramiro Rodríguez ple:ase?
3	C:	Sí con él.=
		Yes speaking.=
4	T:	= A:h [señor]
		=Ah [Mr]
5	C:	= [Sí señor.]
		= [That's right.]
6	T:	Pedro de nuevo de Vacaciones Inolvidables (.) cómo
7		está usted,
		Pedro again from Holidays to Remember (.) how
		are you",
8	C:	Muy bien gracias (.) dígame
		Very well thanks (.) tell" me

The addition of the distinctive politeness marker *por favor* ('please') removes the utterance's ambiguity, with the result that it can be interpreted as a switchboard request, irrespective of the subsequent turns. Likewise, the inclusion of the main verb indicating the intended action, together with modality markers, would make it clear that the request in question is a conventionally indirect request (Márquez Reiter et al. 2005) to speak to the (prospective) client, as shown in Excerpt 20. It should be noted that the answerer in this excerpt is female and that the agent of this call wishes to speak to a male rather than to a female client. This, in turn, may help to explain the preference for a non-elliptical request.

Excerpt 20 [9:1] *First call* (T = telephone agent, A = answerer)

```
1   A:   (Nombre de la organización) buenas tardes
         (Name of the organization) good afternoon
2   T:   Aló::: buenas tardes. quisiera hablar con el señor
3        Vidal ()?
         Hello::: good afternoon. I would like to speak to Mr
         Vidal ()?
4   A:   No se encuentra. quién le llama,
         He is not in. who is calling ,
5   T:   A::::h no se encuentra,(.) le habla Luis Gómez de
6        Vacaciones Inolvidables Latinoamérica.
         A:::h he is not in,(.) it is Luis Gómez speaking from
         Holidays to Remember Latin America.
7   A:   A:::h. déjeme tomarle nota,sí? no se  [retire.]
         A:::h. letᵛ me write it down, sí? don'tᵛ  [hang up.]
8   T:                                         [No:::.] no
9        se preocupe.(.) no está?.
                                           [No:::.] don'tᵛ
         worry.(.) isn't he there? ?
```

While the inclusion of the politeness marker *por favor*, together with the main verb and the modality markers, reflect consideration for the answerer and the called, they leave the agent with fewer cards up his or her sleeve. If the answerer were in fact the called but did not wish to take the call, he could potentially adopt the identity of mere answerer and claim that the called was not available; at which point he could offer to pass on the message or simply put the telephone down. As explained earlier, however, there are no instances of such behaviour in the database. As fascinating a possibility as telephone identity impersonation may be, the data in this study, therefore, do not lend themselves to such scrutiny. What they can confidently tell us is that *por favor* was found in 4 out 95 calls, and conventionally indirect requests, like the one exhibited in Excerpt 20 above, in 10 out of 95 calls. Two of the calls where *por favor* occurred were placed to the (prospective) client's place of work; consequently, they were answered by a third party, typically the company's receptionist, as illustrated in Excerpts 20 above and 21 below.

Excerpt 21 [2:2] *Call-back* (T = telephone agent, A = answerer)

```
1   A:   (Nombre de la organización) Buen dí:a.
         (Name of the organization) good morni:ng.
2   T:   Bu= buenos días con el señor Santa María por
3        favo:r,
         Goo=good morning Mr Santa María plea:se,
4        (0.3)
```

```
5    A:    Discu:lpe?=
           Pardon"?⁼
6    T:    =Con el señor Santa María.
           = Mr Santa María.
7          (0.1)
8    A:    Momentito.
           Just a moment^DIM.
9          (0.3)
```

In Excerpts 20 and 21, it is immediately obvious that the answerers cannot be the called by virtue of their gender and of the fact that they are the company's telephone receptionists, a job that is unlikely to generate the income needed to enjoy the services of *Vacaciones Inolvidables* ('Holidays to Remember'). In Excerpt 21, after the original switchboard request (line 2), at the request of the answerer, the caller reformulates the switchboard request in his next turn (line 6), albeit this time without uttering *por favor* ('please'). This second request is elliptical and, owing to its sequential placement and to the contingencies of the talk, it can only be a switchboard request. The other two calls in which *por favor* ('please') was found were made by Colombian agents to the (prospective) client's home number, and in these two cases the gender of the answerer coincided with that of the called, as shown in Excerpt 22.

Excerpt 22 [2:3] *Follow-up call* (T = telephone agent, A = answerer, C = called)

```
1    A:    Aló.
           Hello.
2    T:    Buenas ta::rdes, (.) por favor la señora Vicky
3          Gonzále:z?
           Good afternoon, (.) Mrs Vicky
           González please?
4          (0.2)
5    C:    Ella habla::,
           Speaking::,
6    T:    A::h como e:stá, le habla el señor Pereira:::,
7          de:::Vacaciones Inolvidables.
           A::h how are you", Mr Pereira speaking,
           from Holidays to Remember.
8          (0.1)
9    C:    A:já::,
           M:m::
10   T:    Señora ayer. Vicky (la llamo con respecto) a una
11         solicitú: que habían hecho en el día de aye::r, (.)
12         con nosotros(h),y queríamos saber qué había
13         pensado:,
```

Ma'am yesterday. Vicky (called you[v] with respect) to a
request you had made yesterday morning, (.) with us, and
we wanted to know what you[v] had decided,

Interestingly, the 10 calls in which the switchboard request was formulated by means of conventional indirectness were also made by Colombian agents. Excerpt 23 is illustrative of this pattern. It may be that conventional indirectness is employed because the answerer is female and thus cannot possibly be the person to whom the agent wishes to talk; however, conventional indirectness was also employed when the answerer's gender coincided with that of the (prospective) client.

Excerpt 23 [9:1] *First call* (T = telephone agent, A = answerer)
```
1    A:    (  )  buenas  tardes,
           (  )  good afternoon,
2    T:    Aló:::  buenas  tardes.  quisiera  hablar  con  el  señor
3          Estefani,
           Hello::: good afternoon. I would like to speak to Mr
           Estefani,
4    A:    No  se  encuentra.  quién  le  llama?
           He is not in. who is calling ?
5    T:    A::::h  no  se  encuentra,(.)  le  habla  Luis  Lorenzo
6          de  Vacaciones  Inolvidables  Latinoamérica.
           A:::h he is not in,(.) it is Luis Lorenzo speaking from
           Holidays to Remember Latin America.
7    A:    A:::h.  déjeme  tomarle  nota,sí:  No  se  [retire.]
           A:::h.let[v] me write it down,sí: don't[v]      [ hang up.]
```

The orientation of the Colombian agents towards negative politeness (Brown and Levinson 1987), even at this early stage of the call, is in line with the results of the research carried out into their politeness behaviour (see, for example, Fitch 1991; Escamilla Morales et al. 2005) and coincides with the perceptions that non-Colombian call centre agents have of their northern neighbours. During the interviews, agents described the Colombian clientele, and in particular Bogotanos, as very formal. For the purpose of this chapter, it suffices to say that, irrespective of the ways in which requests to speak to the (prospective) clients, or requests to establish that the agents are connected to them, are formulated, they are produced at the first available opportunity in an attempt to start the sales pitch as soon as possible.

How-are-yous and the reason for the call
After ensuring that communication with the called has been established and before launching into the reason for the call, in the majority of the calls (92 out of 95) participants exchanged 'how-are-yous'. The 'how-are-you'

exchange was typically initiated by the agent and responded to by the (prospective) client. There were only three calls where the (prospective) clients did not respond to the 'how-are-you' with a second pair part; Excerpt 22 above contains an example of these. Also, in 7 out of the 92 calls in which 'how-are-yous' occurred, they were initiated by the (prospective) clients. These conversations represent a combination of first calls, call-backs and follow-up calls. The common denominator among them is the fact that the (prospective) clients were all from Venezuela. This, in turn, provides interactional evidence to support the comments made by agents with regards to the friendly and affectionate attitude of Venezuelans during the interviews (see Chapter 6).

Contrary to the findings of the bulk of the research into the openings of various kinds of institutional calls (see Chapter 1, Section 1.5) and in line with the interpersonal connectedness (Fitch 1991) reported in earlier studies of institutional calls in Spanish (Márquez Reiter 2005, 2006), these calls exhibit an overwhelming presence of conversational footings (Goffman 1979); and these are reminiscent of the kind of quotidian enquiries found in everyday calls. As I have argued above, this is a reflection of the norms that underlie Spanish business talk and is as basic and socially ingrained as 'please' and 'thank you' are in English. The social exigency of greetings and 'how-are-you' exchanges is encapsulated in common expressions such as *El saludo no se le niega a nadie* ('nobody should be denied a greeting') or *retirarle o quitarle el saludo a alguien* ('stop greeting someone'). While the former makes reference to expected norms of politeness in the sense of what is socially permissible or not, the latter has the metaphorical meaning of to 'stop speaking to someone'. It reflects the importance that greetings and 'how-are-yous' are accorded in the construction of interpersonal relationships even when these are temporary and unlikely to develop any further.

The 'how-are-you' exchange is generally initiated by the agents. It is offered once the agents have established that they are connected to the (prospective) account holder or client (see lines 6 and 7 in Excerpts 18 and 19 and line 6 in Excerpt 22). The fact that there is a high incidence of 'how-are-yous' after recipient identification in the same turn as organisational and self-identification, and before the reason for the call, is significant. 'How-are-you' exchanges in these calls serve as 'greeting substitutes' (Sacks 1992) and as a preliminary to the business in hand, making 'an answer relevant in the next turn' (Schegloff 1986: 129).They are strategically deployed by agents as a way of enabling them to proceed to the sales pitch at the request of the called.

On proffering a first pair part of a 'how-are-you' exchange, the agents are indicating that they recognise the answerer as the called, that is, as the (prospective) client whose identity has been confirmed in the preceding turn and whose name coincides with the one that appears in the company's records. The 'how-are-you' reciprocation offered by the clients, though triggered by the presence of a first pair part, serves to show recognition of the callers as agents of the institution on whose behalf the call is made and indicates acceptance of their proffered identity and, as a result, their acceptance of the call. In those calls where a second pair part was not offered by the client (see line 9 in Excerpt 22), recognition of the caller as an agent of the institution and, by default, of the call as institutional is, nonetheless, proffered. After the agent acknowledges that the answerer is in fact the called (*ah* in line 5), he produces the first pair part of a 'how-are-you' exchange followed by self and organisational identification. With the uttering of *ajá* ('Mm') in line 9, following the silence at line 8, the called indicates that she recognises the caller as an agent of the organisation and the call as unsolicited. This is reflected in the non-effusive nature of the minimal response *ajá* . In uttering *ajá,* the (prospective) client recognises the call as institutional and helps to reconstruct the anchor position, where she expects the agent to give the reason for the call. Mutual recognition is achieved in these calls by the confirmation, or disconfirmation, of the recipient's identity, the proffering of identification by the caller, and the exchange of 'how-are-yous' in those cases where a first pair part is offered by the agents prior to the proffering of self or organisational identification or of both (see line 8 in Excerpt 22). In other words, mutual recognition is accomplished by what Schegloff (1986) calls interlocking organisation, whereby 'some turns have two (or sometimes three) components, combining in the same turn the last part (the second pair part of an adjacency pair or a sequence-closing third) of one sequence and the first pair part of a next sequence' (p. 131).

Schegloff (1986: 131) observes that 'the how-are-you sequence is ordinarily an exchange sequence', which can generate different sequential courses depending on whether it is elaborated or closed. According to the database in this research, it can comprise a two-turn, three-turn or even four-turn sequence. The 'how-are-you' exchange illustrated in Excerpt 19 consists of a minimal adjacency pair, namely the enquiry in line 7 and its response in line 8. In this example the (prospective) client limits himself to the provision of a formulaic answer without reciprocating the enquiry, thus making it difficult for the caller to give the reason for the call. Instead, immediately after offering the second pair part, it is the client who gets down to the business in hand by requesting the reason for the call. Excerpt 24 below is an example of a 'how-are-you' sequence which comprises three turns. At line 10, the agent utters the first pair part of the sequence. This is responded to at line 13, subsequent to the silence (0.3 seconds at line 12) in which the called figures out the institution on whose behalf the call is being made, and then proffers a reciprocal enquiry. This, in turn, generates the kind of response which Schegloff (1986) terms a sequence-losing third turn (*bien bárbaro:* 'fine great'), followed by the reason for the call. In this case, the sequence-closing third consists of a response to the enquiry (*bien:* 'fine') and an assessment (*bárbaro:* 'great').

Excerpt 24 [7:9] *First call* (T = telephone agent, A = answerer, C = called)

```
1    A:    (Nombre de la organización) buenos días
            (Name of the organization) good morning
```

```
2   T:   Sí::buen día:. con Marina (Capa) por favo::r,
3        Yes::good morning:. Is Marina (Capa)there please,
4   A:   Un momentito.
         Just a momentᴰᴵᴹ please.
5        (0.5)
6   C:   Ho:la, [ho:la?]
         Hello, [he:llo?]
7   T:          [Sí:.] buen dí:a. estoy hablando con Marina
8        Capa:?
                [Yes:.] good morning. Am I speaking to Marina
         Capa:?
9   C:   Sí::,
         Yes::,
10  T:   qué tal, le habla Daniela. de la empresa
11       Vacaciones Inolvidables, cómo está:,
         how are you, this is Daniela speaking. from the company
         Holidays to Remember how are youᵁ:,
12       (0.3)
13  C:   Qué tal.
         How are you.
14  T:   Bie::n bárbaro. Marina: sabe que la estamos
15       llamando porque tenemos una semana que es para
16       utilizar en su- e:n en::,está ingresada en
17       su cue:nta::, (.) para utilizar en cualquier
18       desti::no:, y puede ser hasta el dos mil diez? (.)
19       h:asta:::, hasta junio del año dos mi:l diez.
         Fine great. Marina:.well, we are calling you because
         we have a week to be used in your in in:, it's in the
         system in your account::, (.) to be used in a any
         destina::tion:, and it can be used up until 2010, until
         June 2010.
```

Most of the calls where the 'how-are-you' exchange was formulated over three turns consist of a mere assessment as a closing third, as shown in Excerpt 25:

Excerpt 25 [1:4] *First call* (T = telephone agent, A = answerer, C = called)

```
1   A:   Aló
         Hello
2   T:   Aló: buenas tardes hablo con el señor Julio
3        Peña:?
         Hello good afternoon am I speaking to Mr Julio Peña?
4        (0.3)
5   C:   A la orden,
```

```
                    At your service,
6      T:    Qué tal señor Peña. le está hablando Andrea
7            desde (ubicación de la compañía) de Vacaciones
8            Inolvidables Latinoamerica = cómo está.
                    How are you Mr Peña. it's Andrea speaking from
                    (company's location) from Holidays to Remember Latin
                    America = how are you¹¹.
9            (0.3)
10     C:    M::uy bien gracias.
                    Very well thanks.
11     T:    Me a::legro= señor Peña lo estoy llamando
12           porque estoy a cargo de su cuenta, = si aquí en
13           Vacaciones Inolvidables. y quiero verificar los
             da:tos,=
                    I'm glad to hear that= Mr Peña I am calling youu
                    because I am in charge of your account,= here at
                    Holidays to Remember.and I want to verify the
                    details,=
14     C:    =Ajá
                    =Mm
```

In this excerpt, the agent offers the first pair part of a 'how-are-you' (line 6) once she has ascertained that she is connected to the right person. In line with the other calls, the (prospective) client responds once he has had a chance to work out the institution on whose behalf the call is being made (see silence at line 9). The (prospective) client response is a formulaic answer, *muy bien gracias* ('very well thanks' at line 10). This, in turn, generates a sequence-closing third by the agent in the form of an assessment *Me alegro* ('I'm glad to hear that'), after which she launches into the alleged reason for the call.

On the other hand, if we return to Excerpt 18, we notice that, after the identity of the answerer as the called, had been established (line 7) and the called had displayed recognition of the caller as an agent of the institution that had previously telephoned her, the caller utters the first pair part of a 'how-are-you' sequence. The called, for her part, utters the second pair part in overlap as part of her recognition display. The second pair part is formulated as a reciprocal enquiry. This, in turn, yields a response and another reciprocal enquiry by the agent (line 10). This is then responded to by the called with an assessment *bien bien* ('fine fine', at line 11) before proceeding to the first topic slot. The 'how-are-you' exchange illustrated in Excerpt 18 comprises a four-turn sequence, where both participants have a chance to utter an enquiry and provide an answer.

In sum, the analysis of the outbound calls presented so far indicates that, strictly speaking, the only essential sequences in these calls are the summons answer and identification–recognition. The discussion has shown that, unlike in the results of similar research into the openings of institutional calls in other languages and in other institutional settings, in these calls, the agents' first efforts are directed at ensuring communication with the (prospective) clients and at starting the sales pitch as soon as possible. To this end, the agents refrain from providing any sort of identification before establishing that they are connected to the called, that is, before they recognise the answerer as the called. It is only after this that they proceed to provide identification. This is done by flouting the in-house rules for placing calls. Thus, after confirmation that the channel of communication is open, they launch into a request to speak to the (prospective) client or they attempt to identify the answerer as the called. In the overwhelming majority of calls, agents initiated a 'how-are-you' exchange prior to offering the reason for the call. I have argued that they did so in order to proceed to the business at hand at the request of the called.

3.4 Some concluding comments

The analysis of the openings of the inbound and outbound calls has shown that the participants of these calls engage in communicative tasks similar to those reported in earlier research into the openings of institutional calls, despite differences in the languages and institutional settings examined. Specifically, the conversations start with a summons (telephone ring) and the corresponding answer, after which participants proceed to the identification–recognition sequence before the reason for the call is announced.

In the inbound calls, the identification–recognition sequence was mainly achieved by the telephone agents', in this case the call-takers', proffering of organisational identification and the subsequent confirmation by the (prospective) clients, that is, the callers, that they were connected to the right institution. In the case of the outbound calls, contrary to the in-house rules, the agents delayed the provision of both self- and organisational identification until they ensured that they were connected to the (prospective) clients. This conversational manoeuvre responds to the fact that most of the outbound calls are unsolicited; therefore, early identification can maximise the chances of early declination. Nonetheless, answerers can infer early on in the conversation that the call is institutional, given the absence of recognition claims during, or following, the summons-answer sequence (Schegloff 1986; Márquez Reiter 2006). Further support for this lack of recognition, and by default for the institutional nature of the call, is the agents' immediate request to speak to the (prospective) clients or their attempt to ascertain whether the answerers are in fact the called. Additionally, the switchboard request, or recognition attempt, depending on the contingencies of the call, is usually preceded by a neutral-respectful greeting. Although the greetings observed principally serve to confirm that the channel of communication is open, that they are neutral or respectful provides the answerers with further clues as to the non-mundane nature of the call.

The answerers then proceeded to (dis)confirm their identities as 'called'. When the answerers were not the called, the agents were put on hold. In those cases where the answerers were the called, they provided their telephone identity confirmation before gaining self- or organisational identification by the caller. Organisational identification was proffered in the same turn in which 'how-are-you' exchanges were initiated. It is in this sense that the identification–recognition sequence was interlocked with the 'how-are-you' exchange sequence. In offering the first pair part of 'how-are-you', agents skilfully got the answerers to request (implicitly or explicitly) the reason for the call. They thus managed to start the sales pitch with the full approval of the called. This, in turn, provided a warrant for those calls which were unsolicited. Thus, the establishment and ratification of their conversational roles were a prior condition to the introduction of the main business at hand.

In the light of the above, it would seem reasonable to posit that the same communicative tasks identified by Zimmerman (1984, 1992), following Schegloff's (1986) canonical model for the openings of ordinary calls, are pursued in these calls. However, these calls also contain an overwhelming incidence of conversational elements which reflect interpersonal connectedness (Fitch 1991). Significantly, most of the inbound calls comprise (partial) greetings and, in several cases, a 'how-are-you' exchange, despite the fact that this is not prescribed by the company and that the calls are institutional rather than mundane. The overwhelming presence of greetings and how-are-yous is even more notable in the outbound calls.

That greetings and 'how-are-yous' are not, strictly speaking, essential elements for the business to be transacted but are, nonetheless, overwhelmingly present is indicative of the fact that they are a social practice in Latin American business, a practice which possibly extends beyond business environments. In the calls in this study, they were part of the identification–recognition sequence and a preliminary to the business at hand in an institutional setting where the participants do not know each other and are unlikely to be in contact with one another in the future. The social practice of greeting and of exchanging 'how-are-yous' between the mutually unacquainted offers us a window into the social norms that underlie the business of Spanish talk and Spanish business talk: before unacquainted participants can proceed to the main motive of the call, they normally enter into a face management with each other as part of the construction of their (business) relationship.

Notes

1. Unless otherwise stated, in all excerpts C = (prospective) client, A = agent.
2. All first and last names in the excerpts are fictitious.

3. It can be argued that the institutionality of the call started when the caller decided to telephone the company's number.
4. However, Houtkoop-Steenstra (1991) and Lindström (1994) have demonstrated that Dutch and Swedish speakers show a preference for self-identification over recognition in ordinary calls.
5. Although *picardía* does not necessarily entail the expression of *simpatía*, the latter can be craftily deployed. For a definition and explanation of *simpatía* see Márquez Reiter et al. (2005).
6. This conversation was recorded at a family home in Montevideo. The participants' names are fictitious.
7. Escamilla Morales et al. (2005) examined five telephone conversations made to local ironmongers in Cartagena (Colombia). They report that call-takers provide organisational identification as an answer to the summons and that organisational identification may be followed by a greeting (*Buenos días*, 'Good morning') or by an offer of assistance *(a la orden*, 'at your service').

4 The Negotiation of the Business Exchange

4.1 Introduction

In Chapter 3 I examined the ways in which the relationship between the conversational participants is (re-)established at the onset of the calls. I did so by analysing the opening sequences of the telephone conversations. In this chapter, I will turn my attention to the communicative activities participants engage in after the opening is achieved and before they bring the conversation to a close. This chapter will thus look at the middles (Hopper 1992) of the calls. These are also known, and perhaps more appropriately termed in the light of the data examined in this book, as the negotiation of the business exchange (Bailey 1997). The negotiation of the business exchange is typically longer than the opening and closing sequences of the call, and more complex in terms of the various activities it can comprise. It includes the proffering of the reason for the call and a series of adjacency pairs through which participants engage in interactional activities, which orient towards the pursuit of their (sometimes different) conversational goals.

Out of all the aspects of the negotiation of the business exchange I could have selected to explore, I have chosen to focus principally on the practices which, strictly speaking, are not essential for the transaction to be accomplished. They are, nonetheless, recurrently deployed by the participants to enhance their chances of obtaining their interactional goal. The rationale for offering an elaborate treatment of these practices rather than of the range of activities the participants engage in when supplying and demanding a service is based mainly on two reasons. First, these practices are recurrent and, to the best of my knowledge, they have not been reported in similar interactional environments, that is, in other studies of telesales calls. They thus deserve some attention. Second, the examination of these practices is embedded within a general discussion of the steps taken by the interactants to supply and demand a service and couched in the rather scant though incisive research conducted into telesales calls. It thus includes an analysis of the general aspects of service provision, drawing primarily, though not exclusively, on the activities observed by Mazeland (2004) in his study of

Dutch telesales. This is because, procedurally speaking, these participants go about negotiating the business exchange in much the same way in spite of differences in corpora. These include: differences in languages and varieties of a language; in the relationship between participants; in the product being supplied or demanded; and in service operationalisation.

Furthermore, in these calls, there is an existing relationship between the participants. The relationship stretches beyond the realm of one prior interaction and typically encompasses a transactional history between the parties, that is, between the (prospective) clients and the company. This is a relationship the parties build on in each encounter with one another and one they wish to maintain in pursuit of their objectives. The telephone agents have access to the clients' transactional history and use this knowledge to articulate (some of) their moves. The clients, for their part, need to maintain the relationship with the agents to gain access to relevant product or service information, given that service provision is conducted over the telephone; as a result, client up-to-date knowledge of the availability of services and offers is usually dependent on telephone interaction.

In view of the above, it is possible that the practices I discuss here result from the specifics of the type of service calls examined. In these calls a business relationship between the parties was established prior to the telephone conversations and is re-established every time the parties contact one another. Additionally, the participants have to telephone each other to supply and demand a service, as customer services are primarily operationalised via this medium. Thus, the presence of the practices I elaborate on reflects some of the negotiating tactics put in place by the participants to counterbalance some of the limitations of service operationalisation; specifically, the management of restricted access to information by the clients, and the creation of a product or service need when none may actually exist. In short, while these practices are not, strictly speaking, essential for the transaction to be accomplished, they are part and parcel of the type of business interactions examined in this book.

In inbound calls, the negotiation of the business exchange involves clients telephoning the company to: request holiday exchange information, such as destinations and slots available; report the non-arrival of holiday-related documentation; request change of dates or accommodation; and, in some cases, renew their membership and deposit weeks. The database shows that membership renewal and week-depositing are proactively pursued by agents primarily in outbound calls where they telephone (prospective) clients to persuade them to renew and deposit.

The negotiation of the business exchange starts with the reason for the call and it is at this point the participants establish what they will talk about. In inbound calls, an account of the service needed is given by the client, whereas in outbound calls, the agent provides an account of the service on offer. In providing an account of the service required, or intended to be sold, the discursive identities of client and telephone agent are further ascribed. The interaction is thus given a practical frame and direction (Arminen 2005a) and the institutional nature of the encounter is underlined. Following this, participants proceed to negotiate the service needed, or being offered, according to their own agendas, that is, the caller's needs and the agent's goal(s); the latter, in turn, fit with the institution's goals. There are occasions when the participants share a common goal; for instance, in those cases where the client wishes to renew the membership within the realms of what is institutionally possible, and the agent has telephoned the client with a view to persuading him or her to do so. More commonly, however, their interests separate them. Clients want best value for money while agents want to sell them as many products as possible, as this will reflect positively on their performance. The achievements of agents who surpass their sale targets are publicly displayed in the call centre and, in some cases, reflected in their salary.[1]

In the first part of this chapter (Section 4.2), I analyse the occurrence of fabricated ignorance, a tactic employed by clients to request something that they are not contractually entitled to and to enhance their chances of obtaining it. In examining this practice, I delve into the range of activities the participants engage in to supply and demand a service. I then turn my attention to the in-house rules that the agents are required to follow to pitch their sale and negotiate the business exchange (Section 4.3). I follow this with an overview of the patterns observed across outbound calls, with particular attention to the practice of camouflaging, a recurrent agent manoeuvre in angling for the (prospective) clients. Finally, I discuss the role of arrangements and reproachful talk in follow-up calls and offer some concluding comments (Sections 4.4 and 4.5).

4.2 The middles of inbound calls: fabricated ignorance

The inbound calls of this study show that clients principally telephone the call centre to: enquire about destinations, type of accommodation and time slots available; report they have (not) received relevant holiday-related documentation (for example, an accommodation voucher); request change of dates and accommodation; and complain about the service received. To a lesser extent, clients also place calls to renew their membership and to deposit their weeks in the company's database. This should not come as a surprise given that membership renewal and the depositing of weeks are tenaciously pursued by agents in outbound calls and that the clients appear to remember that their membership is about to expire, or that they need to deposit their weeks, just before they want to use the service, that is, when planning a holiday.

A common denominator across the interactions is that, irrespective of the main goal of calls, the overwhelming majority of the agents, almost by default, use the current encounter as a platform from which to pitch another sale. While on the phone to supply a given service, the agents generally attempt to entice the clients to purchase yet another company product. For example, if a client telephones the company to have his or her allotted weeks deposited, the agent may offer a special deal on membership renewals and the clients, for their part, may try to get best value for money.

In this section, I devote my attention to exploring a practice deployed by clients to get best value for money: fabricated ignorance. Fabricated[2] ignorance is observed in more than half of the inbound calls (19 out of 36). Put differently, it is demonstrable at the level of the interaction in more than half of the inbound telephone conversations, including intra- and intercultural calls made for various reasons. Through this practice the clients falsely pretend to be unaware of the balance of their account or of how the system works in order to gain access to information, services or benefits that they are not, in theory, entitled to under their agreement.

I have selected a practice pursued by the clients because the book deals not only with calls made by the agents to (prospective) clients but also with those made by the (prospective) clients. Futhermore, the general literature on negotiation shows an orientation towards selling strategies rather than buying practices in the sense of the activities that clients pursue to obtain best value for money. The practice I explore here is dependent on the environment in which it occurs, in this case mediated service encounters, where participants do not have access to paralinguistic cues. The absence of paralinguistic cues provides some of the right conditions for the practice's emergence given that the risks of it being interpreted as a client 'fabrication' are reduced by the affordances of the medium. Similarly, if the business agreement offered better value for money, there might not be any need for customers to engage in it. Given the existence of institutional rules which dictate what is permissible or not, and the signing of an agreement where the terms and conditions are stipulated, the presence of fabricated ignorance prompts the question: why take the trouble to do it? This is one of the questions that I shall attempt to adumbrate in this section by examining the middles of two telephone conversations (Excerpts 1 and 2) where this practice is prevalent.

In the calls where fabricated ignorance was present, the following pattern was observed. After the opening, the clients provide the reason for the call in the anchor position in the form of a request for information, such as the procedures required to deposit weeks or the requesting of holiday-related documentation. The agents offer a response and take the clients' details, or vice versa. Immediately after locating the clients' details and having had a chance to look at their history, the agents elaborate on the original response given and the topic is typically bounded, thus creating a closing-implicative environment. At this juncture, the clients make a further enquiry which opens up new dimensions of relevance. The enquiry constitutes a second reason for the call, hence a move out of the closing. It is here that the practice is best appreciated as a fortuitously constructed move out of a closing, where the clients mobilise linguistic resources that allow us to look into it.

The client in Excerpt 1, below, has already booked and paid for a unit of accommodation and now telephones the company to see whether there is another unit in the same, or a nearby, resort for the corresponding period without having to deposit another week. A prerequisite for conducting the search is the depositing of weeks and this can only be done if the client is up to date with the resort service charges.

As illustrated at lines 8–16, the client telephones the call centre to report that the accommodation voucher has not been received and thus implicitly requests that it be dispatched. In order to deal with the client's request, the agent initiates a series of interrogative questions to locate the client's details and history in the system. Once the relevant information is obtained, the agent confirms that the system shows that a reservation has been made (line 39). She thus implies that the voucher should have been received and proceeds to place a (new) request, reassuring the client that it will reach its intended destination (see line 45 and contingency questions which follow).

At first, the non-arrival of the voucher seems to constitute the (main) reason for the call. It is proffered at the first available opportunity, immediately after the opening has been achieved and interpreted as such by the agent, who, after double-checking the client's details (line 45 and contingency questions which follow), initiates a potential closing sequence. The agent does this at line 48 by offering a remedy to the complaint expressed at line 16. She confirms that the voucher will be sent to the client and formulates her contribution as an assurance. She utters it immediately after the previous turn, which contains the last pieces of information needed to establish that the client's details in the system are correct. This shows promptness and, in the agent's view, there is, then, nothing else to talk about; the client's request for service has been satisfactorily met and the interaction can thus be brought to a close. The agent packages her closing-implicative contribution in the progressive and in the active voice, *Se lo vamos a estar enviando señora* ('We are sending it to you[u] Ma'am'), including the address term *señora* ('Ma'am') uttered with falling intonation contour in final turn position; thus, she further constructs the turn as a potential first closing (Jefferson 1973; Button 1987). The progressive helps to emphasise service continuity. It brings to the fore the fact that steps to remedy the fault are not just being taken while the participants are co-present, over the phone, but that they are likely to continue during absence, off the phone. The choice of the active, in particular the pronoun 'we', *vamos* ('we are'), displays the agent's footing (Goffman 1979). She is speaking on behalf of the institution, the same institution which did not send the voucher and now offers a remedial action, thus demonstrating duty of care towards its clients.

Excerpt 1 [2:4]

```
8    C:   Tengo hecho una reserva:, que ya me la adjudicaron
9         porque es más ya la pagué. para el veintitres de
10        septiembre (.) al treinta de septiembre (.)
          I have a reservation:,that has already been allocated
          to me because what is more I've already paid for it for
          the twenty third of September (.)to the thi:rtieth of
          September(.)
11   A:   Sí.
          Yes.
12   C    en Bahía Manzano.
          in Bahía Manzano.
13   A:   Sí.
          Yes.
14   C:   =Villa la Angostura.
          =Villa la Angostura.
15   A:   =Sí.
          =Yes.
16   C:   pero nunca me llegó el voucher,
          but I never received the voucher.
17        (0.2)
18   A:   Hace cuánto que hizo la reserva,
          When did you" book it,
          (. . .) (contingency questions)(then the client
          is put on hold while the agent looks for the
          reservation in the system)
39   A:   Tiene acá una reserva hecha bueno ya le hacemos el
40        reclamo entonces de la reserva:. (.) e:h [para:,]
          You have here a reservation okay we will request then
          the reservation for you" straight away(.) u:m  [for:,]
41   C:                                                  [Claro,]
42        en realidad el día ocho de febrero, fue: e:m yo no
43        llame a éste número llamé al cero ochocientos lo
          que pasa
44        que ahora lo había perdido,=
                                                [of course,]
          in fact the eighth of February, it was um: I didn't call
          this number I called 0800 what's happened is that now I
          had lost it,=
45   A:   = No hay problema igualmente ya le va a estar
46        llegando la dirección correcta. es calle treinta y
47        cinco mil cuarto veintisiete↑=
          =no problem in any case it will arrive at the right
```

```
        address. Street thirty five one thousand and twenty
        seven↑=
        (. . .) (contingency questions left out)
48   A:   = Se lo vamos a estar enviando [señora.]
        =we are sending it to you⁰          [Ma'am.]
```

The client's next contribution, however, represents a move out of the closing (lines 49–50 below). In overlap, she acknowledges the information received and takes the floor via the uttering of a minimal response (*m:h*), after which she swallows and starts uttering the next request for service, that is, another reason for the call. It contains elements which are usually associated with dispreference (Pomerantz 1984), in this case the announcement of a new topic via swallowing and the presence of the discourse particle *bueno* ('well'). This is followed by a justification, indicating that the client anticipates that the request may not be granted and that she is aware of its potentially delicate nature. The agent responds in a latching turn with the acknowledgement token *sí* ('yes'), uttered with continuing intonation (line 51 below). In this way, she indicates her understanding that the client has further business to discuss and her incipient recipiency. It is at this juncture that the client starts to disclose the second reason for the call.

At lines 52–3, the client offers an explanation. That an explanation of this kind is proffered to justify a request for information is telling. Strictly speaking, it is unnecessary, as the provision of product information is part and parcel of selling, and is, therefore, one of the things agents have been hired to do. The explanation comprises a self-portrait characterised by uninformedness and lack of planning. It is congruent with the client's request for information, which reflects low entitlement and uncertainty as to its granting. It does, however, stand in contrast with her behaviour so far and subsequent contributions (lines 63–4, 67–9 and 72–4) where her knowledge of how the system works and 'general alertness' become evident. Arguably, her goal, which is to find out whether there is another unit of accommodation without having to deposit her week, has a bearing on the way in which she portrayed herself as someone who is ignorant of how the system works.

The agent responds by stating a mutually known institutional restriction, namely, that slot searches can only be conducted once allotted weeks are deposited (lines 50–1). In so doing, she implies that the client has not yet deposited her week and the participants go over the facts (Pomerantz 1984). The client presents the facts on which her request was based (lines 53–4 and 67–9) and, in doing so, she shows that she is aware not only of how the system works but also of which week and year she needs to deposit her week for: Easter week of 2006; a sought-after week. Essentially, she claims to have deposited the week, which would enable the agent to carry out the search for an additional unit of accommodation. The way in which the client formulates the explanation prior to the request at lines 52–7 vis-à-vis the explanation given at lines 67–9 is noteworthy. The former sounds hesitant, as illustrated by the semantic material deployed: *casualidad, posibilidad, no sé, bastante descontectada* v. *claro, el tema de*; and by the use of the conditional v. the simple past, the observance of self-repair, *p- de casualidad*, together with a few prolonged sounds: *si:::, que::, e::h*. The latter, on the other hand, sounds assertive. What's more, the client limits herself to presenting the facts. In so doing, she relies on the agent seeing the importance of the facts for the issue at hand (Pomerantz 1984). This, in turn, would justify her request and absolve her from any potential interpretations of dishonesty or manipulation.

Excerpt 1 [2:4 continued]

```
49   C:                                      [M::h] (.) ((traga))
50        bueno la pregunta porque:=
                                             [M::h] (.) ((swallows))
          okay the question because:=
51   A:        =Sí,=
               =Yes,=
52   C:   =A veces estoy bastante desconectada de esto. E::h
53        esto salió p- de casualidad.(.) yo no sé si:::
54        está la posibilidad y si tengo alguna semana para
55        que:: poder e::h, (.) de mis semanas usar en el
56        mi::smo o e:n algún otro que ustedes tengan en
57        Villa la Angostura para esa fecha,
          =Sometimes I'm very out of date with this. U:m this
          came out f-of the blue.(.) I don't know if:: there is a
          possibility and if I have any weeks so that I:: can u:m,
          (.) use one of my weeks in the same u:m or another one
          that you have in Villa la Angostura for that period,
58   A:   No. El tema de que tiene que depositar
59        semanas,=sino no le va a dar luga:r.
          No. The thing is that youᵛ have to deposit weeks,=if not
          youᵛ will not get availability:.
60   C:   E:l e:h lo concreto es eso. Yo no tengo
61        deposit[adas]
          T:he u:m that is exactly the case. I don't have weeks
          deposit[ed]
62   A:          [No]
63   C:   porque por ejemplo yo (.) bueno este: voy a tener
64        que reclamar al [complejo]
          because for example I (.) well um: I'm going to have to
          complain to the    [resort]
65   A:                   [Cla::ro] le faltaría la semana
66        dos mil seis que deposite,
```

```
                        [That's right:] youᵛ'd need to deposit
                        the week of two thousand and six,
67    C:    Claro es que el tema de la semana del año dos mil
68          seis de Semana Santa yo no la usé y la deposité.
69          (.) [y no] te figura:,=
            Right the thing is I didn't use the week of the year two
            thousand and six corresponding to Easter and I deposited
            it. (.) [and you don't] have it:, =
70    A:    [M:h]=No me figura no. se la tiene que reclamar a
71          e:llos,
            [M'm]=No it doesn't show no. Youᵛ have to request it from
            them.
72    C:    Sí al complejo exa[ctamente] porque ellos la
73          hicieron el depósito (.) que obviamente se les
74          pasó,=
            Yes from the resort ex[actly] because they made the
            deposit(.)and obviously
            forgot,=
75    A:                      [sí:]=Claro:: por eso tiene que
76          reclamársela porque es una pena porque usted está
77          perdiendo una semana que tiene mucho valor,=
                          [yes:]=Right::that is why youᵛ have to
            claim it because it is a pity because youᵛ are losing a
            very valuable week.=
78    C:    >Sí no si es de Semana Santa.<=y te hago una
79          pregunta porque:: e:m, (.) bueno no↓ voy a tener
80          que llamar a:-a, (.) e::h porque mi papá:( )
81          también es propietario (.) es Sapi Roberto él,=
            >Yes of course it is an Easter week.< =And I ask youᵛ a
            question because: u:m, (.) well no↓ I'm going to have to
            call the:-the, (.) u:m because my dad:, is also an owner
            (.) his name is Sapi Roberto,=
```

Further evidence of the client's knowledge of institutional rules can be found at lines 78–81 when, upon hearing the agent repeating the instruction offered earlier (lines 70–1), she responds by reiterating that the week in question is Easter week. The client's response is triggered by the agent's apparently altruistic instruction; it is constructed as a selfless concern for the client, when, in fact, the depositing of that very week is beneficial to the institutional agent. The client reacts with *Sí no sí* (literally 'yes no yes'; idiomatically 'yes of course') in turn-initial position. In this sequential environment *Sí no sí* appears to reflect the 'obviousness' of what was previously said, thus linking the contribution to the preceding talk and making it function as 'wrap-up' of the current topic.[3] That it is rushed can be taken as evidence for the obviousness of the previous material, and that it is uttered with a falling contour can be taken as a further indication that she wishes to 'shut down' the topic of Easter week. It is now clear to her that there are no more avenues to explore here. Having ascertained that a search for the desired holiday unit will not be made unless the week is deposited, the client now pursues an alternative route. She moves out of the closing by projecting yet another enquiry, that is, a new request for service.

Excerpt 1 [2:4 continued]

```
78   C:    >Sí no si es de Semana Santa.<=y te hago una
79         pregunta porque:: e:m, (.) bueno no↓ voy a tener
80         que llamar a:-a, (.) e::h porque mi papá: (.)
81         también es propietario (.) es Sapi Roberto él,=
           >Yes of course it is an Easter week.<= And I ask youᵛ a
           question because: u:m, (.) well no↓ I'm going to have
           to call the:-the, (.) u:m because my dad:(.) is also an
           owner (.) his name is Sapi Roberto,=
82   A:    =Sí.
           =yes.
83         (0.2)
84   C:    E::h que: bueno el falleció en realidad no sé si
85         está todo a nombre de mi mamá. María Ellis,
           U:m that: well he passed away and in fact I don't know
           if everything is in my mother's name. María Ellis,
86         (0.2)
87   C:    No sé        [cómo se ( )]
           I don't know [how do ( )]
88   A:                 [Ma-]María↑
89   C:    Ellis↓
```

The client projects a new request for service with a preliminary *te hago una pregunta* (literally 'I ask youᵛ a question'; idiomatically 'let me ask youᵛ a question' or 'can I ask youᵛ a question?'), and cuts its flow with the insertion of *bueno no voy a tener que llamar a:-a* ('well no I'm going to have to call the-the') as if she is thinking out loud as to the fittingness of her ensuing request. She does so as if the projected request had not been planned prior to the call and as if she was unaware of the institutional rules. This can be observed in the change of pitch after uttering the discourse particles *bueno no* ('well no') as well as in the self-interruption before she announces who she was thinking of telephoning (lines 59–81 above). These elements suggest that she sees the projected request as delicate and anticipates that it may not be granted. After some more hesitation (*e::h*), she starts providing informational elements about the projected request. The information volunteered by the client can be classified as hints (Weizman 1989), that is, minimal amounts of information needed for the agent to search the database without the client asking the agent directly to do so. Thus, the client avoids running the risk of being accused of requesting the agent to do something against the mutually known institutional rules. The micro-pauses observed after she conveys that the request is related to her father and that her father also owns a time share with the company might be taken as an indication of her pursuing a response from the agent (Pomerantz 1984). In view of the agent's unresponsiveness, the client provides her father's full name. She does so by volunteering his surname followed by his first name. The way in which the information is provided reflects the inferential framework at play here. The client's reasoning is that her request will be speeded up by having the surname first, a conventional requirement across many mediated institutional interactions, for example, in (electronic) form filling. It is only at this point that the agent acknowledges the information, indicating that she is listening to the client, but she does not, as yet, offer to do anything else for her.

Following the silence at line 83, the client reviews the information she has given so far by providing more pieces of information in support of her request. Importantly, these new elements entail her father's death and her ignorance as to whether the account is still in his or in her mother's name. The death of her father is presented in the past tense without any reference to a given time. This would make it difficult for the agent to ascertain whether the inheritance was being processed and, therefore, to judge the potential legitimacy of the request on such a basis,[4] unless, of course, she were to ask the client and, thus, risk slipping into private talk. Yet again, the client presents this hesitantly (*e::h que:, no sé si*) in line with her earlier self-portrayal as an uninformed person and with the low entitlement of such a request. Upon sensing yet another dispreferred response by the agent (see silence at line 86 above), the caller reformulates her uncertainty, and it is then that in overlap the agent projects a search using the mother's name (line 88 above).

Excerpt 1 [2:4 continued]

```
89   C:    Ellis↓
           (0.5) (the agent searches for the information and
           initiates a series of contingency questions)
90   A:    Sí:: figuran e[llos,]
           Yes:           [they] are on the system
91   C:                   [Bue:no] porque e:h ella m:m fue la
92         que me preguntó. me dice fijate que si yo tengo-
93         porque exacta[mente.]
                        [Okay] because u:m she m:m was the one
           that asked me. She says to me find out if I have-because
           exact[ly]
94   A:         [Sí::] e:h mirá justamente hoy habló no-ayer
95         habló con alguien de Vacaciones Inolvidables su
```

```
96            ma[dre:]
                   [yes::] u:m look^{T/V} precisely today she talked
              no-yesterday she talked with someone from Holidays
              to Remember your mo[ther:]
97    C:                          [Sí] porque creo que:: tenemos
98            asignada una semana para irnos a Aruba,
                           [yes] because I think that:: we have
              been allocated a week to go to Aruba,
99    A:      =Sí(.) exactamente [acá está.]
              =Yes (.) exactly     [here it is.]
100   C:                          [en septiembre] el dieciseis por
101           eso lo que te preguntaba. porque e:s, la mujeres a
102           un lugar y los hombres [a otro.]
                           [in September] the sixteenth that's
              why I was asking you^{T/V}. Because it is:, the women to one
              place and the
              men to [another]
103   A:        [A::h bueno]está [bien]
                [o::h okay]that is [fine]
104   C:                          [Bien] organizadas para no
105           pelearnos.=
                           [Well] organised to avoid
              quarrels.=
106   A:      =Pero la semana de Aruba no la tienen con nosotros
107           e:h↑
              =but the week in Aruba is not with us ah:↑
108   C:      E:h no no no no sé si esa la tenía por Top
109           Holidays. por [no sé ( )] porque ella tiene las
110           dos cadenas.=
              U:m no no no I don't know if she had it with Top
              Holidays. With [I don't know ( ) ] because she is with
              both chains.=
111   A:                  [claro]
112           ella sí tiene semanas para usar.
                           [that's right]she has weeks available.
113   C:      Bueno por eso porque ella me dijo vos fijate,
114           (.) que si dentro de mi: cadena e:h tenía
115           disponibilidad, y en esa fecha el veintitrés (.)
116           [al::]
              Okay that's why because she said to me you^{T/V} find
              out, (.) if there is availability in my chain,
              and during that period from the twenty third (.)
              [to::]
117   A:      [no]
```

```
118  C:    trei:nta, (.) de septiembre:. bueno yo la
119        llama[ba]
           thirtieth, (.) of September:. Then I'd
           call [youᵛ]
120        aunque sea ella la propietaria. pagabamos la tasa
121        de [intercambio y todo eso:.]
           although she is the owner. We would pay the fee for the
           [exchange and all of that:]
122  A:    [claro el tema es que: ,] e:h(.) no hay nada
123        tampoco señora por eso↓
           [of course the thing is that:,] u:m (.) there isn't
           anything Ma'am that's why↓
```

After some contingency questions, the agent checks the facts and confirms that both her parents figure in the system (line 90). At this juncture the client reiterates her request. This time she resorts to using direct reported speech (Holt 1996). She constructs her contribution to imply that she is reproducing her mother's, the account holder's, words. She does so to provide evidence in support of her request to search her parents' account; a request which, for legal reasons, should not be granted. In deploying direct reported speech, the client allegedly reports the words of her mother. As a result, she plays the role of the reported (Coulmas 1986; Holt 1996), seeks legitimacy for her actions, and orients her contributions to their shared knowledge of the institutional rules which are meant to be followed. She thus positions the agent as a problem solver who is not requested to do anything against the rules.

The move pays off as the agent discloses institutional knowledge about another client (lines 94–6). She does this in overlap and inadvertently switches to the familiar second person singular *vos/tú*, as in *mirá* ('look^T/V') at the beginning of her contribution. The client confirms the information provided by the agent and reports facts which can be easily corroborated by the agent (lines 97–8) as a way of further legitimising her request to search her mother's account for available weeks. She continues going over facts (lines 100–2), the veracity of which can be easily checked by the agent, and offering a rationale for her original request (lines 52–7). The agent offers a positive assessment at line 103 and, at lines 111–12, after checking out the facts, finally discloses the balance of the mother's account. The client quickly reverts to the deployment of an evidential device, reported speech, to reiterate or rather spell out the reason for the call (see also lines 52–7): another unit at Villa Angostura from 23 to 30 September (see lines 8–10) using her mother's rather than her own weeks. Once it became clear that there is no availability during that period, that is, after the agent has searched for the additional unit of accommodation at the desired resort and time slot, using the mother's available week, and found that there is no availability, the conversation is finally brought to a close.

Excerpt 1 shows how the client seizes the moment to obtain a service and also information to which she is not entitled. Specifically, the client wants to know whether there is another accommodation unit for the destination and time slot where she has booked her family holiday. The search can only be conducted if the client deposits her week. With this in mind, the client claims to be unaware of the state of her account. She does so in a closing-implicative environment as an almost fortuitous enquiry coming from an absent-minded client and arising from the details of the discussion. The request is not granted. In a second closing-implicative environment, the client moves out of the closing by presenting another apparently chance enquiry to obtain information to which she is not entitled. She does this by adding further brushstrokes to her self-portrait, as illustrated by the choice of the semantic material deployed, hesitancy, the explanations offered and the presence of reported speech to justify her actions. In line with the pattern observed in the rest of the inbound calls where fabricated ignorance was found, the reason for the call proffered in the anchor position does not appear to be the main one. The main reason emerges from the details of the discussion regarding the client's ordering state.

Excerpt 2, below, provides another example of how fabricated ignorance may be manifested in interaction. The client in this call telephones 'Holidays to Remember' to cancel the unit of accommodation that she has booked and paid for, and tries to avoid losing the week that she had to deposit in order to make the reservation. According to the rules, the client would have to claim that special circumstances prevented her from doing so for her request to be considered.

After the opening, the client proffers, at the first available opportunity, the reason for the call as a request for information (lines 4–22). The agent offers a response and proceeds to take the client's details (lines 23–4), after which the participants elaborate on the original enquiry and response. During the course of the conversation and contingent on the information received, that is, the cost of the exchanges, the client proffers another enquiry (lines 54–6), which is another request for information. This second request constitutes another reason for the call and entails a request for credit transfer. Essentially, the client had used her additional week, a bonus week which the company gives to its clients when they renew their membership or effect a similar transaction, to book a week's accommodation in Canada. She can, however, no longer make use of it but she does not wish to lose it either. Instead, she wants to use it to book accommodation in Mexico, where she will be travelling to. Later on in the encounter, it transpires that the client had previously contacted the company (lines 70–6 and 79–83) for this purpose, adducing that circumstances beyond her control prevented her from travelling (lines 64–5 and 71–6). In keeping with the Company's procedures (see Chapter 2, Section 2.1), her call was then transferred to the Customer Care department, where it was explained that she needed to send them a letter detailing the reasons for her request so that her case could be considered.[5]

As with Excerpt 1, an enquiry into the procedures for depositing weeks and the cost of the exchanges is presented as the (main) reason for the call. It is offered in the anchor position and responded to by the agent before he initiates a series of interrogative questions (lines 23–4) aimed at locating the client's records in order to offer her further assistance by providing her with information on availability. He also wishes to enhance his chances of further engaging her commercially by exploiting the information, namely destination and tentative date, which the client has given during the reason for the call (lines 4–5 and 7–8).

Excerpt 2 [9:11]   (C = client, A = agent)

```
4    C:    E:::::h yo tengo (.) e:::h estoy afiliada a los
5          hoteles del Royal acá en Colombia.
           E::::h I have(.) e:::h I am a member of the Royal hotels
           here in Colombia.
6    A:    Sí:.
           Yes:.
7    C:    Yo quiero viajar a Puerto Vallarta↑ para el
8          veintiocho de octubre,
           I want to travel to Puerto Vallarta↑ from the twenty-
           eighth of October,
9    A:    Sí.
           Yes.
10   C:    Qué tengo que hacer para depositar las becas que
11         yo tengo con del Royal,(.) y::::: y cuánto le debo
12         de pagar a usted por el intercambio.
           What do I have to do to deposit the points I have with
           Royal, (.)and::::: and how much do I have to
           pay youᵛ for the exchange.
13   A:    Bueno con el intercambio, para usted poder
14         utilizar e:::::h? con becas tendría que pagar
15         trescientos cuarenta y cinco dólares.
           Well with the exchange, for youᵛ to be able to use
           e::::h? with points youᵛ'd have
           to pay three hundred and forty five dollars.
16   C:    Trescientos cuarenta y cinco dólares me vale el
17         intercambio.=
           Three hundred and forty five dollars is what the
           exchange costs me=
18   A:    =Exactamente con becas.
           = exactly with the points.
19   C:    Con becas.
           With the points.
20   A:    Exactamente.
           Exactly.
```

```
21  C:    Eh: tengo que pues mandarle la carta a del Royal para
22        decirles que les transfiera a ustedes las becas,
          Eh: do I have then to send a letter to Royal asking them
          to transfer youᵘ the points,
23  A:    Exactamente.>Tiene usted el número de socio en la
24        mano< señora por favor?
          Exactly.>do youᵘ have your member's number to
          hand< Ma'am please
25        57,
          (client speaks off the mic to another person
          presumably her partner and says
          ' eh: cuál eh el número de socio de nosotros,'
          Um: what is our membership number,')
          (contingency questions)
```

Once the client's details have been located and confirmed, the client initiates a further query based on the content of the information she had received so far (line 35–6 below): whether the cost of the exchange is fixed or varies according to the destination. She prefaces it with *o sea* ('so') thus indexing an inferential connection to the preceding talk (particularly lines 13–15 and 20) and displaying the understanding that all exchanges cost $345; at the same time, however, she makes a further enquiry in the same turn about whether costs are destination dependent. Through this further query, the client paves the way for her incipient action: a request for credit transfer (lines 54–6). The agent responds to the client's enquiry at lines 37–8 with a second pair part and the client confirms her understanding in the subsequent line, where she confirms the approximate cost of the exchange. Following this, the agent provides an assessment of the client's understanding using extreme expressions (Pomerantz 1986) as in, *exactamente* ('exactly)', *siempre* ('always' at line 40), thus strengthening the response he had given earlier (lines 37–8).

Excerpt 2 [9:11 continued]

```
35  C:    >O sea< siempre me va a costar eso el intercambio,
36        o eso depende del destino?
          >so, is it always going to cost that the exchange, or
          that depends on the destination?
37  A:    E::::h siempre le va a costar eso, (.) e:::h
38        internacionalmente en cualquier lugar.
          U::::m it will always cost that,(.) e:::h anywhere
          internationally
39  C:    Trescientos y pico.
          Three hundred and something
40  A:    Exactamente= Siempre le va a [costar-]
          Exactly =it will always      [cost youᵘ-]
```

Reassured of having understood correctly, the client reveals that the information so far received does not seem to coincide with her experience. She does so at lines 41–3, below, in overlap with a contribution projecting a dispreferred action. It is prefaced by *ve* ('you^U see') followed by *y por qué* ('and why'). Like *o sea* ('so'), *ve* ('you see^U') marks a causal link to the material previously talked about and conveys understanding. However, with *ve* the client seeks to engage the agent in her ensuing contribution (Carranza 1997). This is followed by an interrogative, constructed by means of a double conjunction, which is typically heard in the prefacing of complaints, *y por qué* ('and why'), and uttered with rising intonation; thus, the utterance is tinged with the flavour of a complaint, and suggests too that an answer is imminently expected. The agent proceeds to offer a second pair part, an answer to the client's complainable. The answer is constructed as a deduction and, in line with the evidentially oriented contributions initiated by the client, it can be taken to reject any implicit blame in the client's turn. The client confirms the agent's deductive turn with a contribution prefaced by *A:::h* ('oh'). She thus displays that the new piece of information received has produced a change in her state of mind (Heritage 1998)[6] and confirms that she had in fact used a week[7] as opposed to points to make the reservation. Thus, she shows her agreement with the agent and removes the essential condition for her request for information at lines 41–3 below becoming a complaint, despite its being expressed implicitly as such. At line 46, the agent provides an assessment in third position. The assessment is initiated by the extreme adverb *exactamente* ('exactly'), thus connecting back to the first pair part, the implicit rejection of blame he had proffered at line 44 while displaying his stance towards what the client had intimated and offering a confirmation of this understanding by adding a repair (Schegloff 1992). The client did not use a regular week but an additional or bonus week. This, in turn, would explain the higher cost of the exchange.

Excerpt 2 [9:11 continued]

```
40   A:    Exactamente= Siempre le va a  [costar-]
           Exactly =it will always        [cost-]
41   C:                                         [Ve] y por qué y por
42         qué para una reserva que yo hice en el Canadá, me
43         cobraron cuatrocientos sesenta y cinco?
                              [seeᵛ] and why and why
                 for a reservation I made in Canada, they charged me four
                 hundred and sixty five?
44   A:    Porque >me imagino que no utilizó< becas.
           Because >I imagine that youᵛ didn't use< points.
           (.)
45   C:    A::::h no utilicé una semana vacacional.
           O::::h no I used an allotted week.
```

```
46   A:    Exactamente utilizó la semana abono.(.)
           Exactly you used the additional week. (.)
```

Upon hearing a minimal response by the client (lines 47 and 50 below), the agent elaborates on the explanation offered earlier (line 44) by going over the facts that made his deduction possible; by dwelling on the mutually known institutional rules. He does so in a client-oriented manner as illustrated by some of the semantic choices made – *no sacrifica su propiedad* ('you[U] don't sacrifice your weeks'), *un poco más alto* ('a little higher') – which highlight the client's benefits. It is at this juncture, after providing the necessary information to advance her interactional agenda, that is, that she has been charged $465 for a reservation in Canada, that the client shows her hand. She does so with a contribution prefaced by a hesitation marker and followed by *y mira* ('and look[T]'). With *y mira* the client seeks to invite the agent into her own sphere (Carranza 1997; Zorraquino and Portolés Lázaro 1999; Márquez Reiter 2002) and thus to appeal to his sense of affiliation with respect to what will be uttered next: a request to have the additional week refunded (lines 54–6). The request is preceded by an explanation, *y yo esa semana no la pude utilizar* ('and I couldn't use that week'), containing a deictic reference, *esa* ('that') to the preceding discussion (lines 41–3 and 45) and negatively phrased, *no la puedo pasar para Puerto Vallarta* ('can I not use it instead for Puerto Vallarta?'). The negative interrogative expresses the client's low entitlement to the requested action and its low contingency of being granted (Curl and Drew 2008). This is not surprising in the light of the company's rules and her subsequent contributions, where she demonstrates knowledge of the procedural steps needed for her request to be considered and discloses that she had already contacted the right department about this.

Excerpt 2 [9: 11 continued]

```
47   C:    Mmm
48   A:    la semana abono (.) no utiliza becas= no sacrifica
49         sus-su propiedad.(.)
           the additional week (.) does not use points= it does not
           sacrifice your-your week
50   C:    Mmm
51   A:    pero el valor del intercambio es un poco más alto
52         por ese mismo motivo↑ porque no está sacrificando
53         sus becas.
           but the cost of the exchange is a little higher
           for that reason↑ because you[U] are not sacrificing
           your points.
54   C:    M:::= Y mira y yo esa semana no la pude utilizar
55         en el Canadá= no la puedo pasar para Puerto
56         Vallarta?
```

```
         M:::= and look⊤ and I couldn't use that week in Canada=
         can I not transfer it to Puerto
         Vallarta?
57  A:   E:::h si ya está confirmado, >desafortunadamente
58       ya no< puede manejar nada↓
         E:::h if it is already confirmed, >now unfortunately you⊔
         cannot< do anything↓
```

The agent offers a dispreferred second pair part as signalled by, among other features, the semantic material mentioned, that is, an implicit reference to the institutional rules that would make it impossible to grant the request (line 57–8). It is prefaced with some hesitation (*e:::h*), and the main thrust of the rejection is partly rushed and uttered with a lower intonation contour (*desafortundamente ya no*, 'unfortunately not now'). This suggests that there is nothing else to add and that the topic can be 'shut down'. In pursuit of response (Pomerantz 1984), the client utters the negative particle with rising intonation (line 61 below). This triggers the agent's elaboration of the institutional facts, where he reports the information in the system to substantiate non-compliance further (lines 62–3 below). The client confirms the information received via the affirmative particle *sí*, followed by an affiliation-seeking appeal (Davidson 1990). Specifically, she modifies her request and, in so doing, indicates that she does not take the agent's rejection (lines 59–60 and 62–3) as final. Through this appeal, the client seeks to engage the agent further, arguably to engage him at a personal rather than institutional level. This is illustrated by the inclusion of *imagínate* ('imagine⊤') in the familiar second person singular, as if she were talking to a friend. In using *imagínate* ('imagine⊤'), the client literally asks the agent to put himself in her shoes; the use of the extreme adverb *nunca* ('never'), the subsequent self-correction, and the semantic content of the contribution where she explains that she was not granted a visa all further boost her plea for sympathy and indicate heightened affectivity. Further support for the client's affiliation-seeking contribution can be found in the deictic *allá* ('there'). The presence of the stressed deictic emphasises the fact that the client is in Colombia; that she is calling from a country that makes it difficult to travel over 'there'.

Excerpt 2 [9:11 continued]
```
59  A:   E:::h si ya está confirmado, >desafortunadamente
60       ya no< puede manejar nada↓
         E:::h if it is already confirmed, >now unfortunately you⊔
         cannot< do anything↓
61  C:   No↑
62  A:   No↓ usted ya tiene confirmada una en: Harbour Star
63       Resort del 12 al 19 de noviembre no,
```

> No↓ you*ᵤ* already have a confirmation at: Harbour Star
> Resort from 12 to 19 November right,

64 C: Sí. Pero pero imagínate que a mí nunca me dieron-
65   no me dieron la visa para viajar allá,
> *Yes. But but imagineᵀ I was never given-I wasn't given*
> *the visa to travel there,*

66 A: A::::hh (.) ↑guau↓
> *O::::hh (.) ↑wow↓*

Her move pays off, albeit only partially, as we will see. The agent's sympathy does not stretch as far as granting her the credit refund she wants. The agent's response at line 66 shows affiliation with the client as evidenced by empathetic displays, namely, the stretched *a::::h* ('oh') which indexes his realisation of the client's worthwhile motive, followed by an extreme expression of surprise *guau* ('wow') with a rise-and-fall pitch.

On the basis of such an emotionally positive response from the agent, the client continues with her pursuit of response by perservering along the affiliation-seeking road. She reports the facts involved in the issue at hand in a way that would absolve her from any possible blame (lines 67–9 below). Given the agent's comparatively lax response in the subsequent turn (line 70) in uttering an acknowledgement token with low intonation contour, the client revises her position (lines 71–6). She displays heightened affectivity, as illustrated by the deployment of consecutively stressed and negatively phrased constructions (*no me la dieron*, 'I wasn't granted it'; *no voy a poder*; 'I won't be able to'), with which she logically intends to provide a grounder for her request and highlight the fact that she is not to blame for the problem; this she does by using the passive voice in the first of these constructions. It is, however, while displaying such affectivity that she discloses shared knowledge of the institutional rules: she needs to send a letter to the company for her case to be considered. While doing so, she reverts to treating her interlocutor as an agent of the institution, using the respectful form of address *usted/es* (*les tengo que mandar a ustedes*, 'I have to send you'; *para que ustedes.* 'for youᴾ to'; *para que ustedes pues me la tengan allí*, 'for youᴾ then to have it there'). She repositions her interlocutor from an individual to an organisational agent, as evidenced by the switch from the familiar second person singular to the second person plural (see lines 54, 64 above), and finalises her disclosure of her institutional knowledge with a stressed indexical *allí* ('there') and continuing intonation before a micro-pause. At this point, the agent could have offered confirmation of the client's understanding or some other type of response, but he does not. As a result, the client persists with the grounder for request by reiterating the explanations offered earlier.

Such a disclosure means that the client knew that her request for credit transfer cannot be considered by an agent over the telephone. However, her pursuit of response throughout the interaction indicated the contrary, that is, that she was unaware of the mutually known rules. As evidenced by her contributions at this point in the call, she had clearly understood the rules stipulated in the agreement signed with the company and had even discussed them in her previous interaction with the institution. Thus, to pursue her interactional goal, the client pretended to be uninformed.

Excerpt 2 [9:11 continued]

```
67   C:   Yo-yo mandé la reserva que ustedes me dieron y
68        todo, pero todavía no me ha llegado pues el motivo
69        de por qué me la negaron,no lo sé
          I-I sent the reservation you gave me and everything,
          but as yet I haven't been told of the reason why they
          rejected it, I don't know then
70   A:   Ajá.
          Aha.
71   C:   pero no me la dieron↓ entonces no voy a poder
72        viaja:r↓ De todos modos yo les tengo que mandar
73        a ustedes una carta↑para que ustedes esa semana
74        vacacional pues me la tengan allí, (.)para yo
75        luego poderla utilizar porque la verdad es que
76        yo >no la voy a poder utilizar< no fue por mi
          cu::lpa↓ sino porque no me dieron la vi::sa↓
          but I wasn't granted it↓so I will not be able to trave:l↓
          In any case I have to send you a letter↑ for you to keep
          that week there, (.)so that I can use it becasue the
          truth is that I >I will not be able to use it< it wasn't
          my fa:ult↓ it was because they didn't grant me the vi:sa↓
```

At lines 77–8 below, the agent confirms that the disclosure of institutional procedures offered by the client was correct and adds that this is a matter for the Customer Care department. He thus washes his hands of the situation. He aligns with institutional authority by presenting himself as subordinated to the institutional rules that dictate that such a request can only be considered by another institutional body. As a result, the client reformulates her understanding of the institutional procedures by taking the agent out of the equation, as illustrated by her use of the pronoun *ellos* ('they') and reported speech, *de Calidad me dijeron* ('Customer Care told me'). She thus suggests that the agent is not responsible for the bureaucratic steps which she now has to follow for her request to be actioned and implies that talking with him can potentially help to solve things differently.

Excerpt 2 [9:11 continued]

```
77   A:   Cla:ro >sí eso señora< lo maneja directamente es
78        el:-el Departamento de calidad,
```

```
           Su:re >yes that Ma'am< is dealt by the-the Customer Care
           department,
79   C:    Sí. de Calidad me dijeron que les mandara una
80         carta↓ yo ya la tengo allí para mandarla para que
81         ellos- para que ellos me tengan pues presente esa
82         semana que no la voy a utilizar pues por otros
83         mot↑ivos↓ cierto,
           Yes. Customer Care told me to send them a letter↓I
           already have it there to send it to them-for them to
           bear in mind then the week that I will not be able to
           use then for other rea↑sons↓ right,
84   A:    Exactamente= sí señora.
           Exactly= yes Ma'am.
85   C:    Pero entonces yo quería saber si yo esa semana la
86         puedo utilizar en Puerto Valla:::rta↑ porque para
87         eso sí yo ya tengo la visa para México,
           But then I wanted to know if I can use that week in
           Puerto Valla:::rta↑ because for that I do I already have
           a visa for Mexico,
88   A:    >(claro)no la puede utilizar de momento en Puerto
89         Vallarta< y además como-por la cercanía de la
90         fecha con la que usted está solicitándola en
91         Puerto Vallarta, (.) no >creo que le alcancen a
92         dar< una respuesta de aquí a allá.
           >(sure)youᵘ cannot use it for the moment in Puerto
           Vallarta< and besides because-given the proximity to the
           date at which youᵘ are requesting to use it in Puerto
           Vallarta, I don't> think they will be able to< give you
           an answer between now and then.
```

The agent offers with the extreme adverb *exactamente* ('exactly') confirmation of the client's understanding and her repositioning of him (line 84). Thus, he asserts his non-affiliative hearing followed by the affirmative particle and an address term in final position with lower intonation contour (line 84). In doing so, he suggests that the topic should be shut down and creates a closing-implicative environment. The client, however, does not take the agent's contribution at line 84 as final; this is manifested in her redoing of the request for credit refund. Now, however, she has revised it through an appeal which, by inference, helps to highlight the fact that her visa application to travel to Canada was rejected through no fault of her own, and that she was granted one to travel to Mexico (lines 85–7). The new information opens up a new dimension of relevance.

The agent responds at lines 88–92 (above) by going over the facts again, only this time by adding further information. Essentially, the time seems too short for an institutional decision to be taken in time for her trip to Mexico. The client further pursues a response until it becomes evident that the rejection is final and, after the client has checked the costs of the exchange, the conversation is brought to a close.

Like the client in Excerpt 1, this client wants to obtain a benefit which, according to the agreement with the company, she is not necessarily entitled to. Unlike the client in Excerpt 1, however, this client had already been in touch with the company to find out whether it would be possible to have her bonus week refunded and was told that her case would be considered once certain bureaucratic steps had been taken. Excerpt 2 shows the client telephoning the company for what seems to be another reason. In line with the behaviour observed in Excerpt 1, the client in Excerpt 2 seizes the moment to reveal the main reason for the call. She does so in a closing-implicative environment by presenting herself as unaware of how the system works and as a responsible individual who, through no fault of her own, has been denied the opportunity to travel overseas. The client attempts to get the agent to grant her the request by, among other resources, seeking affiliation and repositioning herself and the agent throughout the encounter.

Fabricated ignorance sits well with the role normally associated with clients in these asymmetrical business interactions, where it is the agents who have access to the information that the clients need and who present it in ways which are conducive to achieving their institutional goal(s), irrespective of the extent to which their formulation may have been customer-oriented. In some cases their goals coincide with those of the clients, but in others they do not. Fabricated ignorance is observed when the clients wish to gain access to information, or to a service, that they are not entitled to receive. Through the practice of fabricated ignorance, the speaker proposes solutions which are against the participants' shared knowledge of the institutional rules. In order to have a chance of succeeding, the solutions are proposed as arising from the discussion of the order details rather than offered at the anchor position, that is, as the reason for the call. In going over the facts, the call recipient is put in the position of problem solver, someone who can simply refuse the requests by adducing institutional rules but who is not being requested to do something which may go against them. This I believe I have demonstrated in the discussion of Excerpts 1 and 2. Furthermore, fabricated ignorance can be realised by a range of resources. In Excerpts 1 and 2, it was constructed by the deployment of: explanations, (direct) reported speech, changes in footing, the conveyance of hesitance, seeking affiliation, use of address terms and pronouns, and the pursuit of response.

Two of the interviews conducted suggest that additional weeks are allotted by some of the agents at their own free will. Below is what one of the team leaders had to say while describing her experience of managing Uruguayan agents and what an agent had to say about her experience of working with Argentinean clients in respect of the issue of additional weeks:

Y es mucho de tomar la iniciativa . . . ellos creen que hay otra posibili-dad. Si nosotros decimos 'la política es no le canceles al socio por ningún motivo, ¿qué es lo que no entendiste?' Entonces, 'oye, pero es que se le murió la mamá', 'si se le murió la madre, que no viaje y listo'.

They tend to take the initiative . . . they believe that there is another way. If we say 'the rules say that you cannot cancel under any circum-stance, what part did you not understand?' So, 'listen, but someone's mum died', 'if someone's mother died, they don't travel and that's it'.

El argentino, sobre todo el de capital, saca a flote todo lo horrible, se desa-hoga mucho . . . supongo yo que porque no está muy contento con el servi-cio; también creo que es muy ventajero. Porque por ejemplo, hay semanas que son gratis, que no tienen costos; las cuentas de los argentinos están llenas de esas semanas, las cuentas de otros socios no tienen esas semanas.

The Argentine, in particular the one from the capital city, brings out all the negativity, he rants a lot . . . I suspect that this is because he is not happy with the service; I also think that he is an opportunist. Because for instance, there are free weeks, weeks that have no costs, the accounts of the Argentines are full of these weeks, the accounts of other clients are not.

In addition to these meta-comments, and not surprisingly, given the above remarks, in a couple of complaints calls made by Argentinean clients they attempted to get the agent to look for slots without depositing their week. They did so by claiming that other agents had done so for them. In so doing, they requested the agent to go against the mutually known rules by pretend-ing that this was a common practice. Interestingly, this practice was observed in one of the calls I witnessed during fieldwork.

Service operationalisation, which positions the clients as information-disadvantaged relative to the agents and thus potentially leads them to pursue ways of counterbalancing such an imbalance, is one condition for the emergence of fabricated ignorance. According to some of the interviews I conducted, an additional condition seems to be client experience. Fabricated ignorance is a client's way of sizing up opportunities. Sizing up entails a par-ticipant's assessment of where the interaction is leading, an estimation of the extent to which it is conducive to meeting the participant's goals and the steps that might be needed to achieve them. On the basis of this, participants judge the moment in the encounter when it might be more convenient to make their move in order to gain as much as possible. In the case of the agent this trans-lates into multiple sales per single call made or received; whereas for the client it means getting good value for money, getting the agent to go out of his or her way to help, ideally to get him or her to obviate institutional restrictions.

One avenue for achieving this aim is the acting out of an uninformed stance, for which I assume some planning must be needed.

(Un)conscious planning prior to call placing is essential to telephoning in as much as the caller prepares to speak to someone who is not co-present, and normally has a motive for doing so. Planning is particularly important in the calls that the agents make to (prospective) clients. They typically have to tally the goal(s) of the call – for example, depositing a week; membership renewal and so on – with the client's history and the island's daily, weekly or monthly strategy. The importance attributed to planning is illustrated by the in-house rules for placing calls, to which I now turn my attention before presenting an examination of the activities the agents and the clients engage in when placing and receiving calls, respectively.

4.3 The middles of outbound calls

The calls made by the agents to (prospective) clients can be classified into first-attempt calls, call-backs and follow-up calls. First-attempt calls are those calls in which the agents telephone the (prospective) clients to sell them one of the company's products for the first time; for instance, to get them to renew their membership or to deposit the allotted weeks corresponding to a given year. First-attempt calls share a number of characteristics with tele-marketing calls in which prospective clients have been previously approached by a salesperson, have expressed some interest in the product and have given their contact details. First-attempt calls are unsolicited and unscheduled; they are, however, neither unwarranted nor randomised, given that the (pro-spective) client has previously been a client of the company. The company thus has access to the client's contact details and transactional history. The existence of a business relationship between the parties and a customer inter-face which is primarily operationalised over the telephone entitles the agents and the (prospective) clients to supply and demand a service over the phone, respectively. It also obliges (most) of the clients to take calls, particularly first-attempt calls, even when they may not have any plans to go on holiday. The main justification for this is that the agents have access to information that the clients may not be able to obtain otherwise; hence their call may be useful.

It could be argued that the asymentry which typically characterises the relationship between parties in service encounters is intensified in the case of this company since it runs its operation principally over the telephone, with relatively scant information posted on its webpage or sent to clients by snail post.[8] To be more precise, the agent has access to information, such as up-to-date resort availability, special offers and so on, to which the client does not. This information endowment potentially allows agents to keep their cards close to their chests and make the most out of the hand they have been dealt

– for instance, multiple sales opportunities in a single call – depending on how the encounter unfolds in respect of the larger institutional agenda, that is, the achievement of a sale. On the other hand, it positions the clients behind the starting line in as much as they may not be aware of the potential benefits they can stand to gain – for example, further additional weeks – despite their being, at least in theory, the hierarchically superior party in the relationship. During interviews, a few of the telephone agents revealed that, when the customers are rude, they threaten them with cancelling their booking for a given slot or withdrawing the possibility of gaining an additional week. These are services to which the clients are entitled but that can be accessed and ultimately managed only by the agents. In the words of one agent when generalising about her experience of working with some of the clients:

A mí me llegaron a decir una vez 'escuchame pendeja, vos me tenés que dar lo que yo quiero'. Entonces en ese caso 'señor, usted me está faltando el respeto, esta conversación está siendo grabada, yo en este momento le voy a dar de baja a su semana.' 'No, vos no me podés hacer esto.' 'Sí señor lo puedo hacer porque lo tengo ahora en vista.'

On one occasion I was even told 'listen^v to me idiot, you^v have to give me what I want'. So in that case I said 'Sir, you^U are being disrespectful, this conversation is being recorded and right now I'm cancelling your^U week.' 'No, you^v can't do that.' 'Yes Sir I can because I have it right in front of me.'

Beyond the agent's reference to their differing interactional goals ('give me what I want') and their struggle for power ('listen^v to me idiot, you^v have to'), the agent's description of unequal access to information ('No, you^v can't do that';'I can because I have it right in front of me') and the advantages this may bring supports my characterisation of the clients as information-disadvantaged.

Contrary to most traditional face-to-face service encounters,[9] where services are supplied when demanded by customers and the physical co-presence of the parties at the commercial site is a requisite, in these encounters synchronous interactional presence is mediated by the affordance of the medium, in this case, the telephone. That services are mediated over the phone enables agents to supply services when the parties are physically apart, in a different region or time zone and, importantly, when the services have not necessarily been requested. This last factor allows agents to impose their agenda on clients, particularly in first calls, and gain further terrain to pitch sales. This can be seen in the element of surprise which prevents clients from thinking about whether they are interested in the product offered or about whether, prior to receiving the call, they actually needed it. It is also illustrated by the clients' (in)voluntary disengagement from their ongoing activities to engage in an unplanned activity, at least in first calls, where clients are not the call-takers and agree to take the calls. Call centre operationalisation provides the company with a series of infrastructural financial benefits (see Chapter 2). Its outbound operation, in particular, also helps telephone agents to counterbalance the traditional hierarchical advantage that customers have over service providers. It equips them with access to information that clients do not have and the ability to generate interest, where none may have otherwise existed.

Besides first-attempt calls, the agents also place call-backs and follow-up calls. Call-backs, as the term indicates, are those telephone conversations in which the agents telephone the clients immediately or soon after the first call with some required information, such as further details of the accommodation, confirmation of a transaction being executed, and so on. Unlike follow-ups, in which the agents telephone the clients to learn about their decision with respect to the product offered in the previous call, in call-backs a decision to purchase a product has either been made or needs to be finalised once all the necessary details are obtained. Call-backs are typically made by the same agent who made the previous call, whereas follow-ups may be made by different agents. Frequently, an arrangement for a future call is made in first-attempt calls where a sale is not achieved. When making arrangements, the clients' concerns about convenient times for the agents to phone them again take precedence over the agents' working shifts. For this reason is not uncommon for some follow-ups to be made by different agents.[10]

Follow-ups can be divided into first-attempt, second-attempt and third-attempt calls. This division brings to the fore the importance attributed to the sales agenda vis-à-vis service provision by the agent and the institution. It also reflects the imposing nature of telemarketing, where most of the agents seem unable to take no for an answer. Like first-attempt calls, follow-ups are not unwarranted given that the closings of most conversations contain an arrangement in which the grounds for a future call are established (see Chapter 5, Section 5.3.1). The arrangement typically entails an approximate date and time by which the client should have reached a decision regarding the product originally offered by the agent. The agents thus recurrently refer to the arrangement previously made in the anchor position as a way of legitimising the call and connecting the first encounter with the current one.

4.3.1 In-house rules for placing outbound calls

In spite of the different types of outbound calls, the in-house rules for placing calls do not distinguish between them. Instead, they offer generic advice on the activities that the agents should engage the clients in and the ways in which they should be formulated (see Figure 4.1, given above as Figure 2.2, reproduced here for the reader's convenience).

I. Prior planning

1. Revise the client's details:
   * Deposits made
   * Confirmations made
   * Payments made
   * Special offers
   * Account balance
2. Decide what you want the client to do:
   * Renew for five years
   * Deposit his or her allotted week for 2011
   * Confirm two weeks in Puerto Vallarta during low season, and so on . . .

II. Opening

1. Greet the (potential) client and provide organisational identification:
   Buen día, mi nombre es (Nombre y Apellido), y le estoy llamando de Vacaciones Inolvidables Latinoamérica, su empresa de Intercambio Vacacional
   'Good morning, my name is (First Name and Surname) and I am calling you[U] from Holidays to Remember Latin America, your holiday exchange company'
2. Explain the reason for the call:
   Le estoy llamando porque tenemos una promoción especialmente para usted . . .
   'I am calling you[U] because we have a special offer just for you[U] . . .'
3. Establish the client's interest:
   Es interesante ¿cierto?, suena atractivo ¿verdad?
   'It is interesting, isn't it?', 'it sounds enticing, doesn't it?'
4. Request permission to continue

III. Learn

1. Ask questions in order to: find out what the client is like, develop objectives and establish criteria to select the holiday destination and understand the client's habits:
   * Open questions:
     ¿Por qué eligió ese destino?
     'Why did you choose[U] this holiday destination?'
     ¿Cuál es su plan de vacaciones?
     'What is your[U] holiday plan?'
   * Closed questions:
     ¿Cuántas personas viajan?
     'How many people will be travelling?'
     ¿Le gusta la playa?
     'Do you[U] like going to the beach?'
2. Verify:
   * Summarise
   * Ask confirmation question:
     Entonces quiere viajar a Londres ¿Cierto? ¿Verdad? ¿Es correcto?
     'So you want[U] to travel to London. Right? Don't you? Is this correct?'

Figure 4.1 In-house rules for outbound calls (repeated from Figure 2.2)

IV. Advise

1. Explain your recommendation:
   Sr. (Apellido), la mejor opción disponible en este momento es . . .
   'Mr (Surname), the best available option at the moment is . . .'
2. Explain why the offer is convenient:
   No vendas características, vende beneficios, la forma en cómo estos cubren las necesidades del socio
   'Do not sell[T] characteristics, sell[T] benefits, the way in which these cover the client's needs'

Características	*Beneficios*
Characteristics	Benefits
Grande	*Confort*
'Large'	'Comfort'
Blanco	*Limpieza*
'White'	'Cleanliness'
Distinción	*Lujo*
'Difference'	'Luxury'

V. Agree

1. Ask the client to establish a commitment:
   ¿Entonces le confirmo este espacio en este momento Sr. (Apellido)?
   'So can I book this for you now Mr (Surname)?'
2. Ask the client to perform an action:
   Confirm, deposit, renew, give credit card details
3. Ask if you can be of further assistance:
   ¿Hay algo más que pueda hacer por usted Sr. (Apellido), algo más en que le pueda ayudar . . . ?
   'Is there anything else I can do for you[U] Mr (Surname), is there anything else I can help you[U] with . . . ?'
4. Say goodbye and thank you
   Muchas gracias por su atención, le recuerdo que mi nombre es (Nombre y Apellido) y estamos para ayudarle, que tenga un hermoso día
   'Thank you very much for your time, may I remind you that my name is (First Name and Surname) and that we are here to help you[U], have a wonderful day'

Figure 4.1 (continued)

Prior planning is one the activities the agents have to perform before they contact the (prospective) clients. The script clearly describes what it should comprise. The agents are required to study the clients' history in order to familiarise themselves with their profile, particularly in terms of their spending behaviour with the company, as in special offers purchased, number of deposits made, account balance and so on. This, in turn, should give the agents an indication of the spending power and likely consumer behaviour of the clients so as to establish their interactional agenda in advance. That such a phase figures in the script and is given pre-eminence over others would appear to imply that the agents are allocated time to execute it. This, however, stands in contrast to what happens in practice. While observing agents making calls, it became clear that the goal of the call is given by the island team leader in accordance with the remit of the island, which represents one of the departments of the call centre. It was also evident that, given the volume of calls that the agents need to handle per shift, it is virtually impossible for them to study the clients' history prior to placing calls. In practice, the agents have time only to retrieve the clients' details, including contact numbers, before calling them. While on the phone, the agents typically check the last time the clients were contacted and learn about their profiles. This transpires in some interactions where the clients refer to previous transactions with the company that the agents seem unaware of. It was also mentioned in some of the interviews, as illustrated in the quotation below from an agent describing her experience of working with Argentinean clients:

> *El argentino te dice 'Yo quiero Londres en verano., 'No hay señor Londres en verano, '¿Cómo no si viajo todos los años?' Y te fijas y realmente viaja todos los años.*

> The Argentinean says to you 'I want London in the summer', 'No Sir that is not a possibility', 'Yes it is I go every year.' And you look in his file and it's true he does travel to London every year in the summer.

According to the guidelines, once the agents have considered the clients' history, they place the calls, following the recommendations stipulated in the in-house rules. The script indicates that there is no time to waste as the sales pitch is meant to start at the anchor position, when proffering the reason for the call, and should be tailored to the client: *le estoy llamando porque tenemos una promoción especialmente para usted* ('I am calling you[U] because we have a special offer just right for you[U]'). After such personalisation the agents have to check the client's interest in the offer and seek permission to continue. These are questions that the agents do not always ask, as doing so would make it easier for the (prospective) client to say no.

In the next stage, 'Learn', the agents have to build the clients' profile in terms of their holiday preferences through a series of questions, the answers to which need to be summarised and their accuracy duly confirmed. In the case of first-attempt calls, it is assumed that clients have the time to answer an unsolicited call, dwell on their holiday preferences and, by default, demonstrate interest in the products and a demand for the service, despite not having telephoned the company themselves. Even if this optimistic recommendation were a clear reflection of what takes place, it would apply only to first-attempt calls as the need to learn about the clients' holiday habits in call-backs or in follow-ups decreases, unless their circumstances have changed since they were first contacted. This stage is to be followed by the 'Advise' stage, where the agents are required to offer their professional recommendation in a client-tailored manner, provide a summary of the benefits the clients will gain and ensure that they see it in the same way. Last, but not least, comes 'Agree'; an agreement should be reached before closing the call. Essentially, the agents need to get the clients to agree to some action that is financially beneficial for the company, such as week depositing or giving their credit cards details for a financial transaction to be initiated. Once this is done, the proffering of a topic-initial elicitator (Button 1987) is recommended. This will not only help to announce the agent's intention of bringing the conversation to a close but leaves the door open for another potential sale opportunity. It also highlights the helpfulness and readiness to serve of the agent and, by default, of the institution.

In keeping with the in-house rules for receiving calls, the recommendations for placing calls bear little resemblance to the division of labour at the call centre. They do not distinguish between the different types of outbound calls that the agents have to make, or between different types of clients. While the script preaches client personalisation and tailoring, it does, in its actual detail, the opposite. In other words, it provides generic recommendations as if the interactions with its varied clientele were completely standardised and the clientele homogeneous. In short, while it offers a generic description of some of the activities initiated by the agents in some types of outgoing calls, the descriptions are decontextualised and do not reflect the way in which the call centre is organised. Put differently, it does not take into account the different kinds of calls that the agents have to make or, for that matter, that the agent's goal per call is part of the island's goal, which, in turn, is part of the departmental affiliation of the island and ultimately in line with the overall objective of the outbound sections of the call centre. While many of the steps in the script depict the activities initiated by the agents in both inbound and outbound calls, in actual practice the steps do not always occur in the same sequential environments, or they show marked differences in frequency, as well as in the ways in which they are formulated.

Given my interest in examining the participants' interactional behaviour when being offered a product and when requesting one, I will focus on first-attempt and follow-up calls only. As interesting as call-backs may be in ascertaining how the participants go about sealing the business and whether there are differences in the way the participants' relationship is (re)constituted as a result of a second or third encounter between the same interlocutors, this falls outside the remit of this book.

4.3.2 First-attempt calls: camouflaging

It will be recalled that the database of this study contains a total of 95 outbound calls. More precisely, it comprises 58 first-attempt calls, 26 follow-up calls and 11 call-backs. In the majority of these telephone conversations, the reason for the call was volunteered by the agents after the opening section, although in some of them it was requested by the (prospective) client following the how-are-you exchange (see Chapter 3, Section 3.3.2, 'How-are-yous and the reason for the call').

On examining the 58 first-attempt calls, two patterns were observed, and these depended on how the reason for the call was presented. It was either camouflaged as a detail-updating call or, right from the start, presented as a client-tailored opportunity to purchase one of the company's products. In the first case, following the reason for the call, participants engaged in a series of interrogative questions before the details were fully confirmed and, in a closing-implicative environment, the main reason for the call was proffered by the agent. In both camouflaged and non-camouflaged first-attempt calls, the (main) reason for the call was constructed in a client-oriented manner, bringing to the fore the benefits that the product on offer would bring to the client. Following this, the agents volunteered a (recommendatory) summary of the product and solicited the clients' opinion about (an aspect of) the product. When the clients showed any signs of interest, the agents further elaborated on the product to lure them into buying it; and when little interest or doubtfulness was displayed at this stage, the agents pursued an arrangement for a future encounter. In those calls where clients responded to the opinion query with a negative assessment or expressed doubtfulness, the agents volunteered information on a related product arising from the details of the previous discussion, elaborated on this product, lured the clients into buying it and initiated an arrangement for their next interaction.

In this section I will examine primarily the practice of camouflaging, with the aid of two conversational excerpts. These two calls are illustrative of the ways in which camouflaging unfolds and of the steps deployed to supply an unsolicited product, albeit by mobilising different resources. Specifically, the call in Excerpt 3 shows a rather overt way of selling and the call in Excerpt 4 displays the opposite. As I will demonstrate in Chapter 6, Excerpts 3 and 4 are also characteristic of the ways in which the agents deal with Venezuelan and Argentinean clients, respectively.

In Excerpt 3 after the how-are-you exchange, the agent offers the reason for the call: client-detail updating (lines 7–10). The (prospective) client acknowledges the information in the prior turn (*ahá:* 'mm' at line 11) and offers a delayed agreement *Cómo no* ('Sure' at line 13). He does so after the agent's *bien* ('OK') and concurrently as she utters *digame us-* ('tell[U] me yo[U]-'), at the beginning of the contact detail verification.[11] The agent proceeds to initiate an interrogative series of questions (lines 14–38). Once the client's details have been updated, the agent, instead of bringing the conversation to a close, initiates the proffering of the main reason for the call (lines 38–41).

Excerpt 3 [1:4] (A = agent, C = client)

```
7    A:    Me a::legro señor Mora lo estoy llamando porque
8          estoy a cargo de su cuenta, >si: aquí en
9          Vacaciones Inolvidables, (.)
10         y quiero verificar los da:tos,<
           I'm gla:d Mr Mora I'm calling because I'm in charge of
           yourᵘ account, >yes: here in Holidays to Remember, (.)
           and I'd like to check your de:tails,<
11   C:    =Ahá:
           =Mm:
12   A:    Bien [dígame,us-]
           OK   [tellᵘ me, yo-]
13   C:         [Cómo no,]
                [Sure,]
14   A:    Bien. Usted sigue viviendo en edificio treinta y
15         cuatro: apartamento treinta y cuatro veintiuno:?
           OK.Do youᵘ still live in building thirty four? flat
           thirty four twenty one:?
           (contingency questions - the agent checks the
           address, landline and mobile numbers, work numbers
           and spouse's contact details)
```

The agent projects a new topic, that is, another reason for the call (lines 38–41 below). She does so with *bien* in initial position followed by a deference title, the client's surname and a reference to the topic's ad hoc nature, which can be substantiated by the multimodal nature of the agent's work, that is, on the phone with the client while checking and typing the relevant information into the system. Support for this can be found in the way in which the reason for the call is formulated: in the present progressive and in the choice of main verb *estoy viendo* (literally, 'I'm seeing'; idiomatically translated as 'I've noticed that . . . '); both of these highlight the alleged impromptu nature of the activity. Such formulation also helps to support the agent's claim of this being an unplanned reason for the call, rather than a sales call right from the start.

Before 'noticing' that the client's membership was about to expire, the agent projected a new reason for the call by linking it to the one provided at the call's first available opportunity (lines 7–10) via the uttering of the adverb *también* ('also'). The agent thus constructs the main reason for the call as additional and connects it with the action she had pursued earlier: updating the client's details. The hesitation with which she finally announces that the client's membership is about to expire, as illustrated by the positioning of the hesitation marker *eh* followed by *bueno* ('well'), indicates that the ensuing action may be interpreted as dispreferred. The insertion of the tag at the end with a sharper intonation contour suggests that she seeks agreement from the client, hence the green light to embark upon the sales pitch.

After some mishearing, possibly due to background noise (lines 42, 47–8), the agent offers the fully fledged main reason for the call. The mishearing can be observed in the client's contributions at lines 43, 45, 47 and 48, where he first utters a routine repair initiator to indicate that he cannot hear well; he then confirms that he can hear, requests the additional reason for the call, reiterates that he can hear and requests the agent to redo the additional reason for the call from the start rather than start where she left off. The agent displays understanding of the client's requirement by uttering *ahi está* (literally, 'there it is'; idiomatically, 'OK' or 'will do') followed by the reformulator *como le decía* ('as I was saying') before revising the material offered earlier. She redoes her presentation as the agent responsible for the client's account and reveals the main reason for her call as an opportunity to take advantage of a special offer. Support for this can be found in the course of the conversation, and in the self-correction *y llamo porque- para ofrecer* ('and I'm calling because- to offer'); in other words, in this switch from the logical causal connective *porque* ('because'), which focuses on the prior action and thus indicates speaker-orientedness, to a focus on her agenda as an agent, that is, to *para* ('to'), which signals continuation and focuses on the ensuing action; and, hence, on what can be done for the client.

Excerpt 3 [1:4 continued]

```
38   A:   Bien: (0.2 while agent types) bien señor Mora
39        también estoy llamando porque: e:h bueno estoy
40        viendo que: la membresía con nosotros está a punto
41        de vencerse sí::?
          OK: (0.2 while the agent types) OK Mr Mora I'm also
          calling because: u:m well I see that the: membership
          with us is about to expire yes::?
          (0.2)
          (noises of people talking in the background)
42   A:   aló me escucha,
          hello can youᵛ hear me,
43   C:   = Peldón↑
          = pardon↑
44   A:   Me escucha↑
          can youᵛ hear me↑
45   C:   Dígame.
          Tellᵛ me.
46   A:   Bien como le de[cía,]
          OK as I was say [ing,]
47   C:              [No no] dígame >que no le escuche
48        bien<,=
                     [No no] tellᵛ me >I couldn't hear youᵛ
          well<,=
```

```
49   A:    = A::hí esta cómo le decí:a estoy a cargo de la
50         cue:nta sí:? y llamo porque- para ofrecer una
51         promoción que tenemos, (.) e:: una promoción
           porque bueno la membresía con nosotros está a
           punto de vencerse, (.) y: le ibamos a hacer una
           [promoción]
           =Will do as I was saying to youᵁ I'm in charge of yourᵁ
           accou:nt yes:? and I'm calling because- to offer a
           special deal that we have, (.) u:: a special offer as
           well the membership with us is about to expire, (.) and:
           we were going to
           [offer]
52   C:    [Ahá:.]
           [mm:.]
53   A:    para determinados socios sí::↑(.) La promoción
54         consiste en bueno en renovar la membresía por
55         cinco años, y usted va a pagar simplemente tres
56         años, y Vacaciones Inolvidables se va a hacer
57         cargo de los otros dos,
           certain clients yes::↑ (.) the offer consists of well
           to renew the membership for five years, and youᵁ will
           simply pay three years,= and Holidays to Remember will
           be responsible for the other two years,
           (0.3)
58   C:    Ahá:.
           Mm:.
```

As in the case of those conversations in which there was no camouflaging, the reason for the call is presented in a client-oriented manner. It is constructed as beneficial to the client and available only to clients such as the one on the phone. It is also optimistically constructed as evidenced, among other features, by the choice of the simple future *usted va a pagar* ('youᵁ will pay'), *Vacaciones Inolvidables se va a hacer cargo de* ('Holidays to Remember, for their part, will pay for'). Although the future is generally believed to be uncertain, the agent's grammatical choice of futurity to describe the benefits that the client could enjoy displays her attitude. She represents the future as a fact without any doubts: the client will renew the membership and enjoy its benefits. In her recommendatory summary of the product, she dwells on the advantageous payment plans on offer. Additionally, some of the benefits are described as discretionary; as perks for special clients (see line 53): *Vacaciones Inolvidables se va a hacer cargo de los otros dos* ('Holidays to Remember will pay for the other two years'), *le depositamos en su cuenta dos semanas adicionales* ('we will credit yourᵁ account with two additional weeks'), thus further personalising the encounter (lines 59–67 below).

In spite of the client's discouraging reaction, a delayed acknowledgement token with low contour (line 58 above), the agent expands on the offer while allowing the client to provide an assessment; for instance, after the first micro-pause, where the agent utters the affirmative particle with a marked upward pitch, thus signalling that some reaction from him is expected (line 59 below). As none is given, the agent dwells further on the benefits and, on completing her turn, a pause of 0.1 seconds is observed, after which the client utters an acknowledgement token with descending intonation, thus signalling receipt of the information in a lax manner (line 68 below). This is followed by a micro-pause, which further indexes the client's lack of interest and the agent's determination to pursue her interactional goal against all odds. Put differently, it shows the agent's optimism that, despite the lax reactions to the good news she has given, she can lure the client into buying the product.

Excerpt 3 [1:4 continued]
```
59   A:   Sí:? e:ste:: bueno la promoción consiste e:n:,
60        ya le digo. Serí- usted e: h abonaría nada más
61        que tres años? = en Bolívares lo hacemos en
62        Bolívares con su tarjeta de crédito sí:? (.) en
63        pa:gos. (.) sí:, además e::m:::, (.) las cuotas
64        son sin reca::rgo, (.) y le depositamos en la
65        cuenta dos semanas adicionales >para que usted
66        pueda intercambiar con nosotros sin necesidad de
67        utilizar la semana de propiedad que usted< tiene,
          Yes:? u:m:: well the offer consists o:f:,let me tell
          youᵘ. Youᵘ woul- youᵘ u:m would pay for no more than three
          years? in Bolívares we do it in Bolivares using your
          credit card yes:?(.) in insta:lments. (.) yes:, besides
          u::m:::, (.) the instalments are interest free (.) and
          we credit your account with two additional weeks >so
          that youᵘ can exchange with us without having to use
          yourᵘ own week< that youᵘ have,
          (0.1)
68   C:   Ahá:.
          Mm:.
          (.)
```

Disregarding the client's signs of lack of interest in spite of the benefits on offer, the agent projects the bounding of the payment plan topic and ensues a new one by uttering *bien* ('OK') with descending intonation (line 69 below). Just as there was a delay observed when the agent introduced the topic of the cost, the client expresses a delayed understanding of the benefit-elaboration articulated at lines 59–67 by uttering *ah okey* ('I see'). The agent then and in a latch produces a card from up her sleeve: that the special offer is valid only for this week. She stresses the offer's time line by formulating it with the deictic *esta semana* ('this week'), qualifying it with the extreme adverb *única-mente* ('only') and completing this turn-construction unit with the affirmative particle uttered with a sharper intonation rise before a micro-pause. She thus emphasises the here and now of the opportunity and indicates that a reaction is expected. Faced with another discouraging reaction and in keeping with her communicative behaviour so far, she reiterates her proposal to talk about the cost followed by an opinion query (*a ver qué le parece*, 'let's see what you[u] think') (lines 73–4 below).

In contrast to the way in which the summary of the product and its elaboration were constructed, namely by producing rather beneficial and personalised descriptions, the agent's proposal to move on to the cost and the opinion query are neutrally formulated. However, that an announcement is made before offering the price and that this is followed by an opinion query is, arguably, a way of checking interest and looking for agreement, given that a preferred second pair part is typically expected. It is thus a way of seeking alignment with the next proposed activity and, by default, a way of implicating the client commercially (Mazeland 2004). The agent ignores the lack of an immediate answer. After a considerable silence (0.4 seconds), the client produces an acknowledgement token followed by an enquiry into the cost. This enquiry marks a new stage in the conversation. It shows the client's interest in the product and, thus, opens the door to the bargaining sequence that precedes the closing in which an arrangement for a future contact is initiated by the agent.

Excerpt 3 [1:4 continued]

```
69   A:    Bien.(.)El [costo]
           OK. (.)the  [cost]
70   C:                [A:h] okey:=
                       [O:h] okay:=
71   A:    = E:h: l::a promoción es por esta semana
72         únicamente sí: (.) y::: l::e le paso el precio
73         para que usted e:h lo-lo maneje:, (.) a ver qué le
74         parece,
           =U:m: the offer is for this week only yes: (.)and::: I::
           give you the price so that you⁰ can u:m work-work out:,
           (.) let's see what you⁰ think,
           (0.4)
75   C:    Ahá:. y cuánto es el monto,
           Mm:. And what is the amount,
           (0.1)
76   A:    Serían e::h novecientos cuarenta y un mil
77         setecientos bolí:vares nada más, (0.3) E:se
78         precio:? lo puede hacer <en tres cuotas:> sí,
```

```
79        cada una de ellas de trescientos trece mil
80        novenciento:s, (0.2) sin intereses.
          It'd be u:m 941,700 Boli:vares only,(0.3) th:at price:?
          youᵛ can pay it <in three instalments:> yes, 313,900 per
          instalment, (0.2) no interest.
          (0.4)
81   C:   Ya:h. (.) Bueno dejenmé::, yo pienso que esta-
82        que en esta semana solamente no voy a poder.
          O:K. (.) well letᵛ me::, I think that this- this week I
          will not be able to.
```

Excerpt 4 also illustrates a camouflaged reason for the call. In line with the other camouflaged calls, the reason for the call is offered after the how-are-you exchange in the anchor position and consists of some detail updating. The agent presents the reason for the call as an enquiry for information. Specifically, she wants to know whether the client is aware of the company's change of address and, in keeping with the detail-updating agenda, she proceeds to verify the client's details (line 12). Once this is done, she launches into a new topic, the main reason for the call: the depositing of weeks by the client.The agent does this by enquiring if the client has been receiving the company's weekly offers (line 20). Essentially, she uses the enquiry as a springboard from which to launch into the main reason for the call, as a preliminary (Schegloff 2007), that is, as a pre-sequence to the offer initiated at lines 23–5.

Excerpt 4 [12:4]
```
8    A:   Me alegro. Raúl. ha recibido::eh:: la carta donde
9         Vacaciones Inolvidables le dice que ha mudado la
10        atención al cliente a::: (nombre de la ciudad)
          I'm so glad. Raúl. Have youᵛ received:: um:: the letter
          informing you that Holidays to Remember has moved its
          customer services to::(name of the city)
11   C:   Sí:,
          Yes:,
12   A:   Recibió esa información,
          Have you received the information,
13   C:   Sí.
          Yes.
14   A:   Usted sigue en Lamadrid ocho veinte?
          Do youᵛ still live in Lamadrid eight twenty?
15   C:   Exactamente.
          Exactly.
          (further contingency questions - telephone numbers
          and email address confirmation)
```

```
20   A:   está recibiendo las promociones semanales? con los
21        destinos internacionales que estamos enviando?
          Have youᵘ been receiving the weekly offers? with the
          international destinations that we've been sending?
22   C:   Sí sí. exacta[mente.]
          Yes.yes. exact [ly.]
23   A:             [Vió que] esta semana tenemos como
24        destino Orlando. tenemos como disponibilidad de
25        acá al mes de febrero,
                    [have youᵘ seen] that this week we have
          Orlando. We have availability from now until the month
          of February,
26   C:   =síↄ
          =yesↄ
```

The preliminary is possible given that, previously, it had been ascertained that the correct client details figure in the system. It would then follow that he should have been receiving the relevant publicity and, if interested, would have contacted the company. That he has not contacted the company to take up the seasonal offers, deposit his weeks or make use of the additional week, as it emerges later on in the conversation (see lines 54–6 below), explains the motivation for the call, demonstrating its goal-orientedness and the inferential framework at play.

The client responds with a dispreferred second pair part, in which he confirms having received the seasonal offers by consecutively uttering the affirmative particle followed by the extreme adverb *exactamente* ('exactly') with a final intonation contour (line 22). This motivates the agent to check the details of the offer to ascertain whether the client is fully informed about it or simply not interested. The agent thus pursues response (Pomerantz 1984). She seeks information on the client's perspective on the offer to build his profile and, in turn, use this information as a resource to enhance her sales pitch (lines 23–5). She initiates her contribution with *vió que* ('youᵘ saw that'), thus indicating an evidential connection to the prior turn and her intention of continuing with the same topic. The destination on offer and the time line, particularly the start date of the offer, are brought to the fore by means of emphatic stress. That the deictic *de acá* (literally, 'from here'; idiomatically, 'from now on') was chosen over the actual start date of the offer highlights its recency and thus the beneficial nature of the call to the client given that a first-come first-served policy applies in these cases.

Upon receiving a lax acknowledgement from the client, the affirmative particle with marked downward pitch and in latch (line 26), the agent modifies the offer to include the whole of the USA (lines 27–8 below). Before she completes the modified offer, 'any trip of that kind' (line 30 below) where 'that kind' can be interpreted as any trip overseas, the client expresses a minimal declination (line 29 below) and some personal reservations, after which the offer is completed (lines 31–2 below).

Excerpt 4 [12:4 continued]

```
27   A:    =le interesaría programar algo::para::para los
28         Estados [Uni:dos,]
           =would you like to organise something: for:: for the
           United    [States,]
29   C:    [M::h no no no:]
30   A:    algún viaje de ese tipo,
           or any trip of that kind,
31   C:    Por ahora no tengo nada en vista y no puedo (.)
32         definir por eso que [no::: ₒtomoₒ,]
           For now I don't have anything in mind and I cannot (.)
           decide that is why I [I don't:: ₒtakeₒ]
```

The agent displays alignment as observed in the overlap at line 33 (below), where she repeats part of the client's answer, and starts her subsequent contribution (line 35) with *entiendo* ('I understand') in turn-initial position. However, rather than prepare the ground for topic shutting, after *entiendo* she extends the company's offers. This shows the agent's ad hoc ability to tailor services to clients' needs and demonstrates that her ultimate interactional goal is to sell any product within the range of services available (Licoppe 2006). This triggers a minimal response from the client (line 38), albeit a less discouraging one than some of his previous contributions (cf. lines 26, 29 and 31–2). This makes the agent check the client's interest before continuing (lines 39–40). She constructs her query in a recipient-oriented manner. This is reflected in the expression *le gustaría que le dijera* ('would you[U] like me to tell you[U]'), in which the recipient, through the agent's use of the subjunctive, is made responsible for the hypothetical enacting. It conveys the notion that the client is under no obligation to do so and that, furthermore, its performance will not implicate him commercially – *para que tenga una idea* ('so that you[U] can get an idea') – although a preferred response would mean that the agent had managed to implicate the client commercially (Mazeland 2004). In line with her general helpfulness and service personalisation, she now informs the client of the destinations which she has available, as observed in the choice of the singular person pronoun *donde tengo lugar* ('the destinations I have availability for'). The client reacts by showing some interest. He enquires about the deadline for the offer to take up holiday units within Argentina (line 41).

Excerpt 4 [12:4 continued]

```
33   A:              [No toma]
                     [you don't take]
34   C:              [( )]
```

```
35   A:   Entiendo. y dentro de la Argenti::na, alguna
36        semana completa, o algún fin de sema:na, >tres
37        noches y cuatro días< en algún luga:r,
          I understand. And within Argenti:na, perhaps a week, or
          a wee:kend, >three
          nights and four days< in any pla:ce,
          (.)
38   C:   E::::h.
          U::::m.
39   A:   Le gustaría que le dijera dónde tengo luga::r?
40        para que tenga ide:a?
          Would you like me to tell you⁊ the destinations I have
          availabili:ty for? to get a general ide:a?
41   C:   Hasta cuándo puede ser,
          What deadline,
```

The client's query (line 41 above) enables the agent to do some sales pitching. She thus exerts pressure by elaborating on the benefits that can be accrued if the offer is taken up now (lines 42–7 below). The client reacts showing further interest. He enquires as to the destinations available (see offer made at lines 35–7 and 39–40). The agent proceeds to ask some contingency questions in order to understand the client's needs better (lines 50 and 52 below). Once this is done, she searches the system (see 0.4-second pause at line 54) and engages in unsuccesful fishing (Pomerantz 1980). The agent attempts to gain access to the client's viewpoint, that is to say, to get him to provide feedback on the reason why he has not been using the services, so as to fine tune the sales pitch in pursuit of her interactional goal. The client reacts with a dispreferred second pair part, formulated by means of the extreme adverb *exactamente* ('exactly'). In so doing, he indicates his resistance to cooperating, that is, he is not prepared to dwell on why he has not made use of the service and gives the agent the green light to search for the slot using the additional week.

Excerpt 4 [12:4 continued]

```
42   A:   Mire. eh tenemos- estamos ahora en octubre y ya
43        digamos vendiendo los espacios hasta diciembre.
44        (.) o sea::: nos- nos queda todavía algún espacio
45        bueno de acá a diciembre y estamos digamoh
46        ofreciendo para que lo pueda:::n (.) este: ir
47        tomando. [Verdad,de repen-]
          Look⁊. Um we have- we are now in October and we are
          already let's say are selling time slots for December.
          (.)so::: we- we still have some good slots from now
          until December and we're let's say offering them so that
          clients ca:::n start (.) making use of them.
```

```
                    [Right, so perh-]
48  C:              [Y qué,-] y qué destinos tiene::::,
                    [and what,-] and what destinations do youᵘ
            have::::,
50  A:      Bueno. de semana completa::, le-le digo Raúl?
            Well. For a whole:: week, shall I-shall I tell youᵘ Raúl?
51  C:      A ver,
            Let's see
52  A:      Como no. (.) en qué mes le busco,
            Sure. (.) what month shall I search,
53  C:      Diciembre.
            December.
54  A:      Diciembre. (0.4) bueno. le estoy buscando con una
55          semana abono. Verdad, porque usted no:: no nos ha
56          depositado sus semanas última[mente.]
            December. (0.4) well. I'm searchingᵘ with a bonus week.
            Right, because you haven't:: haven't deposited yourᵘ
                        weeks with us late    [ly.]
57  C:                                        [Exacta]me:nte:.
                                              [Exact]ly:.
58  A:      Tengo, en Bariloche,(.) en San Martín de los
59          Andes, (.) el Patio >es un resort< muy bueno e::h
60          tengo en Mendoza, (.) en Las-Las Leñas, (.) y en
61          Salta.(.) son los destinos que me quedan para
62          diciembre disponibles.
            I have, in Bariloche, (.) in San Martín de los Andes,(.)
            the Patio >is a resort< very good u::m I have in Mendoza,
            (.) in Las-Las Leñas, (.) and in Salta. (.) those are
            the destinations where I still have availability in
            December.
63  C:      Ta bien.
            Fine.
64  A:      Alguno de esos le puede interesar, Raúl:
            Might any of those interest you, Raúl:
65  C:      En principio no.
            Not really.
66  A:      Mh.
67  C:      =Yo consulto y: pero: en principio no.
            =I will discuss it and: but:it's not likely.
68  A:      Ajá:,
            Mm:,
69  C:      De todas formas no es -no era nada seguro porque
70          todavía no puedo: definirlo.
```

In any case there was nothing -there was nothing
confirmed because I'm still not in a position to decide.

Having retrieved the relevant information, the agent lists the destinations available and allows the client to express his interest in them (see micropauses at lines 58–62 above). Upon receiving the lax response *ta bien* ('OK'), she launches an opinion query (line 64) to establish the client's interest and receives a dispreferred response (lines 65, 67, 68–70) through which the client explains that he cannot yet commit to anything. In line with the agent's selling agenda and prior expressions of interest by the client, the agent does not take no for an answer, since she has managed to open a window of opportunity for a sale, as evidenced by the glimmer of interest reflected in the client's responses. She thus exerts pressure by reiterating that taking up the offer now, rather than later, would represent good value for money, at which point the client shows agreement (see lines 74 and 76 below).

Excerpt 4 [12:4 continued]

```
71   A:    Claro. [Digo que -que]
           Sure.   [I mean that -that]
72   C:           [ ()]
73   A:    Queda poca disponibilidad,
           There is little availability,
74   C:    =[exacto.]
           =[exactly.]
75   A:    =[porque ya] estamos vendiendo to: do [después]
           =[because already] we've been selling every:thing
                                                 [later]
76   C:                                          [no seguro]
           seguro.
                                                 [sure] sure.
77   A:    Después, lo que-lo que tenemos son fines de
78         semana, después. que: a esta altura del año mucha
79         gente bueno. No se puede tomar una semana entera:,
80         y toma (.) este fines de semana. >Le voy a decir<
81         estos son en fechas próximas verdad,
           Later, what we-what we have are weekends, later. That:
           at this time of the year many people well. Can't take a
           whole wee:k, and take (.) like weekends. >I'll tell you⁰
           <the dates are close right,
82   C:    Sí:
           Yes:
83   A:    Eh: Le digo. mire tengo. (.) bueno Bariloche,
84         tengo en Buenos Aires en la costa, (.) en costa del
85         este, en Villa Lorena (.) después puedo tener algo
```

```
86            en Córdoba tanto en:: Glenhouse en Villa General
87            Belgrano como en Villa Gessell, (.) eh:::[ ( )]
              Um: I tell youᵘ. Lookᵘ I have. (.) well Bariloche, I have
              in Buenos Aires on the coast, (.) on the east coast, en
              Villa Lorena (.) then I can have something in Córdoba
              in: Glenhouse and in Villa General Belgrano and also
              Villa Gessell, (.) um:::                        [ ( )]
88    C:      [Y:] el fin de semana que
89            incluye,>viernes sábado y domingo:<,
              [and:] what does the weekend include, >Friday Saturday
              and Sunday:<,
90    A:      Bueno depende cómo::: por ejemplo::: en Glenhouse:
91            hay algunos que se entra viernes. otros que se
92            entra sábado. este:: por ejemplo en Glenhouse para
93            darle un ejemplo en Córdoba. tengo para el quince
94            de octubre que es sábado: pasa la noche >del
95            sábado. La del domingo la del lunes< y sale el
96            martes en la mañana.
              Well it depends on::: for example::: in Glenhouse: there
              are some units where occupancy starts on Fridays. And
              others on Saturdays. For example in Glenhouse to give
              an example in Córdoba. I have availability from 15th
              October that is a Saturday: you spend the >Saturday
              night. Sunday night Monday night< and vacate the unit on
              Tuesday morning.
97    C:      ∘Claro∘
              ∘Sure∘
```

The client's understanding of the offer's time line (line 74 above) and his previous contributions in which some interest was expressed would seem to indicate that the time line itself may not be the reason why he cannot commit now (lines 69–70 above). This leads the agent to engage in some fishing (Pomerantz 1980). At lines 77–81, she explains that some people may be able to take only a weekend at this time of the year, thus insinuating that the recipient may be one of them. The move pays off as the client offers a preferred second pair part uttered by means of the affirmative particle with rising intonation contour, thus displaying increased interest relative to that expressed earlier. The agent objectively enumerates what is available (lines 83–5 above) and, on the basis of this, the client enquires as to the details of such availability. These he acknowledges, however, unenthusiastically (line 97 above), thus potentially offering a putative closing.

This triggers the agent to renew her efforts at establishing the client's profile, given that she has now gathered that, if resourceful enough, she might even hook her prey. In pursuit of a positive response, the agent presents the

possibility of a different holiday region within Argentina and attempts to discover whether the client might be interested in more of a city break with access
to the coast or just a city break relative to the more rural areas offered earlier.
Thus, the same process is re-enacted until a potential destination is found.

In contrast to the agent in Excerpt 3, this agent offers only an optimistic
summary of the product, once the client's potential interest has been identified. The participants then engage in contingency questions regarding the
details of the product discussed. The agent thus produces a putative closing
by suggesting that the client should discuss it with his family and proposes
an arrangement for a future encounter (line 110 below). More precisely, she
offers to book it until tomorrow and arranges to call him back the next day
for his decision. In so doing, she is potentially committing the client to the
purchase of the product and making him responsible for the call that will
follow. The client accepts the offer (line 110 below) and commits himself to
a future encounter, albeit not to purchasing the product (lines 120–1 below).
The client thus agrees to a next encounter but rejects any implicit reference to
any contractual obligations. The arrangement for the next call is confirmed
and the participants then bring the conversation to a close.

Excerpt 4 [12:4 continued]

```
                (13 lines omitted)
110  A:     Eso le puede interesa::r Raúl, Consultalo? de
111         repente se lo puedo reservar hasta mañana y usted
112         lo consulta:: con la [familia?]
            Would you be intere::sted in that Raúl, discussᵛ it?
            perhaps I can reserve it until tomorrow and youᵛ discuss
            it:: with the           [family?]
113  C:                             [Está bien.] yo lo consulto::
114         a ver si podría ser si no:::
                                    [Fine.] I will discuss it:: to
            see if it is possible or not:::
115  A:     Bueno. yo se lo voy a reservar, porque me queda
116         sólo una unidad para el cuatro de no[viembre,]
            OK. I will book it for youᵛ because I have only one unit
            left for the 4th No                [vember,]
117  C:                                         [Bueno.]
                                                [OK.]
118  A:     =porque Buenos Aires no::: no es muy común que
119         haya.
            =because Buenos Aires no:::it is not very common.
120  C:     No seguro. y::::: en todo caso::: le confirmo
121         mañana.=
            No sure. And:::::in any case::::: I will confirmᵛ
            tomorrow.=
```

```
122 A:    =bueno. mañana lo llamo entonces,
          =OK. I will call youᵘ tomorrow then,
```

Excerpts 3 and 4 are illustrative of calls where the reason for the call was camouflaged. The main reason for the call emerged in a closing-implicative environment as an opportunity while on the phone with the client and contingent upon the realisation of a given activity, such as an availability search or detail updating. The kind of camouflaging observed is possible when the clients have not made use of the company's services for a given period of time or when the products or services they had purchased from the company are about to expire. Camouflaging is primarily done by means of a detail-updating query at the first available opportunity, which then triggers a subsequent engagement in an interrogative series of questions. It represents a credible excuse to have the clients on the phone, given that the system shows no transactions for the clients in question and that customer services are principally offered over the phone.

Across the first-attempt calls of the database and as observed in Excerpts 3 and 4, the agents engaged in similar activities, although they mobilised slightly different resources to perform them. Overall, the sales pitches display optimism (see Maynard and Schaeffer 1997, 2002a, 2002b) and client personalisation despite signs of clients' lack of enthusiasm. This can be observed in the choice of tenses stressing certainty, which, in turn, projects the act of purchasing as a fact. It is also observed in: the continuation of the sales pitch, including the production of opinion queries to implicate the clients commercially further; tailor-made descriptions of the benefits of the product, where clients are portrayed as special; changes of footing to align with the institution or to seek affiliation with the client; the presence of fishing to guide the recipients towards the agents' institutional goal; and the exertion of pressure when the opportunity arises.

Altough each and every one of these resources deserves at least one section, bearing in mind the aim of this section, this chapter and ultimately this book, it will suffice for now to note that these agents initiate similar activites to those identified by Mazeland (2004) in his incisive analysis of four Dutch telemarketing calls, where prospective clients were gently urged to purchase a savings plan. Unlike the agents in Mazeland's study, 'Holidays to Remember' agents do not seek permission to continue after offering a recommendatory summary of the product; nor do they provide the main reason for the call right from the start. Instead, they check the clients' interest in the product, as the obviousness of the reason for the call is given by the interactional environment in which the encounters take place. There is a transactional history between the parties since the clients and the company have been involved in a business relationship for a given period of time. This type of relationship entitles clients to telephone the company to demand services and, given the way in which customer services are operationlised, it also obligates the agents to make (un)solicited calls to supply services.

4.4 Follow-up calls: honouring arrangements

In follow-up calls, the agents telephone the clients again to learn about their decision regarding a product or services they were offered in an earlier call. Follow-ups are thus triggered by the arrangement made in the previous encounter between the client and the company. Arrangements are typically pursued by the agents when a sale is not achieved but the (prospective) clients showed some interest in purchasing the product or services on offer, or showed no interest but found it difficult to put the telephone down. Although these calls are volunteered under the banner of a personalised customer service, in essence they represent another sales opportunity for the agent. Without fail, all follow-up calls start with a reference to the arrangement made in the previous call between the parties. They start with what Firth (1995) has termed a retrospective tying reference, thus connecting the current encounter to the prior one and orienting it to what will be talked about, namely the decision taken by the client.

Excerpt 5 shows how the agent moves on to the reason for the call by explicitly referring to the arrangement made in their prior encounter. In doing so, she links the current encounter to the previous one and pursues an early response from the client. Faced with the client's discouraging silence, the agent reminds him of their prior encounter and receives an acknowledgement from the client, just as she starts reinvoking the arrangement made (line 11). The client's acknowledgement of this interpersonal commitment gives the agent the green light to enquire as to his decision (lines 13–16). The enquiry, however, is preceded by an account in which the agent explains the reason why she did not fulfil her part of the arrangement when expected. This, in turn, brings to the fore that the client's part of the arrangement remains to be honoured and provides the agent with the right conditions from which to launch her enquiry.

Aware of the interpersonal responsibilities established in the previous encounter and reinvoked by this very call, the client requests a recapitulation of the product details (line 17) and the agent obliges by offering a recommendatory summary of the membership options. Despite the recipient's discouraging signals, his silences during and after the requested summary of the product, the agent redoes her query (line 27). This, in line with the query she voiced earlier, is optimistically formulated. It presumes that the recipient is interested in one of the options. Despite the recipient's signals to the contrary, the conveyance of such a presumption is possible thanks to the arrangement made by the parties'in their previous encounter. The arrangement is thus used to legitimise this second encounter and make the recipient

responsible for it. Such a formulation would make it akward for the recipient
to utter a straight declination given that, after an arrangement for a second
encounter and a summary of the product by request of the client, a preferred
second pair part would be expected. However, the recipient's proffering of
a preferred renewal membership option would mean, at this juncture, that
he is prepared to initiate the commercial transaction and start the payment
process.[12] Instead, he offers a declination (line 28). After this and on the basis
of the details offered in support of his declination, the agent offers a counter;
the client revises his position and the agent initiates an arrangement for yet
another encounter, by which time the client would have had enough time to
make a decision.

Excerpt 5 [1:3]

```
7    A:   =Me ale:gro mu:cho: (.) Señora-e:h señor García yo
8         lo estaba llamando recuerda por lo que estuvimos
9         hablando la:: la:: en:: la semana pasa:da? sobre
10        el tema de la renovación de la membresí:a?
          =I'm ve:ry gla:d: (.) Ma'am-u:m Mr García I was callingᵛ
          remember what we discussed the:: the:: last wee:k? about
          the renewal of your membershi:p?
          (0.3)
11   A:   Recuerda que habla[mos-queda]
          Remember that we ta [lked-we arrang]
12   C:                      [Sí sí.]
                             [yes yes.]
13   A:   =Nos-acordamos de hablar en el día de:: de ayer.
14        yo e:h no pude venir a trabajar y por eso no lo
15        llamé-: p-este:: para ver cuál de las opciones le
16        interesaba tomar?
          =We-arranged to talk yesterday. I u:m couldn't come to
          work and that's why I didn't call youᵛ-: be-um:: to see
          which of the options youᵛ were interested in taking?
          (0.1)
17   C:   Sí.cómo fue las opcioneh que me dijo,=
          Yes. what are the options you told me,=
          (agent offers a recommendatory summary of the
          options over four turns disregarding the client's
          dispreferred responses represented by means of
          silence in 0.2, 0.3 and 0.4-second micro-pauses)
27   A:   No sé cuál de las opciones le intere:sa?
          I don't know which of the options you're interested in?
          (0.3)
28   C:   Es que yo no sé? es que he estado pensando en ni
          renova:rla sa:bes?
```

> *It's just that I don't know? It's that I have been*
> *thinking of not even renewing it you^T know?*

Excerpt 6, below, provides another example of how the agents move to the reason for the call, at the first available opportunity, by referring to the arrangement. Unlike Excerpt 5, where the arrangement was explicitly mentioned, in Excerpt 6 the reference is implicit. The agent's design of this turn reveals that she is aware that the recipient knows the reason for her call and, therefore, that an answer is expected from him. She initiates her turn with an address term, *Señor Carlos* ('Mr Carlos'). The address term is syntactically optional. It helps to personalise the interaction and to signal her ensuing action as potentially face vulnerable for the recipient. This is also observed by the semantic content of the phrase that follows. This includes the presence of the formal second person singular although this is also syntactically optional – *como usted bien sabe* ('as you^U very well know') – and an implicit reference to the arrangement via the uttering of the agreement token *verdad* ('right'), immediately after mentioning what it had been arranged to discuss today.

The way in which the agent alludes to the arrangement is reminiscent of the kind of reproachful talk between people in a close relationship where rights and obligations have been clearly established. While it is true that a relationship exists between the (prospective) client and the company and that a relationship with this agent, no matter how temporary, was established in their previous encounter and re-established in the current one, theoretically speaking, the agent, in her capacity as service provider, is in no position to demand an answer from the client. She positions herself as the party who has honoured the arrangement and, by default, the recipient as the party who has not fulfilled his obligations. Support for this can be found in the client's apologetic response, where he acknowledges the reason for the call by uttering a stretched affirmative particle and adduces an explanation for not having honoured his part of the arrangement (lines 10–13).

The client first admits that no decision has been taken and, upon the agent's lack of reaction when she could have taken the floor, as observed in the micro-pause following the completion of a turn-construction unit, he justifies his explanation. Once again, the agent remains silent and, in so doing, she displays her reproachful stance towards the client and the issue at hand. Following this, the (prospective) client enquires as to the time line to deposit his week. The agent takes advantage of the query to topicalise the urgency of the problem and, by inference, the fact that the recipient needs to take action promptly, that is, deposit the week to ensure that he gets a good unit.

Arguably, by designing the reason for the call in such a way, the agent shows the activity that she wants the client to engage in – that is, to deposit his week – and the means by which she hopes to accomplish the activity. She thus uses the arrangement made in the prior encounter as a tying retrospective reference (Firth 1995), which orients to what will be talked about, and as a wild card or interpersonal weapon, to remind the recipient of the obligations accrued in his endorsing of the arrangement made in their previous encounter. This allows the agent to take the moral high ground in the form of an altruistically constructed and unsolicited piece of advice (lines 20–1), after which and, allegedly for the benefit of the client, she manages to pursue another arrangement for a second follow-up call.

Excerpt 6 [2:1]

```
7    A:   Se:ñor Carlos como usted bien sabe? lo estoy
8         llamando por la semana verdá que se está
9         vencie:ndo:,
          M:r Carlos as youᵘ well know? I'm calling about the week
          right that is expi:ring:,
          (.)
10   C:   Sí::: y sabe que que no hemos decidido nada.
11        (ha::)(0.1)esto::::-quiero decir no he tenido ni
12        tiempo de:-de platicar con mi esposa (0.2) Cómo
13        hasta cuándo tene:mos e:h?
          Yes::: and youᵘ know what what we haven't decided
          anything. (ah::) (0.1) um:::-I mean I haven't had time
          to:-to discuss it with my wife (0.2) so until when do we
          have um:?
14   A:   Okey. e::h no es tanto el problema de la sema:na?
          Okay. U::m it's not so much a problem with the we:ek?
15   C:   =Sí.
          =yes.
16   A:   Sí, sino el problema real de espacios.
          Yes, but a real problem of space.
17   C:   Perdón ?=
          Pardon me ?=
18   A:   =El proble:ma es- es del espacio verda:d?
          =The problem is-is the unit of accommodation ri:ght?
19   C:   =O:key.
          =O:kay.
20   A:   Aparte. fijesé uste:d. no [ha planificado:: sus]-
21        salú: sus vacacione:s e::: (.) para este año?
          Besides. Lookᵘ youᵘ haven't [planned:: yourᵘ]-bless youᵘ:
          your holida:ys um::: (.) for this year?
22   C:                            [(estornuda)]
                                   [(sneezes)]
23   C:   Mire (.) lo que pasa es que en verano-: (.) vamos
24        hacer, (.) un viaje-: (0.2) aca:mpando-: Un viaje
25        por Estados Unidos de quince días aca:mpa:ndo.
26        (.) entonces ya el verano ya:- ya:: fue ahí:↑ (.)
```

```
27           [tene]mos que hacernos de un espa:cio, e:sto::
             [(¿  ?)↓]
             Lookᵘ(.) the thing is that in the summer-: (.) we are
             going to, (.)on a trip-: (0.2) ca:mping-: a trip around
             the United States fifteen days' ca:mpi:ng.(.) so the
             summer is already:-already:: gone there:↑(.) [we ne]ed
             to make roo:m, u:m::
             [(¿  ?)↓]
28    A:     [A:há: y por qué]
             no las toma por ejemplo para diciembre?
             [A:ha: and why]
             don't youᵘ take them for instance in December?
30    C:     °Quizás sí° pero::(.) ()=
             °Maybe yes° but:: (.) ( )=
31    A:     =O:key.
             =o:kay.
32    C:     =Mm::=
33    A:     =Yo le doy el par de días, (.) [Sí:?] señor
34           Ca:rlos (.) e:h no tengo problema.(.) E::h pero
35           más que nada por u:ste:des,     [traten] de::-de::
36           de localizar verda:d, [o-]
             =I'll give youᵘ a couple of days, (.)[Yes:?] Mr Ca:rlos
             (.)u:m I don't have a problem. (.) U:m but it is more
             for yo:u:,                      [try] to::-to::
             decide righ:t,          [o-]
```

Another example in which arrangements can be seen to be deployed in a reproachful manner is given in Excerpt 7 below, where the agent makes explicit reference to the arrangement made in the prior encounter with the recipient and to her efforts to get hold of him. Upon hearing the recipient's dispreferred answer, the uttering of the affirmative particle with rising intonation, thus signalling disbelief, the agent expands on the arrangement and on the steps she took to honour it. She does so by means of reported speech (lines 15–17) to convey the details of the process she went through to honour her part of the agreement. While doing so, she adds a factor to the equation in order to substantiate her claim: the interactional history with the recipient's wife. The agent thus reports that, in her effort to try to get hold of the recipient, she had discussed the issue with his wife and that, according to the latter, the onus for the decision rested entirely (note the use of the extreme adverb *exclusivamente*, 'entirely') on the recipient's shoulders. Upon receiving another dispreferred response by the recipient where he again expresses disbelief or unawareness, the agent repeats, at line 23, the contribution she made. This time, while deploying reported speech to legitimise her action, she also mentions the first name of the recipient's wife. She thus adds more evidence to her claim and further reflects her stance by the presence of another extreme adverb, *solamente* ('only'), before embarking upon the crux of the call: enquiring as to his decision.

Despite the recipient's discouraging reaction, as illustrated by the silence which follows the agent's query (line 25), the agent proffers her enquiry again, albeit this time she modifies it by listing the facts, namely the options available. The enquiry is optimistically formulated (line 26). The choice of the future conveys that she sees the action encapsulated by the utterance as a fact and that the only thing that remains to be considered is the actual purchase option.

Excerpt 7 [2:6]

```
10   A:   =Me alegro mu:cho. he tratado de ubica:rlo desde
11        el día que: habla:mos habíamos quedado que (.) le
12        marcaba el jueves pasado pero no tuve suerte de
13        encontra:rlo,
          =I'm ve:ry glad. I have tried to lo:cate youᵘ since the
          day that: we spo:ke we had arranged that (.) I'd call
          youᵘ last Thursday but I was unable to get ho:ld of youᵘ,
          (.)
14   C:   Sí:?
          Yes:?
15   A:   = He hablado con su esposa en varias ocasio::nes y
16        bueno ella me ha dicho que el tema es <con usted
17        exclusivamente.>
          =I have spoken to yourᵘ wife on several occa:sions
          and well she has told me that the matter needs to be
          discussed <exclusively with youᵘ>
          (0.2)
18   C:   Conmi:go↑
          With m:e↑
          (.)
19   A:   Sí:: [la señora]
          Yes:: [Mrs]
20   C:        [(Sí Sí)]
               [(Yes Yes)]
21   A:   Teresa↑ (0.2) sí:[me dijo]
          Teresa↑(0.2) yes: [she told me]
22   C:             [ ( )]
23   A:   Que era (.) solamente con usted (.) así que
24        bueno:: (.)eh: señor Pérez qué decisión tomó
25        acerca de la renovación?
          That it was (.) only with youᵘ that(.)so well:: (.) um: Mr
          Pérez what decision have youᵘ taken regarding the renewal?
          (0.1)
```

26   A: Va a hace:rla por un a:ño: por tre:s o por cinco?
           Will you rene:w for one ye:ar: for thre:e or for five?

With the exception of the follow-up calls in which (prospective) clients had decided to purchase the product or services which they were offered in the first-attempt call, follow-ups invariably represent another opportunity for a sales pitch. The proffering of the reason for the call is tied to the arrangement made in the first encounter. It connects the first encounter with the current one, announcing, from the outset, its purpose, that is, the reason for the call and directionality in the sense of what will be talked about. It also helps to re-establish the parameters of the relationship which was constructed by the participants in the first encounter. More precisely, it foregrounds the rights and obligations arising from the participants' previous activity. This, in turn, enables the agents to enquire as to the client's decision, the client to delay his negative response, and the agent to overrule such signals on the basis of the arrangement made. By (re)invoking the arrangements, the agents take the moral high ground. This allows them to generate the right conditions to engage in an arrangement sequence for a further call, that is, another opportunity to continue with the sales pitch and enhance their chances of achieving their interactional goals.

The kind of pressure exerted is possible thanks to the infrastructure on which service provision is based and the ability to pursue interpersonal business relationships in which the participants are often reminded of the rights and responsibilities which constitute these relationships.

4.5 Some concluding comments

The examination of the middles of the telephone conversations has concentrated mainly on recurrent practices which, strictly speaking, are not essential for the negotiation of the business exchange to be completed. The high incidence of these practices is, nonetheless, important. I have argued that they represent strategies put in place by the participants to pursue their sometimes differing interactional goals in the light of the environmental business conditions, primarily the way in which the service is operationalised.

I have thus shown how some of the clients went about pursuing their goal(s) by recurring to the practice of fabricated ignorance in calls they made to the company. Through this practice, the clients pretended to be unaware of the institutional rules in order to gain access to a service or benefits they were not entitled to. They thus proposed solutions that went against the mutually known rules, that is, the institutional rules that stipulate what is permissible and that figure in the agreement the client had signed. Importantly, the clients did not do so in the anchor position, as this would have decreased their chances of succeeding. Instead, the proposals arose from the discussion of the details of the order, while the participants checked out the facts, and in closing-implicative environments. By going over the facts, the client assumed the role of information seeker and the agent that of problem solver; t he kind of problem solver who, given the alleged lack of knowledge of the client, is not requested to go against the mutually known institutional rules but who can simply reject the client's proposal by referring to such rules.

The agents, for their part, dealt with the business environmental conditions differently. Essentially, they were shown to engage in camouflaging and reproachful talk in order to maximise the chances of achieving their interactional goal(s). Contrary to the recommendations encapsulated in the in-house rules for placing calls, the agents seem to have devised their own rules of thumb, and camouflaging is one of them. In line with the behaviour observed by the clients engaging in fabricated ignorance, the agents performing camouflaging did not offer the main reason for their call at the anchor position. Instead, the telephone conversation was initially cloaked as a detail-updating call. Once the relevant details had been updated and when the necessary conditions to bring the conversation to a close had been created, the agents launched into the main reason for the call: sales. The agents volunteered an unsolicited recommendatory summary of the product, overruling any reactions of lack of interest by the (prospective) clients in pursuit of their goal.

I have argued that the environmental business conditions enable the flourishing of these practices as the service is operationalised primarily over the telephone, which makes the clients information-disadvantaged relative to the agents, and requires the agents to enlist the participation of uninterested clients in an unsolicited sales pitch. Camouflaging thus allows the agents to keep the (prospective) clients on the phone, allowing the main reason for the call to emerge as a result of the discussion.

The fact that the service provision is primarily offered over the medium of the telephone allows the agents to place several calls to the same clients over given periods of time in order to inform them about offers, alert them to service expiry dates, confirm purchasing orders and so on. In short, it puts the agents in a powerful position inasmuch as they have access to information to which the (prospective) clients do not, and are, in practice, given a carte blanche to contact the clients whenever they want to with the valid and agreed grounder of providing an individualised service.

While a good customer–service provider relationship is normally part and parcel of any good business, relationship management is integral to this type of business. Put differently, besides the functional benefits that the clients receive from their membership to 'Holidays to Remember', it would seem that further benefits may be gained from the way in which the participants manage their relationship. More precisely, the data suggest that a functional benefit, such as additional weeks, may be gained or granted according to the way in which the participants constitute their relationship and manage the interaction.

The type of relationship management observed here can be seen in the way in which the making of arrangements is mobilised to establish another encounter, that is, another sales opportunity, or to provide time to think about the product on offer. Thus, the arrangement can be seen as a symbol of the rights and obligations of the participants in the relationship, obligations that should be observed, as failure to do so would entitle the other party to take the high moral ground.

While the practices explored in this chapter may well occur in other business interactions, I argue that their occurrence here reflects the interactional environment examined.

Notes

1. This information was provided by the Human Resources department.
2. The term 'fabricated' comes from Goffman (1974).
3. To the best of my knowledge, there are no discursive studies of any sort that have examined this particle. The observation made is thus open to empirical investigation; the kind of research which is out of the scope of the present chapter though essential for studies of this kind to be conducted.
4. Under the terms and conditions of the agreement, allotted weeks may be used by family members provided that authorisation is given by the account holder, in this case, the caller's father. Further, the law in Argentina, where the client comes from, stipulates that unless a will exists to the contrary, the spouse of the deceased inherits half of the inheritance and the children the other half in equal parts (Código Civil de la República Argentina, http://www.infoleg.gov.ar/infolegInternet/anexos/105000–109999/109481/texact.htm, accessed on 19 September 2010).
5. Under the terms and conditions of the agreement signed by the parties, a partial refund is offered in case of death or severe illness of a member of the client's immediate family (for example, death of spouse or children), and other (special) circumstances are considered at the discretion of the company. Clients have to book their accommodation at a different time or place and are reimbursed with 50 per cent of the costs incurred. The case of this client is somewhat different. Her visa to Canada was not granted and she claims not to know the reason why. While this would constitute mitigating circumstances, the circumstance itself is by no means special. As unfortunate as this may be, this is often the case with the Colombian clientele.
6. Although Heritage (1998) examined 'oh' and not *ah*, and changes in the state of mind of a speaker may be reflected by other particles (e.g. *mmmm↑, ajá↑*) or expressions (e.g. *ya veo* 'I see'), in this interactional

context, *ah* indicates precisely this, as evidenced by the prior turn and the material subsequently presented in the speaker's contribution.

7. The client's expression *una semana vacacional* ('a holiday week') potentially includes all the different types of weeks offered by the company, those owned or leased to clients in or by a given resort and for which they are responsible for the service charges, and bonus weeks or additional weeks. The latter are given to clients by the company when renewing their membership, in the case of special offers and so on. Bonus or additional weeks entail a slightly higher exchange cost but have no service charges attached to them.

8. Clients normally receive the directory of resorts and accommodation vouchers by snail post.

9. An exception to this is door-to-door selling.

10. This adds to the feeling of institutional facelessness sometimes reported by the clients and to the feeling of being pressured into buying, which often emerges in the conversations themselves.

11. The delay observed in the client's agreeing to engage in the contact detail verification is also observed in other parts of the call and in other intercultural calls between Argentinean or Uruguayan participants and Venezuelan participants. It is likely to be the result of the faster pace at which speakers of River Plate Spanish speak. The fast pace of speakers of River Plate Spanish was also noted by Mexican and Venezuelan agents. During the interviews I conducted, they explained that Argentinean and Uruguayan agents speak too fast and do not always listen to clients.

12. It is customary to telephone clients to confirm that their payment has been received and that their credit cards will be debited accordingly.

5 Closings

5.1 Introduction

In this chapter, I examine the sequences found in the closings of the inbound and outbound calls. I draw on Button's (1987) taxonomy of the English archetype closing, given that these calls were procedurally closed in much the same way. The analysis demonstrates that the participants engage in very similar activities to those observed in the closings of other languages, in particular those of English. The data do not show any differences in the ways in which inbound and outbound call closings were achieved whether the main goal of the calls was to complain about the service, make a service request, solicit information or achieve any other goal. For this reason, the two types of closings are not discussed separately.

In the first part of the chapter, I examine the in-house rules for bringing conversations to a close and relate these recommendations to what takes place in the actual interactions (Sections 5.2 and 5.3). In the analysis, I first examine the most recurrent ways in which conversations are closed, and then look at less prevalent closings in the data (Sections 5.3 and 5.4). Finally, I offer some concluding comments (Section 5.5).

5.2 In-house rules for closing calls

The discussion of the in-house rules for bringing conversations to a close is based principally on document analysis, supplemented with data from interviews with call centre employees and notes from non-participant observation.

During training, the telephone agents are shown how to bring conversations to a close and are required to follow a script. The script for closing inbound and outbound calls is exactly the same. In contrast to the recommendations for the openings (see Figure 3.1 in Chapter 3), the recommendations for closings are listed under the title *Acordar* ('Agree'), rather than under 'Close' as one might expect. Thus the title highlights the fact that,

---

ACORDAR
AGREE

Stage 1
Ask the client to establish an agreement
¿Entonces le confirmo este espacio en este momento Sr. (Nombre)?
'So shall I confirm this slot for you[U] now Mr (Name)?'

Stage 2
Ask the client to perform an action
Confirmar, depositar, renovar, dar tarjeta de crédito
'Confirm, deposit, renew, give credit card details'

Stage 3
Ask the client if there is anything else you can assist him or her with
¿Hay algo más que pueda hacer por usted Sr. (Apellido), algo más en que le pueda ayudar?
'Is there anything else I can do for you[U] Mr (Surname), anything else I can help you[U] with?'

Stage 4
Say goodbye and offer thanks
Muchas gracias por su atención, le recuerdo que mi nombre es (Nombre y Apellido) y estamos para ayudarle, que tenga un hermoso día
'Thank you[U] for your time, my name is (Name and Surname) and we're always here to assist you[U], have[U] a wonderful day'

Figure 5.1 In-house rules for closing calls

once an agreement, preferably a sale, has been reached, there is nothing else to talk about; hence, the agent should bring the conversation to a close. The instruction under 'Stage 1' indicates meta-pragmatically that an agreement should be established, and endorsed by the client. Conveyed in this way, the recommended steps are somewhat optimistic, as they do not include any provision for cases of non-agreements or of arrangements to telephone the client again for a final decision. Similarly, the script does not account for the fact that, in many cases, it is the client rather than the agent who proposes a move towards closure. The suggested steps represent a disengaged view of the daily work reality of the telephone agents, who have to make various calls before an agreement, that is, a sale can eventually be reached.

Once an agreement, in the form of a confirmation, a deposit, a renewal, has been reached, the agents are told to: express their gratitude through topic-initial elicitators (Button 1987), as in, 'Is there anything else I can do for you?'; thank the clients for their time; remind them of the agent's name and willingness to be of service; and wish them a wonderful day. The number of idioms in this courteous, customer-service-oriented closure, which is common in many Western service encounters, at least in those conducted in English, makes the closure sound slightly formal and 'perfunctory'. Although topic-initial elicitators and appreciations occur, they are constructed differently, both sequentially and verbally.

From interviews with telephone agents and Human Resources person-nel and from my observations, it became evident that, rather than being based on what takes place at this particular call centre, the script had been modelled on scripts from other call centre operations. Although it contains a description of some of the tasks agents perform as part of the activity of closing a conversation, it demonstrates, at the same time, detachment from the daily communicative reality of these particular agents and reflects the way in which Management perceives communication, that is, as a relatively unproblematic, natural and spontaneous phenomenon. It then follows that, from Management's point of view, the extrapolation of a standard script to a new call centre, irrespective of the specifics of its operation, will suffice to meet their needs, provided that the script is sufficiently generic and courteous.

Although the linguistic ability of the agents is taken as one of the essen-tial factors for setting up a call centre for the company's various Latin American clients, communication with the clients is not seen as a resource from which to observe and improve procedures or services in general. It is normally ignored unless there are complaints or other types of potentially problematic talk. Even when this is the case, the agents rarely recurred to the records of what had been said or done. We thus have a scenario where the main business tool – communication – is ignored as a potential source of product improvement and is regarded only as a means of product delivery.

For the most part, the participants organised the closings in four distinc-tive turns, comprising a pre-closing adjacency pair and a terminal exchange (Schegloff and Sacks 1973; Button 1987). They thus engaged in similar tasks to those observed in the closings of English telephone conversations.

That closings have received little attention vis-à-vis openings in this area of research is perhaps a reflection of the fact that bringing a conversation to a close can be a delicate matter. According to the rules of turn-taking, after a turn completion, turn transfer becomes relevant (Sacks et al. 1974). It then follows that post-turn silences may be indicative of the wishes of one of the participants to stop talking about a given topic but not necessarily of his or her wish to end the encounter. Thus, arriving at the point in an encounter in which nothing else remains, or is expected, to be said by either party, and transition relevance is suspended, has to be a joint activity. However, agree-ing collaboratively, at a given conversational juncture, to do so is not always straightforward.

A solo closing may bring in undesired social effects, such as perceptions of abruptness, given the unidirectional way of bringing the conversation to a close. Participants, thus, try to coordinate their actions to suspend turn-transitional relevance collaboratively. In doing so, silence can be interpreted as ending the encounter rather than as an interactional gaffe; or it can be attributed to the desire of one of the participants to disengage from a given topic or, for that matter, from the relationship that had been (re-)established through the encounter.

Using Button (1987) (see Chapter 1, Section 1.5) as a point of departure, I offer below a discussion of the ways in which the agents and clients brought conversations to a close. In spite of the fact that the calls examined are institutional and conducted in Spanish, interactional closedown was achieved in much the same way as in mundane calls in English.

5.3 Practices for closing Spanish service calls

The data for this book reveal that both the agents and the clients tended to bring the calls to a close in a four-turn sequence. Instead of proposing closedown primarily via the deployment of pre-closing tokens, they did so principally by the production and subsequent confirmation of arrangements.

5.3.1 Arrangements

Arrangements were observed in 96 out of 131 calls. Through the practice of arrangement making, the conversationalists indicate that a future action will be accomplished after the current encounter is terminated. Arrangements are, therefore, fundamentally last topics, which are perceived as last conversational topics, signalling that their completion will constitute a closing-relevant environment (Robinson 2001), after which participants can proceed to the closing sequence. Similarly, Sigman maintained that:

> [T]erminations of interaction may establish *agendas* or *programs* subsequent to the closing . . . These projections establish, among other things, a schedule for the next co-presence, its time frame and definition of the situation (e.g., what the circumstances of the return will be like), as well as expectations for the meaning and duration of the non-co-presence (especially that the physical separation will most likely be temporary). (Sigman 1991:113)

Arrangements involve the execution of a number of 'programmes', such as telephoning the client again in the future, doing further research on product availability and ringing the client back, as well as telephoning another member of the family to ascertain their holiday interests and liaising back with the client. In all the cases where arrangements were present, closings were formulated immediately afterwards. The arrangement sequence consisted of the future arrangement proposal and its confirmation, as illustrated in Excerpts 2 and 3.

Excerpt 2 [4:4]

```
87   C:   M::.(.) bueno está::. Llámele y hable con mi
88        esposo. Ya::? Y le propo- y le propone[e:so.]
          M::. (.) well OK::. Call⁰ him and talk⁰ to my husband.
          Right::? And you⁰ sugg- and you⁰ suggest    [th:at.]
90   A:                                            [có::mo] no?=
                                                   [su:]re=
91   C:   =e:h. é:l va a estar aquí a     [la una.]
          =u:m.h:e is going to be here at[one o'clock.]
92   A:                                  [cómo no?]
                                         [sure]
93   C:   Si quiere puede e:ste:: intentar al celula:r?
94        (.) o si no lo llama a la una aquí.=
          If you⁰ want you⁰ can u:m:: try his mobil:e?
          (.) or if not call⁰ him here at one o'clock.=
95   A:   =a la una yo lo llamo a su casa.
          =at one o'clock I will call him at home.
96   C:   Yo le voy a decir que:-que:: (.) va a llamar a la
97        una?=
          I'll tell him that:-that:: (.) you⁰ are going to call at
          one o'clock?=
98   A:   =Sí:. Cla:ro. A la una yo llamo para ahí.
          =yes:. Of course. At one o'clock I'll call him on this
          number.
          (0.2)
99   C:   Yo le digo que espere la llamada.
100       (.)llámelo sin falta entonce:.
101       (.) [bue::no.]
          I' ll tell him you're going to call.
          (.) call⁰ him without fail then:.
          (.) [ok:ay.]
102  A:      [Si:n falta] a la una.
          [Wi:th out fail]at one o'clock.
          (0.2)
103  C:   Bueno.(.) yo le digo que espere la llamada.
          Okay. (.) I'll tell him to expect the call.
104  A:   =pe::rfecto.
          =fi:ne.
105  C:   Hasta luego pues.
          Talk to you later then.
```

```
106  A:    Hasta lueguito.
           Yes, talk to you laterᴰᴵᴹ.
```

Excerpt 3 [2:5]
```
60   C:    Me manda de toda esa información que usted me dio
61         por telé:f[ono-con la semana que tengo:?]
           Will youᵛ send me all the information youᵛ gave me over
           the tele:ph[one-with the week I ha:ve?]
62   A:    [claro que le voy a mandar absolutamente]
           [of course I'm going to send youᵛ absolutely]
63   C:    E::ste reservada [( )]
           U::m booked       [( )]
64   A:                      [claro.] claro que sí.
65         (.)quédese tranquilo que yo le mando toda la: la
66         información.
                          [sure.] sure yes.
           (.)restᵛ assured that I will send you all the: the
           information.
           (0.1)
67   C:    Yo le agradezco mucho.
           Thank youᵛ very much.
68   A:    =estoy para servirle hasta luego.
           = I'm here to help youᵛ talk to you later.
69   C:    Hasta luego¹
           Yes, talk to you later.
```

In Excerpt 2 at lines 87–8, the client requests that the agent telephone her husband after the current encounter is terminated so that he can make the final decision. This triggers, at line 90, an acceptance by the agent, in other words, a confirmation for the requested future action. This is followed by an insertion sequence (lines 91–8), where the details of the future action, that is, the time of the call and telephone number where the client should be contacted, are established, and confirmed by the agent. At lines 99–101, the details of the future arrangement are restated and reaffirmed by the participants. The client then initiates the closing sequence by producing a pre-closing token, *bueno* ('okay'), with falling contour before summarising the outcome of the topic (Button 1987) (see line 103), and this constitutes a first close component. The agent accepts with another pre-closing token, *perfecto* ('fine'), with falling intonation, thereby producing a second close component before the participants engage in the terminal exchange at lines 105–6. The terminal exchange is initiated by the client via the formulation of a goodbye token, followed by the conclusive particle *pues* ('then') with falling intonation. The inclusion of the conclusive particle emphasises the client's intention to terminate the encounter and, given its pragmatic meaning, helps to endorse the preceding arrangement. The production of the first pair part of a goodbye exchange dictates the production of a second pair part by the agent.

Similarly, in Excerpt 3 at lines 60–1, the client proposes a future arrangement, which is fully confirmed by the agent at lines 64–6 before the latter summarises the upshot of the topic. In doing so, the agent (re)creates an environment in which bringing the conversation to a close can be seen as the next most relevant activity. The client offers a second close component at line 67 in the form of an appreciation, which obligates a response by the agent, *estoy para servirle* ('I'm here to help you[U]'). The agent's first pair part of the terminal exchange contains a response to the appreciation offered by the client, followed by a goodbye, which, in turn, triggers a response from the client, and at this point the conversation is terminated.

Arrangements are call related, and emerge from the ongoing conversation. In both calls, arrangements are confirmed and, in this way, the conversationalists jointly create a closing-relevant environment. The initiation and confirmation of the arrangement endorse the preceding talk and establish the grounds for future contact between the participants; thus, the arrangement is something the agents will recur to in justification for the call in the initial stages of a follow-up call (see Chapter 3, Section 3.3.2). The arrangement sequence establishes a warrant for proposing closure. While it makes clear that there is nothing else to talk about, it potentially prevents the addressor from infringing upon the addressee's rights to continue talking (Schegloff and Sacks 1973). In order to avoid offence, interactional disjointedness and other potentially distasteful interactional episodes, and in an effort to steer their conversation towards a close, pre-closing tokens are deployed. Pre-closings allow for the other party to continue with the talk or introduce a new topic. It is after the exchange of pre-closing tokens, of which there may be several, given that they leave open the option of (re)topicalisation, or immediately after the confirmation of the arrangement, that participants display that they no longer have anything else to discuss. At this point, the closing is effected. Excerpts 2 and 3 above illustrate cases where the confirmation of the arrangement constitutes a first close component.

Excerpts 2 and 3 are, at first sight, also information-redundant. For instance, in Excerpt 2 after the insertion sequence (lines 91–8), where the details of the future action were ascertained and further confirmed, there is a 0.2-second silence. The client then initiates the reaffirmation of the arrangement (lines 99–101) and the agent subsequently proceeds to restate her commitment to do so (line 102). The initiation of the arrangement reconfirmation and its subsequent response follows from an activity withdrawal (Duranti and Goodwin 1992). At line 98, the arrangement details had been confirmed, thus making the closing the next most relevant activity. At this juncture, however, neither the agent nor the client initiates the closing activity. Instead, there is a 0.2-second silence, after which the confirmation of the arrangement is (re)initiated and restated. Likewise, after the agent has restated her commitment to telephone the client's husband at one o'clock without fail (line 102), one would assume that the client would be satisfied with the response received and that the participants would immediately proceed to the closing activity. Instead, there is another 0.2-second silence, where the first component of the closing could have been uttered. Similarly, in Excerpt 3 at lines 64–6, the agent restates his commitment to send the requested information to the client, *[claro.] claro que sí* ('[sure.] sure yes'),in overlap and emphasises it with the production of a subsequent turn-construction unit formulated as an expression of reassurance, *quédese tranquila* ('rest[U] assured'), followed by a summarised upshot of the topic. Instead of agent and client engaging in the next most relevant activity, the closing, there is a 0.1-second silence. It is after this silence that the client produces a first close component and the participants engage in closing the conversation.

The repetitiveness observed in Excerpts 2 and 3, as illustrated by the clients' restating of confirmed arrangements and by the reassurances provided by the agents, is a recurrent feature of the calls in the corpus. This feature was most conspicuous in calls between speakers of different varieties of Spanish – in other words, in intercultural calls – and appears to convey the participants' different levels of expectations as to what do next. As we will see later in this chapter, the picture that emerges from intra-cultural calls, that is, from calls between speakers who share the same variety of Spanish, is rather different. Intra-cultural closings (see Excerpts 7, 13 and 15 below) were shorter, contained very few, if any, silences and were essentially non-repetitive.

Arrangement confirmation also contained closing-implicative elements, such as titles and first names with falling intonation, as illustrated by *sí señorita* ('Yes Miss') at line 127 in Excerpt 4 below. It should be noted, however, that *sí señorita* ('Yes Miss') is a minimal response (Stivers 2008)[2] and that, at this conversational juncture, may be ambiguous. It may be treated as attending to the call-closing import of the prior utterance (line 126) and thus be indicative of the willingness of the client to collaborate in closing the call, or of the client's acceptance of the agent's proposal of an additional charge. '[P]roducing an ambiguous and minimal response after some proposal or re-iteration of the proposal may be a client's technique for withholding agreement with the organization's proposal' (Davidson 1978: 125). Following the client's minimal response at line 128, the agent produces a sequence-closing third (*okey*), endorsing the client's response and signalling that she understood that the client had understood that there would be an extra charge. The agent then produces a first close component, which comprises the warrant *bueno* ('fine'), followed by an expression of good wishes with the title and first name of the client in final turn position, and the participants then proceed to the next steps of the closing activity.

Excerpt 4 [5:4]

```
126 A:   Eso será: con un costo pero lo va a poder hacer
127      (.)sí?
```

```
                 That will be: at a cost but youᵛ will be able to do it
                 (.)right?
128  C:          Sí señorita.
                 Yes Miss, I will.
129  A:          Okey.(.)bue:no. que pase muy buena tarde señora
130              Marta.
                 Okay.(.)fi:ne. haveᵛ a good afternoon Mrs
                 Marta.
131  C:          O::key bueno. Que esté bien pues=
                 O::kay fine. Take care then
132  A:          =Hasta luego.
                 =Bye for now.
```

Arrangement confirmation was also displayed by the presence of conclusive
particles followed by first names in final turn position (Jefferson 1973), as
illustrated at line 171 in Excerpt 5.

Excerpt 5 [5:6]
```
171  A:   Yo la llamo mañana [entonces María.]
          I'll call youᵛ tomorrow[then María.]
172  C:                       [bueno bue:]no. Muchas gracias y
173       [perdo]ne la molestia e::h?=
                             [fine fi:]ne. Many thanks and sorry
          for any inconvenience a:h?=
174  A:   [tamos?]= no:. no se preocupe María=
          [okay?]= no:. don't worryᵛ María=
175  C:   Gracias  [hasta luego.]
          Thank you [Bye for now]
176  A:            [hasta] mañana.
                   [Until] tomorrow.
```

In the calls in this corpus, the arrangement sequence is the most recurrent practice used to negotiate closure of the current business encounter,
prepare the way for a future business encounter, and proceed to the activity
of closing. Arrangements are, thus, employed to provide an orderly relationship between the current encounter and the next one. They propose that the
current encounter can be appropriately concluded and that further topics
may be 'reserved' for the next encounter.

That arrangements are prominent in these calls reflects the kind of institutional context examined. In this context, the agents telephone the clients
on repeated occasions before a sale can be finalised. The clients need to
know what is available for their holiday plans, including the type of accommodation on offer, prices and related services, the period during which the
accommodation is available and how this affects their existing company

membership. Given that the clientele of this company is mainly constituted by families, clients typically have to consult with other members of the family before a decision can be reached. In those cases where the clients decide to buy the product offered – for example, a week's accommodation in a given holiday destination, renew membership, deposit their timeshare weeks with the company to exchange them in the future and so on – they will also have to provide their credit details. Subsequently, a follow-up call is normally made to confirm that payment has reached the company's account and that the clients will receive written confirmation of this together with any relevant accommodation vouchers. When a sale is not achieved during a telephone encounter, the agents propose future arrangements for telephoning the clients again. Arrangements are thus part and parcel of the sales process. Decisions are rarely made within a single call, even in those cases where the clients telephone the company with a fixed holiday idea in mind.

Other practices observed for bringing calls to a close include a summarised upshot of the conversation topic, the production of prior turn repetition, prior material reiteration, and the reiteration of the reason for the call. These all function as a way of proposing closing initiation (Button 1987). Unlike arrangements, which were present in calls where the clients expressed interest in the product, as well as in those cases where a lack of interest was evident, most of these practices, with the exception of a summarised upshot of the topic, were found in calls where the clients explicitly expressed their lack of interest in the products offered and in those cases where there was no product availability.

5.3.2 Summarised upshot of the conversation topic

This practice was observed in 7 out of 131 calls. In Excerpt 6, after the client has paid for her holiday, the agent offers a summary of the outcome of the encounter before the participants proceed to the closing activity.

Excerpt 6 [9:10]
```
147 A:   Y es importante que:::,(.)que realmente que
148      descanse(.)ok[ey?]
         And it is important that:::,(.)that you really relax
         (.)ok        [ay?]
149 C:              [Sí] señora.
         [Yes] Ma'am.
150 A:   Que aproveche la inversión que tiene,(.)ya?
         That youᵛ take advantage of the investment youᵛ have
         made,(.) right?
151 C:   Perfe:cto.
         Indeed.
152 A:   Gracias por su tiempo Blanca estoy a sus órdenes,
         Thank you for yourᵛ time Blanca I'm always here to help,
```

153 C: Adiós muchas gracias Doña María.
           Goodbye many thanks Donya María.
154 A: Bai bai,
           Bye bye,
155 C: Que Dios la bendiga chau y gracias.
           May God bless you^v bye and thank you.
156 A: No:: estoy a sus órdenes llame cuando quiera.
           No:: my pleasure call^v whenever you want^v to.
157 C: Gracias.
           Thank you.
158 A: Bai bai.
           Bye bye.

After the sale has been achieved and the payment details and process confirmed, instead of proceeding to close the encounter, the agent offers a summary of the outcome of the call in terms of the benefits that membership of this company brings to the client in question. Put differently, the agent produces 'a proverbial or aphoristic formulation of conventional wisdom which can be heard as the "moral" or "lesson" of the topic' (Schegloff and Sacks 1973: 306), followed by a micro-pause and the uttering of a tag (*okey*) with rising intonation. In doing so, the agent indicates that she is waiting for some response from the client. The 'lesson' is acknowledged by the client at line 149 via the production of the minimal response *sí señora* ('yes Ma'am') in overlap with falling intonation, proposing, thereby, a move towards closure. Instead, the agent, whose variety of Spanish is different from the Colombian Spanish spoken by the client, interprets it as an agreement token. She thus proceeds to expand on the upshot of the conversational topic, which she follows with yet another micro-pause and a tag, *ya* ('right'), uttered with rising intonation. In doing so, she signals her expectation of receiving a response in line with the 'lesson' offered. The client restates her acknowledgement of the lesson, at line 151, via a pre-closing device, *perfecto* ('OK'), with falling intonation, which functions as a potential first close component. This, in turn, triggers the appreciation offered by the agent at line 152 as a potential second close component, after which the participants exchange goodbyes (lines 153–4). The call is not closed at this point, however, because the client moves out of the closing activity by producing an extension (Button 1987) at line 155, *Que Dios la bendiga chau y gracias* (' May God bless you^v bye and thank you'). Pragmatically speaking, the additional turn is congruent with the moral earlier offered by the agent. Only after this do the participants re-enter the closing activity. The agent offers the second pair part of an appreciation by stating her willingness to be of help, after which the terminal exchange is achieved. Excerpt 6 is an extended closing; I shall deal with extended and foreshortened closings in Section 5.4.

5.3.3 Prior turn repetition

Prior turn repetition, prior material reiteration and the reason for the call were found to propose closure in those calls which were unsuccessful from the agent's or client's perspective.The practice of prior turn repetition, which was observed in 6 out of 131 calls, is illustrated in Excerpt 7.

Excerpt 7 [2:4]

```
89   A:    [no claro el tema es que::?](.)no hay nada tampoco
90         señora por eso.
           [no sure the thing is that::?](.)there is nothing
           available either Ma'am that is why.
91   C:    No hay    [nada en esa fecha.]
           There isn't[anything on that date.]
92   A:              [no hay nada] de nada.=
                     [there's nothing] nothing at all.=
93   C:    =bueno. (.) bueno. Listo veremos [cómo hacemos
94         entonces,]
           =okay. (.) Okay. Fine let's see [what we can do,]
95   A:                                     [bue::no bárbaro.]
                                            [oka::y great.]
96   C:                                     [tamos] gracias.
                                            [okay] thank you.
97   A:    =no de nada.
           =not at all.
```

At lines 89–90, the agent creates a closing-relevant environment by producing an upshot of the topic, in this case that there is no availability on the dates requested by the client. This can thus be perceived as a possible last topic, given its closing-implicative content and the inclusion of the title *señora* ('Ma'am') followed by the deductive marker *por eso* ('that's why') with falling intonation and in final turn position. The client then repeats the outcome of her enquiry at line 91 and the agent in overlap confirms and emphasises it via the inclusion of an intensifying device, *de nada* ('nothing at all'). In doing so, the agent re-establishes the closing-relevant environment, in which nothing else remains to be discussed. The client acknowledges the lack of product availability with *bueno* ('okay') with falling intonation in a latched utterance and, following a micro-pause, initiates the first close component (line 93). The first close component is formulated via the production of another instance of *bueno* ('okay') with falling intonation, followed by yet another pre-closing device, *listo* ('Fine'), and the closing-implicative comment *veremos cómo hacemos entonces* ('we'll see what we can do, then'), which also includes the conclusive particle *entonces* ('then'). The production of the second *bueno* ('okay') by the client followed by *listo veremos* ('we'll see'), triggers a second close component by the agent at line 95, *bueno bárbaro* ('okay great'), in overlap with the client's last closing-implicative contribution. The participants thus move to end the encounter via the production of a terminal exchange. Specifically, the client thanks the agent at line 96 and the agent offers a second pair part at line 97.

The call in Excerpt 7 is an intra-cultural call, that is, a call between participants who share the same variety of Spanish; in this case, it is between a client from Buenos Aires and an agent from Montevideo, both of whom speak River Plate Spanish (Lipski 1994). In this call, the client requests a slot that is not available. Upon learning about the lack of availability, she requests a different slot but discovers that new slot is not available either; this is due to the demand for slots during the high season and the lateness of the client's request. The repetition of the prior turn by the client at line 91 displays her understanding of the situation, and the subsequent turn by the agent (line 92) endorses the client's understanding and proposes closure as the next most relevant activity. This is understood as such by the client, who in a latched utterance (lines 93–4) initiates the closing activity. Unlike Excerpts 2 and 3, this call, like others in the corpus, shows the participants' mutual understanding as to what is expected from one another. In other words, these participants display a shared understanding of how the context, namely a service call, and the relationship with each other, namely that of service provider and client, should be constructed, and of how they should go about their business, that is, of pursuing the goal-oriented nature of the call.

5.3.4 Reiteration of the prior turn

Reiteration of prior material was present in six calls and is illustrated in Excerpt 8.

Excerpt 8 [8:6]

```
93   C:   [yo no quiero ser pretenciosa] ni fastidiosa. Pero
94        ahora mismo estoy bien copada de mis tarjetas. Yo
95        hasta que no pague todo lo que me gasté en dólares
96        (.)no puedo hacer cargo a un peso más. Sí? Me da
97        pena. Es que yo quise poder desocuparme y avanzar
98        los pagos para tener más libertad en ella.(.) pero
99        no lo pude avanzar. Porque aquí hay una situación
100       en el pueblo? En el país? En que todo el mundo
101       atrasa sus compromisos y lo atrasan a uno también.
102       Sí?
```

[I don't want to be heavy] or fastidious. But right now
I'm well over the limit on my cards. Until I pay what
I spent in dollars(.)I can't spend another single cent

more. *Right? I'm sorry. I wanted to free up the cards*
and make my payments so as to have more credit available
on it(.)but I haven't managed it Because here there is a
situation in the nation? In the country? Where everyone
delays their commitments and one gets behind too.

103 A: Ya:.
           Right:.

104 C: le agrad[ezco muchísimo,]
               Thank [you very much]*

105 A: [le agradezco] su tiempo. Lamentablemente
106   señora,(.)[va a tener un costo de reactivación.
107   verdad?]
                      [Thank you] for your time. Unfortunately*
           Ma'am, (.)[there is going to be a reactivation cost.
           right?]

108 C: [bueno. bueno gracias María por llamar
109   y] quede por ahí porque estamos pendientes, [muy
110   amable pues]
                      [okay. Okay thank you María for calling and]
           let's leave it at that and see what happens   [very
           kind of you then]

111 A: [gracias.]
           [thanks.]

112 C: Hasta luego.
           Bye for now

In Excerpt 8, faced with the insistence of the agent and her lack of interest in the product being offered, the client interrupts the agent and offers a justification (Scott and Lyman 1968) of a personal nature in order to create a closing-relevant environment. This is finally acknowledged by the agent by the uttering of *ya* ('right') with falling intonation, thus giving the client the opportunity to initiate the activity of closing. The client does so at line 104 by offering an intensified appreciation as first close component. This is responded to by the agent at lines 105–7 in overlap and is followed by the reiteration of prior material in an effort to move out of the closing. Support for this can be found in the final turn tag *verdad* ('right') with rising intonation; thus, the agent is inviting a response from the client in the hope of continuing the sales pitch. Instead, the client acknowledges the prior material reiteration by the agent (the first *bueno*, 'okay') by interrupting the agent; in this way, she claims the floor back and initiates the terminal exchange by thanking the agent for having called. She follows this with a closing-implicative comment and an appreciation with the conclusive particle *pues* ('then') in final turn position. The agent is then obligated to offer a second pair part, in overlap, of the appreciation offered by the client at line 111. This also constitutes the first component of the terminal exchange, after which the client offers the second and final component of the terminal exchange.

5.3.5 Reasons for the call

Reasons for the call closures were likewise present only in those cases where the clients expressed their lack of interest in the product offered, and amounted to 16 out of 131 calls, as illustrated in Excerpt 9.

Excerpt 9 [1:4]
```
94   A:    entiendo.
95         (.)bien señor eh:: Mera entonces de todas maneras
96         usted se puede comunicar a::1 0800200?=6868?(.)
97         sí::?
98         (.)e:ste::= para [poder tomar] esta promoción.=
99         sí:?
           I understand.
           (.) okay Mr eh:: Mera so in any case youᵘ can call
           0800200?=6868? (.) right::?
           (.)u:m::= to [take up] this offer.=right:?
100  C:                [ajá::.](0.1) ajá
                       [mm::](0.1) mm::  .
101  A:    Bien.= muchísimas gracias entonces por haberme
102        atendido. Sí::? Y que tenga buenas tardes.
           Fine.= many thanks then for having taken the time to
           talk to me. right::? and haveᵘ a good afternoon.
103  C:    H:asta luego. bai:.
           Bye for now. bye:.
104  A:    Chau chau.
           Bye bye.
```

At line 94, the agent acknowledges the client's lack of interest with *entiendo* ('I understand') and proceeds to reiterate the reason for the call after a turn-transitional place. Essentially, the agent had telephoned the client to entice him into purchasing a special offer. Given that, initially, the client does not show any interest in taking the floor, the agent proceeds to reiterate the fact that there is a special offer for clients and that the client can telephone the call centre to make use of it, should he decide to do so. The client indicates that he has understood the information at line 100 with an acknowledgement token (Jefferson 1983), *ajá* ('mm'), uttered with falling intonation following a hearable silence. In doing so, the client re-establishes the grounds for a closing as the next most relevant activity. This prompts the agent to proceed to the closing activity by offering another acknowledgement token, *bien* ('fine'), through which he signals understanding of the client's lack of interest in the product and that nothing else remains to be discussed. The acknowledgement token is in fact a pre-closing device, after which the agent offers the first close component comprising an appreciation and an expression of good wishes. The client then offers the first pair part of the terminal exchange and this, in turn, triggers a second pair part by the agent. Excerpt 9 also constitutes a foreshortened closing.

5.4 Foreshortened and extended closings

Button (1987) argues that the archetype four turn-closing may be shortened or extended. Foreshortened closings comprise the packing of more than one closing component within a closing turn, thereby producing a three-turn closing. Extended closings, on the other hand, consist of 'the production of a further close component in a third turn that displaces a first terminal component' (p. 137). The database contains both foreshortened and extended closings.

5.4.1 Foreshortened closings

The database contains 27 foreshortened closings. They were foreshortened by producing two-turn and three-turn closing sequences.

In Excerpt 10 below at lines 70–1, the client produces a closing-implicative turn, where she thanks the agent and explicitly expresses her lack of interest in the product offered. She thus creates a closing-relevant environment, in which closure is the most relevant activity. The agent then proceeds to offer a first close component and a first terminal component in the same turn. The first close component is formulated by a compound pre-closing token, *bueno perfecto* ('okay fine'), a closing implicative comment, *no hay ningún problema* ('No problem'), followed by the conclusive particle *entonces* ('then') and the client's title and surname. Following a micro-pause, the agent then offers another turn-construction unit, comprising his good wishes and the first pair part of a goodbye exchange with falling intonation. In other words, the last component of the agent's turn – that is, the first terminal component – could have occupied a second turn, had the client taken the floor. That it is offered in the same turn as the first close component, and hence foreshortened, allows the client to provide a second terminal in the next turn. This is perceived by the client, who, in overlap, thanks the agent and produces the second pair part of a goodbye exchange. In doing so, the client shows sensitivity to the agent's prior turn, in which an intention to terminate the encounter was displayed. The client's final turn is also foreshortened in that it comprises a second close component and the second component of the terminal exchange. The client's offering of a close component in turn-initial position, followed by a second terminal, preserves the mutual accomplishment of closings (Button 1987).

Excerpt 10 [1:8]

```
70   C:   Cla:ro (.) no yo: yo le agradezco mu:cho su: su
71        amabilidad pero no: no queremos nada.
          Of course (.) no : thank you⁰ ve:ry much for your:⁰ your⁰
          kindness but no: we don't want anything.
72   A:   Bu::eno:: perfecto no hay ningún problema entonces
73        señora Cáceres,
          (.) que pase muy bien hasta [luego.]
          O::kay:: fine that's not a problem Ma'am Cáceres, (.)
          bye                         [for now]
74   C:   [muchas] gracias hasta luego.
          [many] thanks bye [for now].
```

Excerpt 11 below provides yet another case of a closing which is foreshortened by both conversational participants. At line 85, the agent produces the pre-closing token *perfecto* ('fine') followed by a closing-implicative comment, *no se preocupe* ('Don't worry⁰'), and an expression of good wishes. After a silence of 0.1 seconds, and upon not hearing the agent say anything else, the client responds with a second close component, *okey* ('okay'), followed by a second terminal exchange, *hasta luego* ('bye for now'), in response to the client's good wishes. Had this closing not been foreshortened, the client's *okey* ('okay') would have occupied a second turn, followed by the agent's *no se preocupe que tenga un buen día* ('Don't worry⁰ have⁰ a good day') in a third turn and the client's *hasta luego* ('Bye for now') in the fourth and final turn.

Excerpt 11 [4:9]

```
85   A:   Perfecto. No se preocupe que tenga un buen día.
          Fine. Don't worry⁰ have⁰ a good day.
          (0.1)
86   C:   Okey (.) hasta luego.
          Okay (.)bye for now.
```

In Excerpt 12 below, the agent creates a closing-relevant environment by thanking the client and apologising for the potential inconvenience of the call. He then offers a first close component in the form of good wishes. The formulation of the apology includes the tag *sí* ('yes'), uttered with rising intonation, and followed by a micro-pause, after which the client could have taken the floor. Given that she does not, the agent proceeds to offer the first close component, in this case, the good wishes. The client, in response, offers a second close component and the first pair part of a goodbye exchange in the same turn (see line 94). The first component of the client's turn at line 94 shows sensitivity to the ritualistic apology proffered by the agent also at lines 92–3, *no es ninguna* ('no bother at all'). The client thus offers a second close component and a first terminal exchange in the same turn, foreshortening, in this way, the closing. The production of *hasta luego* ('bye for now') triggers the agent's response, upon which the call is ended.

Excerpt 12 [3:7]
```
92   A:   Muy-.Mariela muy amable, y le repito, disculpe la
93        molestia sí?
          (.) Que tenga un buen día.
          Very-.Mariela you're very kind, and I repeat, sorryᵀ to
          have bothered you yes?
          (.) haveᵛ a good day.
94   C:   No es ninguna hasta luego.
          No bother at all, bye for now.
95   A:   =hasta luego.
          bye for now.
```

In Excerpt 13 at lines 31–2, the client confirms the arrangement and the agent proceeds with the closing routine. Specifically, in one turn, the agent offers a first close component formulated with the closing token *bueno bárbaro* ('okay great') followed by the client's first name and a micro-pause. Given that the client does not take the floor immediately after the micro-pause, the agent then offers a first terminal exchange comprising thanks and the first pair part of a goodbye exchange. The client responds with the uttering of *muy bien* ('very good'), which, in this call, serves as a second terminal partly because the client subsequently puts down the phone. That the second terminal is not preceded by a second close component makes this closing appear slightly abrupt (Button 1987). Nevertheless, this call shows that the participants know what to do next in respect of each other's contributions and thus displays intersubjectivity. In view of the foregoing analysis, it should not come as a surprise to learn that the participants are male speakers of the River Plate variety of Spanish.

Excerpt 13 [5:7]
```
31   C:   Quedamos así entonces=La otra semana yo te pego un
32        tubaso.
          Let's leave it like that then = next week I'll give youᵀ/ᵛ
          a bell.
33   A:   Bueno bárbaro Jorge.(.) gracias [hasta] luego.
          Okay great Jorge.(.) thank you bye for now .
34   C:                                   [muy bien.]
                                          [very good ]
```

5.4.2 Extended closings

As Button (1987) observed, extended closings comprise the production of a further close component in a third turn. The presence of a further close component displaces and delays the production of a first terminal. It allows for the continuation of talk and, given its closing implicative nature, precludes the possibility of (re)topicalisation because 'extensions do not exploit an opportunity to move out of closings, nor do they project the relevance of closing reinitiation. They are both closing implicative and terminal elicitive' (p. 139). Extensions were more prominent than foreshortenings. The corpus contains 38 extended closings.

In Excerpt 14 below at lines 51–2 and 53, an arrangement for a future call is proposed and confirmed. Following this, at lines 54–5, the agent produces a closing-implicative comment by offering the upshot of the arrangement, followed by good wishes, thereby offering a first close component. This, in turn, triggers the client's appreciation at line 55, which serves as a second close component and elicits the first terminal by the agent at line 57 via the formulation of the first pair part of a goodbye exchange. At line 58, the client responds in a latched utterance to the good wishes proffered by the agent at lines 54–5, *que pase muy bien* ('all the best'), due to the overlap observed at lines 56–7. Following this and in overlap, the agent produces a further goodbye token (line 59). The extended closing in this call is produced not by delaying or displacing a first terminal but by the addition of a further turn (line 58). Arguably, the extension responds to the fact that overlap is built into this closing.

Excerpt 14 [7:4]

```
51   A:   Entonces nos comunicamos más adelante con usted le
52        parece bien Marí::a?
          so we will call youᵛ later is that okay Marí::a?
53   C:   =sí::? me parece bien.
          =yes::? That's fine.
54   A:   =estamos hablando más adelante que pase muy
55        bie::n,
          =so we'll talk later all the be:st,
56   C:   Bueno gracias. [muy amable.]
          Okay thank you.  [very kind.]
57   A:                   [hasta luego] adiós,
                          [bye for now] bye,
58   C:   =igual[mente.]
          =like  [wise.]
59   A:         [Adiós,]
               [Bye,]
```

Excerpt 15 below constitutes a call-back conversation between the agent and the client. At lines 97–8, an arrangement for a future call is restated and confirmed. At line 99, the client produces a putative first close component via the uttering of the pre-closing *bueno* ('okay') with falling intonation. It is possible, however, that the agent interprets this as a further confirmation of the arrangement made, rather than as an initiation of the closing routine. The production at line 100 of the pre-closing token *perfecto* ('fine'), which elicits a second close component by the client at line 101, would appear to bear this out. In a latched utterance, the agent then produces a candidate first terminal (see line 102). Rather than trigger a second terminal, however, this generates a response to the agent's *un beso grande* ('a big kiss') proffered at line 102. Subsequently, the participants engage in the terminal exchange via an exchange of goodbyes. It is, therefore, after the additional sequence at lines 102 and 103 that the participants enter the terminal exchange and the encounter is completed. The additional sequence arguably responds to the pace of the talk and to the uttering of quick, short turn-construction units in overlap.

Excerpt 15 [12:10]

```
97   C:   Bueno. Eh:: avisame entonces?
          Okay. Um:: let^{T/V} me know then?
98   A:   Sí.
          Yes.
99   C:   =bueno.
          =okay.
100  A:   =perfecto.
          =fine.
101  C:   =bárbaro.
          =great.
102  A:   =bueno: Un beso grande,  [hasta] mañana.
          =okay: a big kiss,       [until] tomorrow.
103  C:                            [Gracias.]
                                   [Thank you.]
104  A:   Chau.
          Bye.
105  C:   Hasta luego.
          Bye for now.
```

Despite the additional sequence, this closing also displays the participants' mutual understanding as to what is expected from one another. Unsurprisingly, this is also a call between speakers who share the same variety of Spanish: River Plate Spanish.

Similarly, Excerpts 16 and 17 are illustrative of extended closings. In Excerpt 16 at lines 140–2, the client expresses his lack of interest with a closing-implicative comment in which he explains that he will telephone the company should he decide to renew his membership. The comment functions as an excuse signalling his intent to bring the conversation to a close. This is understood as such by the agent, who, in the subsequent turn (line 143), acknowledges it with *bueno* ('okay') and produces a first close component via the formulation of the compound pre-closing token *okey perfecto* ('okay fine'). The client then offers a second close component, formulated via the production of the agreement token *(excelente*, 'great'), and followed by the first pair part of a thank-you exchange. The agent reciprocates the appreciation with *por favor* ('not at all'), followed by an expression of willingness to help and of his good wishes, which includes the client's title, 'Mr', and first name in final turn position, thereby formulating a first terminal (line 145). In overlap, the client offers the first pair part of a goodbye exchange (line 147) and the agent reciprocates the goodbye at line 148, after which the encounter is terminated. Given the overlap observed at lines 147–8, Excerpt 16 is also illustrative of an extended closing via the production of an additional turn (line 148), namely, a further goodbye token.

Excerpt 16 [1:6]

```
140  C:   Bueno: e:h yo voy a:.>en este: es deci:r< (.) si
141       este:: es lo que renovamos después te aviso. (.)
142       e:h?
          Okay: u:m I am going to a:. >in um: that i:s< (.) if
          um:: if we renew it I'll let youʳ/ᵛ know later. (.)
          u:h?
143  A:   Bueno. Okey perfecto,
          Okay. Okay fine,
144  C:   =excelente,gracias.
          =great, thank you.
145  A:   Por favor.(.) a las órdenes que pase bien [señor
146       Roberto.]
          Not at all. (.)I'm here to help haveᵛ a good day [Mr
          Roberto.]
147  C:                                              [ta luego.]
                                                     [Bye for now.]
148  A:   Chau chau.
          Bye bye.
```

In Excerpt 17 at line 199, the client offers a first close component via the uttering of *bueno* ('okay'), which functions here as an indexical, followed by an appreciation in which the title and name of the agent appear in final turn position. This then triggers the agent's reciprocation of the appreciation *Por favor ha sido un placer* ('Not at all it's been a pleasure'), followed by an expression of good wishes with the inclusion of the client's title in final turn position. This, in turn, helps to sow the seeds for the next task: the terminal exchange. Instead, the participants engage in a further thank-you sequence (lines 202–3). In the light of the absence of any further contributions, the last thank-you sequence is interpreted by the agent as the terminal exchange; this is not the case with the client, however, as she then offers, at line 204, what she considers to be a first terminal, namely, the first pair part of a goodbye exchange. Given the subsequent silence and the absence of any sound indicating that the agent had hung up, the client reiterates the goodbye token, albeit followed, on this occasion, by the conclusive particle *pues* ('then'), after which she puts the telephone down. The additional sequence observed is yet again the result of overlap talk, while the 0.2-second silence observed after line 204 suggests that the client did not interpret the agent's thank-you at line 203 as a second terminal. Instead, she seems to have expected a second pair part to her goodbye exchange. It is difficult to tell whether this responds to different conversational expectations or merely to the fact that the agent had contacted the client on her mobile phone and that the latter was on the phone while attending a patient during her obligatory A&E shift. Given this contextual information, the additional turns may have resulted from intermittent attention focus and from the background noise affecting the communication line.

Excerpt 17 [4:7]

```
199  C:   Bueno: muchas gracias señor Eduardo,
          Okay: many thanks Mr Eduardo,
200  A:   =Por favor ha sido un placer y que tenga un:-una
201       Buena tarde:: doctora eh?
          =Not at all it's been a pleasure and have a:-a good
          afternoon: doctor uh?
202  C:   Bueno [gracias.]
          Okay  [thank you.]
203  A:         [gracias.]
                [thank you.]
204  C:   Hasta luego.
          Bye for now.
          (0.2)
205  C:   (chau pue:..)
          (bye then:..)
```

5.5 Some concluding comments

The foregoing analysis has shown no fundamental differences in the ways in which inbound and outbound calls were brought to a close. It has also shown that the task of discontinuing an encounter is a joint activity. Essentially, participants have to arrive at a point in the conversation where 'one speaker's completion will not occasion another speaker's talk, and that will not be heard as some speaker's silence' (Schegloff and Sacks 1973: 294–5) or interpreted as a sign of impoliteness.

Despite differences in languages (the shared language of the participants in this study being Spanish) and differences in the interactional environment examined (mediated service talk), these conversationalists have been shown to engage in tasks similar to those reported by Schegloff and Sacks (1973) and Button (1987) in English mundane calls as well as those observed in the closings of English institutional calls (see, for example, Robinson 2001; Maynard and Schaeffer 2002a, 2002b). The analysis thus provides yet further evidence in support of CA as a methodology for research into languages other than English and offers the first analysis of Spanish institutional closings in a pervasively modern mediated institutional environment.

The examination of the closings demonstrates that, to mark their beginning and end, they are constructed with recursively applicable routine formulae, such as goodbye exchanges and general good wishes. Thus, formulaic language plays an important part in the performance of the closing. The fixed and recurrent nature of idioms makes them ideal contenders for the delicate job of jointly exiting mediated presence. The clarity and formulaic nature of the sequences may respond to the potential difficulties of coordinating closure. Formulaic language comprises socially recognised expressions (Coulmas 1986) with clear socio-cultural meaning, which trigger conventional responses. They are thus semantically and pragmatically unambiguous, at least for those participants who share a language and culture. In such cases, formulae offer an opportunity for the other participant to 'agree to depart' and, thus, politely and collaboratively to bring the conversation to a close.

However, some of the conversational excerpts examined showed a lack of understanding regarding what the participants expected from one another on the basis of such formulae. A case in point is the use of *sí señor/a/ita* ('yes Sir/Ma'am/Miss') as a putative pre-closing device by the Colombian participants. The analysis demonstrates that non-Colombians did not understand the expression as a routinised way of signalling a move towards closure in spite of its sequential placement - after the arrangement confirmation. Instead, the expression was interpreted as an acknowledgement token indicating receipt of information and allowing the other participant to continue expanding on the topic. Similarly, the *como no* ('of course') uttered by agents from Buenos Aires and Montevideo, who speak River Plate Spanish, was not heard by Colombian and Venezuelan clients as an endorsement of the arrangement proposal, so they proceeded to seek arrangement reaffirmation.

It was further observed that, as evidenced in the subsequent silences, a summarised upshot of the conversational topic on its own was insufficient to convey a move towards closure. Instead, participants in intercultural calls seem to have expected that a recognised pre-closing token, such as *bueno* ('okay') or *okey* ('okay'), would follow. These tokens, unlike the ones mentioned earlier, appear to have similar meta-pragmatic meaning across varieties of Spanish. Also noteworthy is the fact that in some intercultural calls where the first pair part of a terminal exchange was formulated not with a goodbye token but with an expression of appreciation, addressors appeared uncertain as to its function as a terminal exchange. On the one hand, this corroborates the status of goodbye exchanges as a prototypical device for lifting transition relevance (Maynard and Schaeffer 2002a, 2002b) and, on the other hand, it foregrounds the importance attributed to goodbyes as markers of interactional cessation. It seems, therefore, that the safest way of collaboratively achieving closure in intercultural calls is via the production of tokens and expressions that are not language- or culture-specific, that is, of pre-closing tokens which are common across varieties of Spanish and goodbye exchanges.

A notable feature of the closings of this corpus is their general verbosity. Essentially, there is an observed tendency by the participants, telephone agents and clients alike, to repeat closing elements, that is, arrangement reaffirmation as well as closing elements within turns; there is also, in some cases, the tendency to include affective terms normally associated with close relationships – *un beso* or *mi amor* ('my love')[3] – and to reiterate goodbye tokens. The cumulative effect of these elements results in more verbose closings vis-à-vis those observed in English institutional calls. This general tendency towards verbosity has previously been observed in studies of Spanish mediated service talk, as has a propensity for a relatively informal and friendly style between participants who are not in close relationships (see Márquez Reiter 2006, 2009). In view of this, we should question the extent to which this verbosity may be related to language, or to culture, or to both. Before doing so, it is apposite to dwell briefly on the type of stylistic verbosity observed, bearing in mind that the sequences which comprise the closing respond to the contingencies of the talk and that, in most cases, closings were triggered by the proposal and later confirmation of an arrangement for a follow-up call. The participants thus constructed their relationship as continuing; the closing therefore represents the end of the current encounter, confirms the interlocutors' relationship and paves the way for the participants' next encounter.

The participants tended to construct their closing components by repeating lexical items and offering supportive terminal exchanges. Essentially, while some closings contained individual pre-closing tokens, in most calls pre-closing tokens comprised the production of compound pre-closing tokens, such as *bueno bárbaro* ('okay great'), *okey perfecto* ('okay fine') and *bueno listo* ('okay then'), when, strictly speaking, the production of one of these could have sufficed. It is important to note also that, in those cases where single pre-closing tokens were deployed, the calls were extended (see, for example, Excerpt 15 above). Consecutive pre-closing tokens of the kind observed here should be regarded as one rather than two pre-closing tokens. Although they consist of two lexical items, they constitute one recognisable action, in most cases a warrant for closing, and were intonationally packaged as one. Further support for this can be found in the absence of a micropause between the two lexical items or the presence of overlaps and the fact that they were uttered with the same intonational contour. The presence of

compound pre-closing tokens is thus suggestive of a language-related preference: specifically, a tendency in Spanish service talk for compound pre-
closing tokens over single ones, as well as a language variety preference for
certain warrants over others.

Similarly, the terminal exchange was generally achieved by the production of two consecutive goodbye tokens, such as *hasta luego chau* ('bye for
now bye'), *chau chau* ('bye bye') or *chao chao* ('bye bye'),[4] *adiós* ('goodbye'),
within the same turn, or of intensified leave-taking utterances, such as *un beso
grande* ('a big kiss'), or of both. This would suggest a language preference
for consecutive goodbyes while, at the same time, signalling the importance
of goodbyes in conveying 'members' reciprocal respect for identity' and
'the import of the interactional cessation for the social relationship' Sigman
(1991: 113). Further support for this can be found in Excerpts 11 and 17,
where the agent neither formulated the terminal exchange with a goodbye
token, nor reciprocated the goodbye token proffered by the client. In both
closings, a perceivable silence immediately followed and this, in turn, was
interpreted by both clients as imminent call cessation.

In addition, most closing turns contain more than one turn-construction
unit, such as an expression of appreciation, accompanied by good wishes, or
expressions of willingness to serve the client, or both. It will also be recalled
that extended closings comprised the production of an additional turn and
that this turn generally consisted of a further goodbye token. This would
appear to reflect the findings of Coronel-Molina (1998), who reports the
occurrence of 'triplet goodbyes' as widespread in a relatively small corpus
of recorded intra-cultural telephone conversations between Hispanic family
and friends (Chile, Cuba, Mexico, Panama, Peru and Puerto Rico). Although
additional goodbye tokens were also observed in some of these closings,
their presence has been attributed to contingent features of the calls, such as
built-in overlap, rather than to a language or socio-cultural preference or to
a culture-specific way of organising talk-in-interaction.

The repetition of verbal elements within the turns indicates a willingness
to continue interacting and shows that there are no additional topics to talk
about. The closing sequences observed – *que tenga un buen día* ('have[U] a good
day'), *gracias por su amabilidad* ('thank you for all your[U] help') – were oriented to the face concerns of the participants in their respective roles of client
and service provider. These sequences consisted of expressions of appreciation as a valued customer and of good wishes, which together allowed for the
possibility of conversational reciprocation. In most cases, reciprocation was
immediately offered and participants departed from each other's presence
politely. The repetition of verbal elements, thus, helped the participants not
only to confirm their intent to bring the conversation to a close, but also to
reassure each other of their relationship.

The contributions of the participants show that, from the point of view
of both parties, this is a relationship worth investing in and one that will

continue in the future. It is worth recalling that, in the inbound calls, it is the client who telephones the company and that, although many of the outbound calls, in particular first call attempts, are unsolicited, they are not unwarranted and, in many cases, they are welcome. When closing, participants reaffirm their roles: the service providers by offering further assistance and making other suggestions, and the clients, for their part, by expressing their appreciation of the service and agreeing on a future point of contact. It is at this point that the participants exchange goodbyes. The preference for *hasta luego* ('bye for now'), *chau* ('bye') and *bai bai* ('bye bye') over the more neutral *adiós* ('goodbye') reflects the general degree of informality and relational orientedness of the preceding talk and sums up the type of relationship established through the encounter. The choice of *hasta luego* ('bye for now'), the goodbye token *par excellence*, is semantically suggestive of a potential future encounter between the participants. Put differently, these expressions indicate that the break in social contact is temporary, that the participants are still acquainted with one another and that contact is likely to be resumed at some time in the near future. According to Goffman (1967), farewells 'sum up the effect of the encounter upon the relationship and show what the participants may expect of one another when they next meet' (p. 41).

The interviews conducted with these telephone agents reveal that the interactions are consonant with their everyday expectations and experience of telephone-mediated services where further contact at some point in time is almost a given. The talk examined here, though institutional, is primarily service-based and service-oriented, and is both private and business-related. Despite its goal-oriented nature, it contains several elements which are usually found in mundane talk, in particular personalisation elements aimed at reducing social distance. The pursuit of a friendly image is motivated by the main goal of the interaction: to secure a sale by the agent and a good deal by the client. Given the more negotiable nature of these interactions, namely that prior to the call a relationship between the participants, the client and the company had existed and that it will probably continue in the future, relationally oriented elements should not come as a surprise.

Telephone agents have to try to sell a product over the phone and this normally takes more than one call. An interpersonally oriented closing, thus, helps to build a friendly relationship and, in cases where clients show little interest, enhances the chances of future contact. These closings reflect the preceding talk and are conducive to the agents' receiving the green light from the clients to telephone again. They provide the agents with another opportunity to do their job, obtain a sale, and the client with a more tailored service when service availability may be insufficient elsewhere.

Although my intention is not to paint a picture of service talk that is purely strategic and underpinned merely by the potential for financial gains, relationally relevant elements are salient in the closings and in the conversations as a whole (see Chapters 3 and 4). Strictly speaking, they are not essential for the service to be completed, but their occurrence is nonetheless important. Given the lack of regulation, that is, call monitoring, I argue that this is an example of one of the strategies put into practice by the agents from their experience on the job – from their hearing other agents doing the same as well as from their own experience as clients.

Some evidence in support of the goal-oriented nature of this type of relationally oriented talk comes from the closings of calls where the called, that is, the client, was unavailable. Agents interacted with answerers, usually housekeepers, when telephoning the clients' homes, or with secretaries when ringing the clients at work. As these calls were limited to obtaining further contact details for the clients, closings were characteristically short. They were closer to those identified in the English literature (see, for example, Button 1987; Maynard and Schaeffer 2002a, 2002b) and contained less relationally relevant information; this is illustrated in Excerpt 18.

Excerpt 18 [8:10] (H = housekeeper, A = agent)

```
32   H:    Anotó bien?
           Did you⁰ jot it down correctly?
33   A:    Sí.(.)gracias,
           Yes.(.)thanks,
34   H:    No::. Hasta luego.
           No::. Bye for now.
35   A:    Chau.
           Bye.
```

The conversational footings (Goffman 1979) and interpersonal investment observed are thus attributable not only to the language in which the conversations are carried out, and the type of talk per se, namely service talk, but also to how the footings and investment find their way into this talk. This is done via the new space that they occupy, that is, a mediated service encounter obtained from the comfort of one's home, or at work, on one's landline or mobile phone, in real time without recourse to paralinguistic features.

Despite the relative newness of the medium and mode, in the sense of the replacement of the more traditional face-to-face service encounters, the core activities that the participants in this research have been shown to engage in to bring a conversation to a close are fundamentally the same. Essentially, there are close correspondences, albeit not necessarily precise fits, between the categories identified in English mundane and institutional closings and those observed here. That such correspondences exist provides yet further evidence in support of the basic tenets and findings of CA, that is, the orderliness and apparent universality[5] of the sequential organisation of everyday human actions. Similarly, that exact matches were not found is suggestive of cultural differences, in terms of both the language of the interactions and the way in which the institutional context is constructed; for example, as mediated service talk where single calls are seen as one in a series of potential future encounters.

Notes

1. Normally, *hasta luego* is translated as 'goodbye' and, in other cases, as 'see or talk to you later' or 'bye for now'. My decision to prefer the last two possibilities is two-fold. First, it distinguishes this goodbye token from others. Second, goodbyes encapsulate the relevance of the encounter termination for the kind of social relationship that had been (re-)established by the participants during the interaction, and *hasta luego* signals the possibility of a not-too-distant future encounter between the participants.
2. The client is from Bogotá, where expressions such as *sí señor/a/ita* are used as minimal responses which acknowledge prior utterances. This information was gathered from interviews with Colombian personnel, non-participant observation and repeated listenings of calls with Colombian participants.
3. This is particularly salient in calls with Venezuelan female clients.
4. Chileans, Argentineans and Uruguayans employed *chau* while Colombians, Peruvians and Venezuelans used *chao*.
5. It should be noted that the search for universals is not part of the CA agenda despite an implicit tendency to describe certain conversational practices as if they were universal – for example, telephone openings.

6 Some Final Reflections: Towards an Understanding of Intercultural Communication in Spanish

6.1 Introduction

In the foregoing chapters I have examined the various activities that conversationalists from different Spanish-speaking regions perform in order to supply and demand a service in a modern mediated interactional environment. These activities are mediated by the technological medium which constitutes them, that is, the telephone, and by means of the language that unites them: Spanish. The analysis has demonstrated that, in spite of the relative recentness of telephone service provision in real time, twenty-four hours a day, seven days a week, and the varieties of Spanish spoken by the participants, the core activities that the participants engaged in are fundamentally similar to those which have been reported in face-to-face service encounters of a similar kind. Furthermore, the findings reveal close correspondences between the core activities reported here and those that have been identified in English institutional calls, as well as in other unrelated languages. The similarities in the coordination and ritualisation of specifically located activities, such as openings, middles and closings, provides further evidence for the orderliness of human action.

Besides similarities in the core communicative jobs performed to achieve given task-based goals, the analysis has shown differences in the ways in which socio-cultural practices are interpolated into action. We have thus witnessed an overwhelming presence of greetings and how-are-you exchanges, as well as other conversationalisation elements, when, strictly speaking, these are not essential for the business transactions pursued in these calls to be completed. I have argued that some of this communicative behaviour is oriented towards the business of Spanish talk and Spanish business talk. I have also contended that the environmental business conditions which help to constitute the interactions examined enable the flourishing of service practices which might, otherwise, not exist. These include the enactment of fabricated ignorance by information-disadvantaged clients, and the tendency of the agents (1) to refrain from offering institutional identification before ascertaining that they are talking to the right person, and

(2) to camouflage the reason for the call in order to enhance their chances of enlisting the participation of (prospective) clients in unsolicited sales pitches. Contextual conditions, such as the way in which the service is operationalised and managed, coupled with the need for good customer-service relationships, seem to result in certain practices being endowed with more relational importance than would normally be the case in other interactional environments. One such practice is the making of arrangements for a future encounter. The recurrent presence of arrangements is a result of service operationalistion. The ways in which they are constructed and evoked in the initial stages of follow-up encounters to legitimise communicative behaviour offers a window into the rights and obligations accrued by the participants in this type of business relationship. Differences were also observed in the ways in which the participants managed interculturality and in some of the patterns observed across interactions with clients from certain Latin American nationalities. Thus, while engaging in the interpersonally delicate task of mutually coordinating interactional cessation, participants who speak different varieties of Spanish performed rather long and verbose closings, as a result of differences in routine formulae, among others. Put differently, the ways in which the interlocutors constructed the closings indicated differences in the knowledge on which the communication was based, and this was evidenced in the different symbolic behaviour of familiar linguistic forms. This, in turn, led many conversationalists to repeat and redo closing elements until the intention of bringing the conversation to a close was mutually ascertained.

In this final chapter, I examine segments of some of the calls in which intercultural issues surface and have an effect on the ensuing interaction. I also report on some of the recurrent patterns observed, across interactions, with clients from given Latin American backgrounds. In doing so, I explore some of the communication patterns at the heart of commonly held stereotypical views of Latin Americans by Latin Americans and offer a discussion of the meta-communicative views obtained by means of interviews. The discussion presented in this chapter thus brings together the analyses offered so far by considering the significance of differences which surface from these analyses despite fundamentally close correspondences in activity. In so doing, the discussion seeks to contribute to the body of knowledge in intercultural and cross-cultural communication, where Spanish has received little attention and the contact between native speakers who speak different standard varieties of Spanish, for primarily transactional purposes, has received significantly less.

6.2 Mediated intercultural communication across Spanishes

Until now, research that has indirectly focused on intercultural communication in Spanish[1] has principally examined languages in contact. Scholars in this area of inquiry (see, for example, Zimmerman and de Granda 2004) have investigated the intercultural patterns that emerge when Spanish is in contact with other languages, rather than contact between native speakers of Spanish from different backgrounds in naturally occurring (business) interactions. Owing to the nature of the cultural groups examined, that is, different linguistic and cultural groups who do not share similar communicative norms, and to an overemphasis on the analysis of 'critical incidents', the picture of the field presented is one characterised by problematic talk. Furthermore, little importance seems to have been attached to the fact that intercultural communication is located at the interactional level (Blommaert and Verschueren 1991) and, thus, best examined interactionally (see, for example, Gumperz 1982) rather than by the sole means of surveys and experiments, in which culture and intercultural communication are often treated as variables that can be objectively measured and controlled.

The view of intercultural communication[2] as problematic is based on the assumption of important differences between communities or cultures who speak different languages; an assumption which also lies at the heart of most research into cross-cultural pragmatics and one I was very much aware of when initially embarking on this project. Specifically, I wanted to shed light on the ways in which mediated business interactions are constructed in Spanish given that, to the best of my knowledge, there are no studies in this area and that, what is more, the kinds of service provision represented by the calls examined in this book are an everyday modern occurrence that many of us have to live with. Admittedly, not everyone leases a holiday unit overseas or wishes to do so; however, service provision through the medium of the telephone is prevalent across many private and public institutions in Latin America and the days of face-to-face service provision are becoming increasingly rare. The way in which services are provided by 'Holidays to Remember' represents, thus, a type of interactional environment in which many consumers and service providers are regularly immersed.

Assuming that differences in the production of everyday activities would emerge in the contact between different communities who speak different varieties of standard Spanish, it follows that a point of reference would be provided by studies of service talk in Spanish(es). In other words, research into the ways in which participants from different Spanish-speaking communities construct task-oriented activities of the kind examined here could help to ascertain the significance of any patterns observed. Given that these studies do not yet exist, an initial and somewhat implicit point of comparison has been made in this book with the activities that have been reported for speakers of English in similar interactional environments. The reason for this is that a rich body of evidence exists in this language and, importantly, the research on which it is based brings to the fore the social conduct that is accomplished by conversationalists through language rather than the language itself.[3] A point of comparison is, nevertheless, provided in the corpus itself. The supranational nature of the telephone conversations examined in this book has resulted in the regular contact between culturally and dialectically different speakers of Spanish, who typically have had very little contact with one another and are unaware of each other's customs (Márquez Reiter in press) and, in a very small number of cases, in the contact between dialectically similar participants. This, in turn, provides us with a small number of intra-cultural calls which can be used as a point of comparison to help us understand the significance of the patterns observed across intercultural calls.

Equipped with my training in cross-cultural pragmatics, my initial intention was to discover whether the interactional activities and practices observed here were culturally significant, that is to say, whether they were regularly oriented to Spanish linguistic and cultural features, and whether there were any differences between the varieties of Spanish. My initial fieldwork at the call centre suggested such differences. More precisely, while observing the agents at work, I noticed differences in the ways they approached clients from different regions and the ways in which the latter reacted. These first impressions were confirmed by the interviews I conducted with the agents and other employees of the call centre. The interviews are a testimony to some of the stereotypes that Latin Americans commonly hold about each other. Interestingly, too, they are consonant with many aspects of the actual telephone conversations. In fact, the data show that, inasmuch as the agents put into practice different strategies to deal with different Latin American clients, these views of the other are often demonstrable at the level of the interaction. Likewise, the clients perform their activities in ways which are congruent with those of other clients who, as far as language variety is concerned, come from the same background. Clearly, these patterns cannot be taken to describe accurately the cultural traits of the other as if the other were homogeneous, devoid of the ability to evolve, and programmed to display the same interactional behaviour across different environments irrespective of the interlocutors. The patterns can, however, offer a window into the values of the perceivers, into what they think is socially expected. In other words, they allow us to look through the keyhole of perceived socially appropriate conduct. It is only in those cases where interactional misfires take place, are verbalised, and have an effect on the ensuing interaction that these values come to the surface, providing us with the opportunity to examine them.

Returning to the earlier characterisation of intercultural communication as problematic interaction, the stance taken here is not necessarily one of problematic talk. Inevitably, interactional 'coarseness', hypothetically speaking, is more likely to emerge during encounters between cultural groups who have had little contact with one another, or are unfamiliar with each other's ways, than between groups that speak the same language variety and have had regular contact with one another. The ability to repair interactional problems is, however, one that most competent speakers have developed inasmuch as human beings are endowed with language ability. Therefore, the misfires or elements of interactional friction observed in intercultural encounters allow us to see the ways in which the tools of interaction are deployed by different participants to resolve potential problems and, at the same time, throw light on their expectations of appropriate interactional conduct.

Upon close inspection of the calls in this research, however, more similarities than differences were revealed. As I have shown in the preceding chapters, these conversational participants engage in similar activities to those that have been reported in similar interactional environments by speakers of unrelated languages. Irrespective of the variety of Spanish, they perform similar interactional tasks and resolve interactional problems in remarkably similar ways to speakers of other languages. The previous chapters have also shown a preference for certain ways of going about resolving interactional problems. In particular, a number of recurrent though, strictly speaking, non-essential practices have been identified and linked to standing business practices in Latin America and to contextual features of the interactional environment examined; namely, a mediated business environment, which deprives its users of non-paralinguistic information, and which endows some of them with unequal access to (information) resources and both of them with the ability to supply and demand a sometimes unsolicited, but instant, service.

Intercultural communication in the sense of bringing together people who share the same native language but who have different linguistic and cultural characteristics and have had, in most cases, little contact with one another has hardly received any attention (see Márquez Reiter 2010). Arguably, and particularly in the case of Spanish, this is because such contact is the result of globalisation and thus a relatively modern communicative phenomenon. More precisely, the kind of intercultural contact represented in the data examined in this book is becoming, for many Latin Americans, an everyday experience so far as the provision of certain services is concerned. In addition to the relative newness of the interactional environment examined here, the participants are all native speakers of Spanish, though they speak different varieties of that language and come from nations with rich cultural differences, from their ethnic composition to the languages spoken beyond Spanish, and in terms of music, dance, political and socioeconomic indicators, membership in trading blocks and so forth.

The varieties they speak, to a greater or lesser extent, represent different varieties of standard Spanish. Such identification, however, is typically effected by speakers of those same varieties, who can easily recognise each other, by those versed in the most salient features reported by dialectologists and sociolinguistics, and by those who have had enough contact with the varieties in question and have somehow developed some degree of Spanish heterodialect interactional competence. Research into Latin American Spanish dialectology (see, for example, Lipski 1994) and, to a lesser though not insignificant degree, into sociolinguistics, has revealed how 'astoundingly diverse and incredibly unified' (Lipski 1994: x) Spanish is. Such research has, however, mainly focused on written communication and within the realm of spoken communication it has concentrated on speech, in particular educated speech. The data examined in this book also constitute spoken communication, although they are primarily talk rather than speech. The talk discussed here is also diverse but united under the banner of a commonly understood language: Spanish. Such an understanding would, in theory, allow its participants to resolve problems quickly *in situ*, as they do when faced with lexemes to which are attributed different semantic meaning in different varieties of the language.[4] On the other hand, the very sameness of language and, in particular, the presence of familiar linguistic devices performing unfamiliar actions can bring in potential misunderstandings.

Intercultural communication is understood here as an instance of interpersonal communication between participants who are culturally different (Scollon and Scollon 1981) – who share the same basic language but are not necessarily familiar with each other's language variety in interaction or with one another's interactional practices. So far, the wealth of studies that have explored intercultural communication focus on problematic situations, miscommunication and critical incidents, which, by definition, are not the commonplace events in which cultural differences can be readily overlooked and where, in the end, they become more consequential. The examination I present here, in contrast, is of everyday differences in the context of modern business interactions as they become relevant to the interactional participants themselves.

While the data examined in this book are rich and contemporary enough to write at least one chapter per variety of Spanish in its various contact combinations, it must be obvious by now that the aim of the book and space constraints prevent me from doing so. Instead, the discussion which follows will concentrate on the most salient patterns of interactional behaviour observed in the calls, the views reported by the employees of the call centre and behaviours observed by me during fieldwork. Consequently, in the next section I shall discuss some of the communicative behaviour attributed to the Argentinean and Venezuelan participants. The decision to focus mainly on these two groups is based on the saliency of their communicative behaviour vis-à-vis that of other Spanish-speaking participants and the number of comments made about them. It is, however, instructive to bear in mind that calls to and from Argentina and Venezuela represent a very large percentage of the call centre's business. With this mind, it is possible that the comments made about participants from these countries are partly sustained by the frequency with which the agents and call centre staff interact with clients from these countries.

In what follows I examine a few conversational excerpts in which inter-cultural communication is relevant, and consequential for the ensuing talk (Section 6.2.1). Next, I offer an analysis, based primarily on interview data, of some of the communicative patterns observed for dealing with some Latin American participants (Section 6.2.2). Finally, I conclude the chapter with some reflections (Section 6.3).

6.2.1 On ambivalent *sí* and unequivocal *no*

The selected excerpts discussed below are illustrative of those calls in the database where perceptions of interculturality were explicitly voiced. Excerpt 1 represents a first-attempt outbound call in which an Argentinean agent telephones a Venezuelan client to get her to deposit her weeks. In spite of the client's explicit expressions of a lack of interest, anchored in the fact that 'Holidays to Remember' do not offer any accommodation units in the city the client wishes to travel to over the Christmas period, the agent does every-thing within her power to coax the client into purchasing; in this case, either to deposit her weeks or to renew her membership. The agent thus tries to persuade the client to take a different type of holiday, and suggests that she should visit her family at a different time and that her family should use the client's week to visit her instead. Throughout the call, the client limits herself to expressing her lack of interest in the various products offered through the uttering of discouraging signals, including grounders, in which she states the reasons why the services offered by the company do not meet her needs. In spite of this, the agent succeeds in keeping the client on the line for more than twenty minutes. During that time, she manages to make an arrangement for a follow-up encounter, in which she will not only discuss the client's mem-bership renewal, but will also let her know whether an accommodation unit in her desired destination at the time required has been found.

Excerpt 1 [2:8]

```
311 A:    A:h okey↓. bueno lo que voy a hacer es lo
312       siguiente, voy a ponerla en una lista de espera
313       por si entra alguno de estos espacios para el mes
314       de diciembre, le parece?=
          O:h okay↓. Well what I'm going to do is the following,
          I'm going to put your" name in a waiting list just in
          case a unit in December is freed up, what do you" think?=
315 C:    =Está bien.
          =that's fine.
316 A:    Me parece yo voy a hacer eso. >y bueno la semana
317       que viene< la llamo para que hablemos de la
318       renovación,
          I think tha's what I'm going to do. >and so next week<
```

```
            I will call you^v to talk about the renewal,
            (0.3)
319  C:     Corre:cto. (.) Tú me está llamando fuera de
320         Venezue::la↑
            Righ:t. (.) are you^T calling me from outside Venezue::la↑
321  A:     Sí::. desde (place where call centre is) le estoy
322         llamando,=
            Yes::. From (place where the call centre is) I'm
            calling^v,=
323  C:     =↑A::h:: oke::y↓ sí: es que sentía como que:: no
324         era de aquí,=
            =↑O::h:: oka::y↓ yes I felt like like:: you were not
            from here,=
325  A:     =No yo soy [argentina.]
            =No I am    [Argentinean.]
326  C:                [(Uds manejan eso ahora)] desde
327         afue:ra↑
                       [(do you run that now)] overseas↑
            (.)
328  A:     Perdó:n↑
            Pardo:n↑
            (0.3)
329  C:     Ahora manejan Vacaciones Inolvidables desde afuera
330         no↑
            You now run Holidays to Remember from overseas
            right↑
331  A:     Sí ahora trabajamos desde (place of call centre.)
332         >tenemos todas las oficinas de Latinoamérica y el
333         Caribe aquí< y México.
            Yes now we work from (place of call centre) >we have all
            the offices for Latin America and the Caribbean here<
            and Mexico.
            (0.2)
334  C:     A::h↑ está bien. [(¿?)]
            O::h↑ that's fine. [(¿?)]
335                          [Bueno] señora Marianella yo
336         la voy a estar llamando sí:? quédese tranquila::,
337         (.) E:h a lo mejor la semana que viene por ahí ya
338         tenemos alguna novedad en cuanto a::h↑ al mes de
339         diciembre.
                            [Okay]Mrs Marianella I'm going to
            be calling you^v right:? Rest assured::, (.) u:m maybe
            next week round that time we have some news with respect
            u:m↑to the month of December.
```

The agent ignores the client's discouraging signals. Once she realises that the client will not budge as far as her Christmas holiday is concerned, she proposes putting the client on a waiting list in the event that a slot is made available. The agent seeks permission to do so via an opinion query oriented to elicit a positive response from the client, given its beneficial and non-committal nature for the client (lines 311–14). The client thus offers a preferred second pair part which helps to shut down the topic and pave the way for the closing sequence (line 315). However, in responding positively, the client, by default, agrees to a future encounter, something that the agent quickly proceeds to propose. That the agent insists throughout the interaction on overruling the client's signs of uninterest, and does so again in the enacting of the arrangement for a future encounter (see lines 316–18 and 334–8), is possibly the result of the lukewarm behaviour of the client, which, despite its unenthusiastic displays, allows the agent to continue with the sales pitch. That the agent pursues almost obstinately the road of insistence is echoed by some of the views that most agents seem to hold about the Venezuelan clientele, whereby their 'yeses' appear to be a source of potential misunderstanding. According to one of the Venezuelan agents, *'un venezolano no insiste de esa manera ya que entiende cuando el sí es sí y cuando es no'* ('a Venezuelan would not insist like that as he or she would understand when yes means yes and when it means no').

The agent in Excerpt 1 makes it clear that the next encounter will centre on the client's membership renewal and not necessarily on the client's Christmas holiday needs. Logically speaking, and judging by the client's needs which cannot, as yet, be met by the company, there would be no point in renewing her membership unless a slot were made available by the time of the follow-up call. After a significant silence (0.3 seconds), indexing a dispreferred response, the client acknowledges the proposed actions by the agent and makes relevant the distance between her and the agent by evoking a national category (lines 319–20). The agent confirms that she is calling from an offshore destination (lines 321–2). On the basis of this, the client reaffirms her perceived sense of cultural difference: the agent is not local (line 324, use of the deitic 'here'). The agent confirms this by bringing up yet another national category (line 325), through which she explains that she is neither from there, that is, Venezuela, nor from the country where the call centre is located (see lines 321–2). This, in turn, brings to light the international nature of the service operationalisation and triggers the client's request for clarification. After a micro-pause and the uttering of a repair device by the agent indicating audible difficulties, the client makes a deductive query (lines 326–7 and 329–30). The agent expands on the explanation offered earlier (see lines 321–2 and 331–3) by evoking supranational categories, which bring to the fore the international nature of service provision and of the call itself. After a significant silence, the client offers an assessment with low rise intonation indicating her acceptance of this interactional reality and topic boundness; thus, she recreates a potential closing-implicative environment. The agent takes this up by reinitiating the arrangement for their next encounter before the participants bring the conversation to a close. In this excerpt, therefore, perceived communicative differences are associated with national categories and this is mobilised to explain perceptions of interculturality.

Excerpt 1, in line with many of the calls made to Venezuelan clients, is too long to include in its entirety; it suffices to say that it encapsulates many of the comments made by call centre staff about the Venezuelan clientele, in particular their inability to say no directly or put the phone down. In what follows, I will discuss some of the comments made by employees of 'Holidays to Remember' during the interviews I conducted. Several call centre agents commented on this precise point and the advantages it can bring to them:

Es como una vergüenza decir que no, como que tienen pudor de enfrentar y decir 'no, eso no me sirve, consígueme otra cosa' como por ejemplo lo hace un argentino o un uruguayo. Son así, dicen 'ah, bueno sí llámame entonces de nuevo, mija' pero después igual no te atienden el teléfono. Muy cariñosos pero nada cumplidos.

It's like shameful to say no, like they cannot face you and say 'no, that doesn't suit me, find me something else' like an Argentinean or Uruguayan would do. They would say 'ah, okay yes call me again then, darling' but then they don't answer the phone. They are sweet but very unreliable.

In the words of another agent who has been dealing with Venezuelan clients for more than three years:

Alguno te puede decir que no, pero empieza que no y ya te deja la puerta abierta como para que vos le puedas ofrecer otra cosa. Pero en realidad en el fondo esa conversación termina en eso, es como que da vuelta para no enfrentarte y decirte que no. Y después pueden pasar semanas que ni siquiera te atienden en el celular ya que ven quién los está llamando.

Someone may say no, but he or she starts with no and leaves the door open for you to offer something else. But in reality, deep down that conversation closes like that; it's like beating about the bush so as not to face you, not to say no to you. And then you can spend weeks trying to get hold of them on their mobile and they don't answer as they can see who is calling them.

She then adds:

Venezuela se tiene como lo que es fácil de vender en el call centre, no sé si es por el perfil del socio venezolano en cuanto a su situación económica

*o qué, te escuchan te dicen mi amor', 'amigo' y finalmente al cansancio
puedes venderles algo.*

Venezuela is seen as easier in the call centre, I don't know if it is because
of the profile of the Venezuelan client as far as their financial situation
or what, but they listen to you, they call you 'my love', 'friend' and
finally, at the end by wearing them down you may be able to sell them
something.

According to a Venezuelan team leader this is because:

*Ay mira mi amor, aquí la gente es muy directa y confianzuda. Si bien aquí
también se marca poco las diferencias entre la gente y a todo mundo se lo
trata de tú, aquí conoces a alguien y no existe la formalidad ya directa-
mente es 'hola' y con un beso, allá no. Allá se dan la mano y ya. Y será por
eso es no tienen reparo alguno en llamar a los clientes dos, tres y las veces
que sea, hasta que les atiendan el llamado, insisten hasta que los cansan y
la verdad es que lo logran porque nosotros no podemos decir que no.*

'Look, my love, here people are so direct and very informal. While differences between people are not really marked here either and everyone
addresses you with 'tu', here you meet someone and there is no formality they say 'hello' directly and give you a kiss, over there that is
not the case. They shake hands. And probably this is why they don't
think twice about ringing clients twice, three times or as many times as
necessary, they insist until the clients take the calls and in the end they
achieve a sale as we cannot say no.

We do not know whether the client in Excerpt 1 has honoured the arrangement made by answering the follow-up call, given that the interaction in
question does not form part of the database. Her inability to terminate the
encounter after having conveyed a lack of nterest is a recurrent pattern in the
calls with Venezuelan clients and was reported as rampant in the interviews
I conducted with those agents who have experience of working with them.
It was also evidenced, in second- or third-attempt calls, after the agents had
difficulties in trying to get hold of the clients, in the reproachful tone with
which many agents reminded Venezuelan clients of the arrangements made
in previous encounters.

An almost diametrically opposing picture is observed in the interactions
with the vast majority of Argentinean clients who unambiguously express
their lack of interest in the sales pitch. They do so by means of extreme formulations (Pomerantz 1980), unpadded direct expressives (Austin 1969) and
explanations which directly point out their needs in relation to the inadequacy
of the product or services on offer. The explanations are typically requested

by the agents to establish the client's profile better and thus enhance the chances of securing a sale. They tend to centre on the clients' needs and reflect the ways in which they, vis-à-vis other clients, understand and exercise their rights in this type of business relationship. Excerpt 2 is illustrative of the level of directness and explicitness with which they express their lack of interest.

Excerpt 2 [8:9]

```
11  C:   =pero la puedo tomar yo en el mismo::: complejo,
12       sin gasto?
         =but can I use it in the same:::resort, without
         incurring any expenses?
13  A:   No. para retomarla (¿) tiene que pagar la cuota de
14       intercambio,
         No. To use it (¿) youᵛ have to pay the exchange fee,
15  C:   Bua entonces no. le agradezco.
         Mm then no. Thank you.ᵛ
16  A:   Usted está yendo a su complejo,
         Have you been using your resort,
17  C:   Yo no pero mi personal sí.
         Not myself but my staff has been.
18  A:   O sea ta-usan el(Vacaciones InolvidablesT?).
         So the-use the (Holidays to RememberT?).
19  C:   Sí [sí. por] eso le digo. si está:: vencida y
20       uste:d me la:: da:: para mi complejo::: bien. y si
21       tengo que pagar no.
         Yes[yes. That] that is why I'm saying. If it has::
         expired and you:: give it:: to me for my resort::: fine.
         If I have to pay no.
22  A:        [Cla:::ro.]
23            [su:::re.] Claro.y usted no piensa hacer ningún
24       intercambio con Vacaciones Inolvidables,
              [su::re.] And are youᵛ not thinking of making an
         exchange with Holidays to Remember,
25  C:   Bajo ningún punto de vista.
         Under no circumstance.
26  A:   Y por qué? Dígame,
         And why? Tellᵛ me,
27  C:   Porque:::: no::: suelo hacer intercambios. me
28       voy donde yo quiera y en el momento que yo lo
29       necesito.
         Because:::: no::: I don't generally engage in exchanges.
         I go where I want to go when I need to.
30  A:   Claro. y:::=
         Sure. And:::=
```

```
31   C:   =no programo nada de mi:s salida.=
          =I don't plan any of my: holidays.=
32   A:   =Pero paga la: membresía y todo al día, no tiene
33        mucho sentido. No? o sea (.) no piensa usarla
34        más?o sea nunca la usó. empezando por eso no?
          =but you pay for the: membership and everything is up to
          date, it doesn't make much sense. Right? So (.) are you
          thinking of not using it any more? I mean youᵘ never used
          it. Let's start from there, right?
35   C:   Jamás la usé y no la pienso usar tampoco. No me:::
36        no me resulta::: grato usarla porque consigo los
37        mismos valores que ustedes me dan en los lugares
38        que yo voy (.) y:: voy al lugar que yo quiero,
39        I never used it and I have no intentions of using it in
          the future either. I don't:: I don't find it of use:::
          because I manage to pay the same for the same places
          that you offer (.) and:: I get to go where I want to go,
```

Although at first sight, the reactions of the client would seem rather direct due to the absence of tentativeness (Márquez Reiter 2002), exemplified among other things by the use of extreme formulations (Pomerantz 1980), and thus potentially perceived by those who are not used to dealing with Argentinean clients as impolite, they are not necessarily so. Support for this can be found in the agent's reactions. There is nothing in this short conversational excerpt through which we, as analysts, can demonstrably claim that the client's contributions have been interpreted as offensive or rude. In fact, the client provides an explanation as to the reason why he will not deposit his week (see lines 15, 17 and 19–21) and further dwells on it (see lines 22–4, 31 and 35–9) at the request of the agent; a request which at line 25 is made via the depicting of the client as contradictory. The client's behaviour can thus be characterised as cooperative, albeit straight to the point and transparent, and in line with the behaviour of those of his compatriots who are not interested in the product that the agents are trying to get them to buy. This type of behaviour is reported time and again by the agents with experience of working with Argentinean clients. In the words of a Uruguayan agent with vast experience of working with Argentinean clients and with an impressive record of sales, as displayed in one of the call centres boards:

> *El argentino es muy puntual. Sabe lo que quiere y por lo general quiere dominar la situación. Hay que dejarlo y depende obviamente de la perspicacia que tengamos para poder rebatir eso y traerlo para el campo de nosotros a fin de poder venderles. Yo por ejemplo, les planteo la venta sin mucho adorno pero obviamente les doy las herramientas para que ellos mismos se piensen que es buen negocio el comprar.*

Argentineans are very precise. They know what they want and generally want to control the situation. You need to leave them and it depends on our perspicacity to refute their points and bring them to your point of view if you sell them something. For example, I explain the basic things about the product without too many details. I give them the tools for them to think whether the business is worth their while.

The words of this agent reflect familiarity and alleged mastery of the strategies that, according to her, work well with the Argentinean clientele. Her comments also show some stereotypical perceptions of Argentineans. This can be seen in the way in which given characteristics, such as being precise, are attributed to a national category, that is, that of being Argentinean, via the production of assertive acts. Similarly, the Colombian agent interviewed below refers to some of the national stereotypes held about Argentineans – 'They are not easy to deal with' – and projects these onto the type of relational management that can emerge in interactions with them:

No son fáciles de tratar. Pueden ser irrespetuosos y pueden decirle a uno pues cualquier tontería. Luego de trabajar ni un mes con Argentina pedí cambio y listo. En una oportunidad estaba describiendo los beneficios del producto que estaba vendiendo y el socio me respondió 'no necesitas explicármelo, me doy cuenta solo', 'dime lo que te pregunto y no me cuentes más'.

They are not easy to deal with. They can be disrespectful and say anything to you. After working for a month with Argentinean clients I requested a transfer and that was it. I was once describing the benefits of a product I was trying to sell and the client said to me 'you don't need to explain to me, I can work it out without your help', 'answer what I ask you and don't add anything else'.

Interestingly, in the majority of the telephone conversations with the Argentinean clients, when the agents present a summary of the product, the summary though client-oriented does not contain much adornment. Essentially, the agents tend to limit themselves to enumerating the benefits of the product on offer without adding any information, such as adjectives, which may be seen as subjective or judgemental. Put differently, a summary of the products tends to lack some of the personalisation elements we have seen in Chapter 4, particularly elements which may reflect the agent's interpretation of the client's ensuing reaction or generic personalisation elements, such as *'es una muy buena oportunidad para poder pasar con la familia y descansar un poquito'* ('it's a very good opportunity to spend time with the family and relax a little') or *'tenemos una promoción especialmente para socios como usted, si renueva en el correr de las próximas semanas le damos dos semanas gratiutas sin que tenga que usar las suyas o pagar cuota de mantenimiento*' ('we have a special offer for clients like you[U], if you[U] renew the membership in the next couple of weeks we will give you[U] two additional weeks free of charge without you[U] having to make use of yours or to pay the service charges'). Instead, when dealing with the Argentinean clients, this agent claims to leave the inferential process to them and thus offer similar descriptions to the ones before:

> *El condominio tiene buenas comodidades, una pileta para chicos y otra para adultos, sauna con hidromasaje; en este momento hay una oferta que si renueva en el correr de las próximas semanas estamos dando dos semanas adicionales.*

The resort has good facilities, a children's swimming pool and one for adults, sauna with hydro massage; right now there is an offer that if you[U] renew the membership in the next couple of weeks we give two additional weeks.

Upon hearing this type of information, the Argentinean clients typically enquire as to the conditions under which the perks are given and whether they would need to pay anything at all. This, in turn, is believed to give them the impression of having conversational control.

Excerpts 1 and 2 show the ways in which 'yes' and 'no' are negotiated in pursuit of a task-based goal; more precisely, how an ambivalent 'yes' or inexplicit 'no' is interpreted as a potential relational commitment and how an unequivocal 'no' as potentially offensive. This, as Gumperz (1982) and Scollon and Scollon (1985), among others, have explained, represents a potential source of misunderstanding between speakers of the same basic language owing to a lack of mutual common ground. In essence, the same interactional resources convey different cultural presuppositions; presuppositions which are not necessarily shared among speakers of different varieties of Spanish or with which they are not familiar due to the (historically) infrequent contact between them.

6.2.2 Hiding behind the name of 'difference'

Excerpt 3 below represents an inbound call between a Venezuelan client and a Colombian agent. The client telephones the company to request written confirmation of the accommodation unit she had booked but for which she has now managed to misplace the confirmation. Her trip is imminent and hence a new document is needed. The agent proposes he could send an email confirming the details and, to this end, he checks the client's email address. During this process, the fact that the participants do not come from the same region becomes relevant and generates a side sequence (Jefferson 1972). In the case of Excerpt 3, potential errors in the spelling of the email address might impede successful goal achievement. Similarly, the spelling of certain parts of the email address are potentially delicate at an interpersonal level in that confusion as to the correct graphemes can imply lack of knowledge of the rules of orthography, which, in turn, is associated with a poor education.

Excerpt 3 [9:5]

```
15  A:  Señora Lucinda, >Tiene confirmación del siete al
16      catorce en el Royal Suite<. Usted tiene algún correo
17      electrónico donde yo le pueda enviar inmediatamente
18      una copia de esta confirmación señora,
        Mrs Lucinda, >you⁰ have a confirmation from 7th until
        14th in the Royal Suite<. Do you⁰ have an email address
        where I can send a copy of this confirmation straight
        away Ma'am,
19  C:  Sí. Ah: sí cómo no.       [este::]
        Yes. Um: yes of course[um::]
20  A:                            [Cuál] sería?
                                  [So what] is it?
21  C:  ‗este::=
        =um::=
22  A:  tengo un letri (.) arroba cal te ve punto net,
        I have a letri (.)@ cal t b dot net,
23  C:  Bueno envíelo:::::. ah no no. ese letri no. envíelo
24      a:: lucysanchez (.) be,
        OK send⁰ it:::um no no. That letri no. Send⁰ it to::
        Lucysanchez (.) b
25  A:  Permítame. Lu:ci con ce.     [Sánchez,]
        Bear with me. Lu:ci with c   [Sánchez,]
26  C:                               [Con be y griega]
                                     [with b and y]
27  A:  la última con zeta, -ah con y griega?
        The last is z, -um with y?
28  C:  No con y griega Lucy.
        No Lucy with y.
29  A:  Sí Lucy Sánchez y Sánchez con zeta,
        Yes Lucy Sánchez and Sánchez with z,
30  C:  Ajá:. OK.
        Right:. OK.
31  A:  Sí,
        Yes,
32  C:  Sí. Lucy Sánchez be
        Yes. Lucy Sánchez b
33  A:  Be de bata?
        B for Bobby?
```

34   C: Sí.
           Yes.

35   A: Sí?
           Yes?

36   C: Todo pegado >arroba calteve punto net.<
           So all one word >@ caltv.net.<
           (0.3)

37   A: Calteve punto net,
           Caltv.net,

38   C: Punto net.
           .net.

39   A: Perfecto.
           Right.

40   C: Calteve con ve pequeña,
           Caltv with small b,

41   A: ↑Sí claro↓ (.) Permítame un segundo.
           ↑Yes of course↓ (.) bearᵘ with me one second.

42   C: Bu:eno. es que pensé que usted este::: que esto no
43   e::s, ustedes no están aquí en Venezuela verdad?
           We:ll. The thing is that I thought that youᵘ um::: that
           this i::s not, you're not here in Venezuela right?

44   A: No no señora. En (nombre de la ciudad seguido por
45   nombre del país)
           No no Ma'am. In (name of the capital city followed by
           the name of the country)

46   C: ↑A:::h ve↓ por eso decía. <u>Claro</u> Porque dije a lo
47   mejor no:::,
           ↑Youᵘ see↓ that is why I was saying. <u>Sure</u> because I said
           maybe no:::,

48   A: =No >pero no se preocupe< que igual atendemos al
49   día <u>muchísimos</u> socios venezolanos que tienen el-
50   [el cal te ve↓]
           =No >but don'tᵘ worry< in any case we deal daily with
           <u>lots</u> of Venezuelan clients who have the -
           [the caltv↓]

51   C: [↑A:::::h sí↓ ya sabe claro claro.]
           [↑O:::h yes↓ youᵘ already know sure sure]

52   A: Quédese tranquila.(.) señora a ver (.) permítame
53   un segundo ya se lo envío,
           Restᵘ assured. (.) Ma'am let me see (.) bearᵘ with me a
           second and I will send it to you,

In view of the reason for the call, the agent requests the client's email address (lines 15–18 and 20).While doing so he seeks confirmation of whether the information should be sent to the email address which figures in the system (line 22) and the client responds by offering a different email address (line 23–4). The agent thus proceeds to check the correct spelling of the new email address, a common practice when email addresses are exchanged (over the telephone).The spelling activity is directly related to the achievement of the participants' interactional goals; in this case, for the client to receive a confirmation by email of the accommodation she had booked and for the agent to ensure that the email reaches its destination. The importance of the spelling activity as a source of potential miscommunication is evidenced by the fact that it is initiated by the agent on whose shoulders the responsibility for the confirmation of the accommodation unit now rests, and who, most probably, has been in this kind of situation before. It is also observed in the elements of the email address which are seen by the participants to require confirmation, namely those that allow for a different spelling such as proper names and surnames and those that may need clarification as a result of regional differences or educational level. The first part of the user's name is clarified by the client (line 26) given that the spelling of her abbreviated first name, Lucy, with final 'y' does not coincide with the spelling of her first name in full, where there is an 'i', not a 'y', after 'c'. The clarification is necessary because the graphemes in question, 'y' and 'i', are represented in Spanish by the same phoneme and the choice of 'y' over 'i' represents an Anglicism. Similarly, the surname *Sánchez* can be spelt with a final 'z' or final 's' and, in the varieties of Spanish spoken by the participants, these graphemes are represented by the same phoneme, though the choice of 'z' follows a pan-Hispanic norm. Likewise, the 'b' and 'v' in the varieties of Spanish of these participants are distinguishable only on the basis of orthography and not at the level of pronunciation. It is worth pointing out that a spelling mistake regarding the use of 'v' or 'b', outside the confines of proper names, may be seen as an indicator of a poor education.

The participants thus engage in a spelling activity in which the spelling of the client's user name is double-checked by the agent but not its domain of use (lines 36–9), in spite of the fact that the latter contains the phoneme /b/, which can be graphically represented as 'b' or 'v'. This triggers the client to clarify its spelling (line 40). The agent reacts immediately by stating the obviousness of the client's prior contribution with *sí claro* ('yes of course'), uttered with a marked difference in intonation, and continues with his current task: entering the new address in the system. His dispreferred reaction triggers the client to initiate a side sequence (Jefferson 1972). The side sequence constitutes a break from the detail-updating activity. This temporary departure from the main business at hand comprises the participants' engaging in a secondary shared activity; an activity which helps to visualise aspects of the interactional context in which the principal business is conducted.

The side sequence starts at lines 42–3 with an account in which the client explains the rationale for having proffered what turned out to be an unwelcome, albeit not necessarily unwarranted, spelling clarification. Such a remedial account shows the client's interpretation of the agent's reaction to her spelling clarification (line 41) as offensive and threatening to his professional face (Márquez Reiter 2009), as an adequately educated person should know when to use 'v' or 'b'. Added to this, the 'v' in the domain of use of the client's email address does not stand for the nation where the client comes from, that is, Venezuela. From the agent's perspective, however, this information should, theoretically speaking, be known, given that the email address which already figures in the system has the same domain of use and that this had been articulated earlier (line 22).

The client's remedial account (lines 42–3) indicates her interpretation of her prior turn (line 40) as face-threatening to the agent's face given his reaction (line 41). It also reminds us of the technological mediated form of the interaction, which does not give the participants visual clues as to each other's concurrent actions or setting. The client's account is based on the distance that separates her from the agent. In other words, if the agent were in Venezuela, there would have been no need to clarify the spelling of the domain of use given that this is a common domain among Venezuelans.[5] That she clarifies the spelling of 've' indicates that the client is aware that the agent is not Venezuelan and that he is not calling from Venezuela either. She thus uses differences in nationality to justify her interactional gaffe.

The client's remedial account is packed with elements typically associated with dispreference, thus indicating her interpretation of the situation as interpersonally delicate. It comprises *bueno* ('well') in turn- initial position, followed by some hesitation and a query in which what is asked is common knowledge (lines 42–3). In doing this, she invites agreement from the agent as if to absolve herself from her gaffe. The agent confirms that the interaction is geographically remote (lines 44–5) and the client uses it as ammunition to justify her earlier conduct (lines 46–7); this is illustrated by the evidential construction with which she initiates her contribution. In doing so, she conveys that no offence was intended. Nonetheless, the remedial account does not seem to be embraced fully by the agent. He proceeds to explain that, despite the linguistic and geographical distance between them, as an agent of the institution (notice the use of the institutional 'we' in *atendemos*), he deals with many Venezuelan clients who have the same domain of use. In so doing, he reaffirms his participant role as institutional agent, and his professional face as a competent and experienced agent who does not need to live in Venezuela or indeed be Venezuelan to be able to deal competently with what for him is a minor spelling challenge (lines 48–50). In overlap, the client acknowledges the agent's professional face (line 51) and the participants return to the main activity.

The side sequence helps the participants to verbalise aspects of the interactional context which would otherwise remain unsaid. In the case of this call, it offers a key insight into what the participants think is shared understanding, or what they think should be shared understanding, in this case, that adequately educated speakers of Spanish should know when to use 'v' or 'b'. Importantly, it shows how national differences are deployed to manage relationships; specifically how they are mobilised to redress offensive behaviour when they are seen as a potential source of misunderstanding. Thus, something incidental and peripheral to the main business at hand becomes significant in helping us to understand how the participants themselves conceive and co-construct interculturality in interaction.

Excerpt 4 below is a follow-up call in which an Argentinean agent telephones a Mexican client, as previously arranged, to find out what decision has been taken with respect to the depositing of the client's week. In line with the previous excerpt, the client evokes their different nationalities as an explanation to redress behaviour which he thinks has been interpreted as offensive by the agent. After the summons, the agent proffers a switchboard request to speak to the client and the call-taker identifies as the called. It is then, at line 5, that the agent offers self- and organisational identification and that the client reacts discouragingly. He proffers recognition via the uttering of the affirmative particle followed by a neutral greeting with a sharper intonation rise (cf. line 4). In so doing, he indicates that the call is unwelcome. Further support for this can be found in the long micro-pause that follows before the agent returns the greeting with falling intonation. With this, the agent projects the end of a sequence and the beginning of the next activity; the activity which can be inferred by the proffering of self- and organisational identification in the context of an arranged follow-up call being the reason for the call; in this case, to find out his decision about the depositing of the week.

Excerpt 4 [2:1]

```
4    C:    Sí buenas noches,(.) dígame,
           Yes good evening (.) tellᵛ me,
5    A:    Señor Juan le habla Claudia Charo de Vacaciones
6          Inolvidables latinoamé::rica,
           Mr Juan I'm Claudia Charo from Holidays to Remember
           Latin Ame::rica,
           (.)
7    C:    ↑Sí::: buenas noches:↓
           ↑Yes::: good evening:↓
           (0.2)
8    A:    Buenas noches.
           Good evening.
9    C:    [laughs nervously]
10   A:    [Laughs] (.) que era yo:
                     (.) it's me:
11   C:    [(¿qué?)]
           [(pardon?)]
```

```
12   A:    su peor-
           your wor-
13   C:    =(qué?)=
           =(pardon?)=
14   A:    =Su peor pesadilla.
           =your worst nightmare.
15   C:    No:::↑ no me hablan- no me hablan m:uchas
16         compatriotas suya:s,
           No:::↑ I don't get- I don't get to talk to m:any of your
           compatriots
17         (they both laugh)
18   A:    A::h↑ Oke:y↓
           O::↑ Oka:y↓
           (.)
19   A:    Se:ñor Juan lo estoy llamando por la semana verdad
20         que se está vencie:ndo:,
           Mr Juan I'm calling about the week right which
           is runni:ng out,
```

In line with his interactional behaviour so far, the client laughs nervously, thus conveying further dispreference. This is understood as such by the agent, who laughs simultaneously, albeit not with the client (line 10), as evidenced by her verbalisation of what she thinks triggered his laughter. In saying *que era yo* ('Yes, it's me') the agent displays her interpretation of the client's communicative behaviour so far as discouraging. After the uttering of the almost indecipherable repair device *qué* ('pardon?') by the client (line 11), the agent starts dwelling on what she thinks caused the client's laughter and is interrupted in full flow by yet another repair device (line 13). In latch, the agent proceeds to offer her assessment of the client's reaction (line 14). A positive response by the client to the agent's assessment would result in a blatant act of rudeness, given that an arrangement had, after all, been made for this call and the client had agreed to it. Thus, the client is put cleverly into the position of welcoming the call and, by default, of accepting what he and the agent will talk about. The client justifies his previous laughter on the basis of perceived differences (lines 14–15). This triggers both participants to laugh simultaneously and the agent to accept cunningly the explanation offered, as manifested in the marked intonation with which the justification is accepted, before she reconstructs the anchor position by explicitly providing the reason for the call; in so doing, she also reminds the client of the arrangement made.

While the agent's assessment of the client's dispreferred behaviour is based on an individual trait and indicates the relational history between the participants in so far as this is not their first encounter (line 14), the client justifies his behaviour at a social rather than individual level, invoking perceived communicative differences, as in *compatriotas suyas* ('your compatriots', lines

15–16). Essentially, communicative differences, based on different varieties of Spanish, are (stereotypically) linked to different nations, and these are once again mobilised to redress face-threatening behaviour. There is nothing in the excerpt itself that would allow us to identify the communicative features which the client identifies as different, and we do not have access to the previous encounter between the participants; yet the agent's convergence (Giles et al. 1991) efforts are noticeable. The agent speaks River Plate Spanish, where there is no differentiation between /ʎ/ and /y/. Thus, the corresponding phonemes to graphemes 'y' and 'll' in *yo* (line 9) and *pesadilla* respectively (line 13) are pronounced in the same way. Notwithstanding, the agent pronounces *pesadilla* with /ʎ/. In the client's variety, Mexican Spanish, such phonemic differentiation is also absent (Lipski 1994), and this makes the agent's convergence futile. That the agent changes her pronunciation in this way indicates her perceived views of some of the differences between her linguistic variety and that of others.

Excerpts 3 and 4 are illustrative of the ways in which many of the conversationalists use linguistic and national differences as ammunition to justify behaviour which they think has been interpreted as offensive and how this, in turn, momentarily distracts them from the substantive business at hand. This then makes relevant certain features of the context which would otherwise have remained intangible at the level of analysis. The characteristic of the interactional context which transpired from these temporary activity departures was the distance between the interlocutors. This distance was realised by reference to the nationality of the agent vis-à-vis that of the client and by the fact that services are no longer provided onshore. In both cases, the agents' reactions to such perceptions of interculturality reflect the volume of calls with speakers of other varieties of Spanish that they handle on a daily basis, and the limited contact that some of the participants seem to have with non-nationals in the provision of services.

6.3 Some final reflections

The foregoing discussion has principally looked at the way in which the participants construct interculturality in interaction and at their commonly held perceptions of one other. Unlike the trend of research into intercultural communication, intercultural issues were examined here in an everyday contemporary interactional environment: a mediated business context which is increasingly prevalent in the way certain services are provided and very likely to be even more widespread in the near future. In other words, it is very likely that speakers of different varieties of Spanish will, in the not-so-distant future, be interacting with each other over a variety of business matters, including more pressing ones such as emergency calls. In the increasingly globalised world in which we live, the potential for growth of call centres is immense. It is thus important for companies such as this one, or others that might entertain the idea of service operationalisation via the setting up of onshore or offshore call centres, to take into account the activities performed by telephone conversationalists when supplying and demanding a service; at the same time, the companies need to consider the potential sources of miscommunication between speakers of different varieties of the same language.

We have seen that intercultural communication is not inherently or necessarily problematic. As contended by Gumperz (1982) and colleagues, one of the difficulties that some of these conversationalists faced was the deployment of shared linguistic devices to perform different actions. The unfamiliarity of familiar linguistic forms performing different actions and attending to different socio-cultural norms resulted in some interactional misfires. These primarily had relational implications inasmuch as they showed the vulnerability of the participants' face in interaction. In order to redress potentially offensive behaviour, these participants construed national differences in the light of their perceived communicative differences emanating from the different varieties of Spanish they speak. We have thus looked mainly at how the same interactional resources may be given a different interactional meaning and how the absence of common ground may lead to undesired communicative effects such as needless insistence and offensiveness. We have also learnt, primarily based on the interviews conducted with call centre employees, that some of the views held about certain clients are stereotypically extended to the nation the clients come from and may have repercussions for some of the strategies put into practice to deal with them by the agents.

A world in which consumers increasingly expect the availability of services twenty-four hours a day, seven days a week, within the comfort of their homes means a smaller world, that is, one which brings together people from different cultures. In this world, we should start reflecting upon preconceived conceptions of cultural differences, focusing on what makes us similar and fine tuning our ears to the wonderful world of diversity. My hope is that this book has laid the foundations for such work and that it will motivate other researchers to pursue and develop even further the lines of inquiry which I have initiated.

Notes

1. There is a very large body of theory and research on intercultural and cross-cultural communication from a variety of perspectives. Even a modestly comprehensive overview would generate a reference list longer than this chapter, and would not be productive given the aim of the book and the type of corpus it examines vis-à-vis those generally used to investigate intercultural communication. Instead, in this section I explain the stance

I have taken in the light of the data examined and the kind of claims that can be made on such a basis.

2. The terms 'cross-cultural communication' and 'intercultural communication' are sometimes used interchangeably. They are also employed to refer to the contact between different groups of participants who do not normally interact with one another or to the forms that emerge from the contact between these different groups. 'Cross-cultural communication' is also found to denote studies which compare the communicative patterns of one group of participants with a different group in similar environmental conditions, and 'intercultural communication' to refer to the communicative contact between different groups of speakers. This last is the meaning of intercultural communication adopted here.

3. This does not preclude the possibility that the resources of a given language may shape the possibilities for the actions that can be accomplished through talk (Sidnell, 2009) (see Chapter 3, Section 3.3.2).

4. Examples include the verbs *cancelar* and *pagar* ('to pay'), nouns such as *carro* and *coche* ('car'), adverbs like *siempre* ('after all' or 'always') and many more.

5. Besides the agent's comment to this end (line 42), this domain of use figures prominently in calls with the Venezuelan clientele.

Appendix: Transcription Conventions

(adapted from Schegloff 2007)

[	beginning of overlap
]	end of overlap
=	latching
-	cut-off of the prior word or sound
underscoring	emphasis
::	pitch rise
CAPITAL LETTERS	volume
.	falling intonation
?	rising intonation
,	continuing intonation
> <	talk between the symbols is rushed
< >	talk between the symbols is slowed
°	talk following the symbol (or between symbols where there are two degree signs) is markedly soft
( )	no hearing could be achieved for the talk or item
(0.3)	silence represented in tenths of a second

Grammatical glosses

T/V	use of the familiar second person singular *tú* and/or *vos*
U	use of the formal second person singular *usted*
DIM	use of a diminutive
P	use of the plural form of address *ustedes*

References

Amthor Yotskura, L. (2002), 'Reporting problems and offering assistance in Japanese business telephone conversations', in K. K. Luke and T. S. Pavlidou (eds), *Telephone Calls: Unity and Diversity in Conversational Structure across Languages and Cultures*, Amsterdam/Philadelphia: John Benjamins, pp. 135–70.

Antaki, C. (2002), '"Lovely": turn-initial high-grade assessments in telephone closings', *Discourse Studies*, 4(1): 5–23.

Arminen, I. (2005a), *Institutional Interaction: Studies of Talk at Work*, Aldershot: Ashgate.

—— (2005b),'Sequential order and sequence structure: the case of incommensurable studies on mobile phone calls', *Discourse Studies*, 7(6): 649–62.

Arminen, I. and M. Leinonen (2006), 'Mobile phone call openings: tailoring answers to personalized summonses', *Discourse Studies*, 8(3): 339–68.

Atkinson, J. L. and P. Drew (1979), *Order in Court: The Organisation of Verbal Interaction in Judicial Settings*, London: Macmillan.

Austin, J. (1969), *How to Do Things with Words*, Harvard University, William James Lectures 1955, Oxford: Oxford University Press.

Avila Muñoz, A. M. (1998), 'Aproximación a la estructura de las secuencias de apertura y cierre en las conversaciones telefónicas en español', *ELUA*, 12: 45–68.

Bailey, B. (1997), 'Communication of respect in interethnic service encounters', *Language in Society*, 26: 327–56.

Baker, C., M. Emmison and A. Firth (2001), 'Discovering order in opening sequences: calls to a software helpline', in A. McHoul and M. Rapley (eds), *How to Analyse Talk in Institutional Settings: A Casebook of Methods*, London: Continuum, pp. 41–56.

Blommaert, J. and J. Verschueren (1991), *The Pragmatics of Intercultural and International Communication*, Amsterdam: John Benjamins.

Brown, P. and S. Levinson (1987), *Politeness: Some Universals in Language Use*, Cambridge: Cambridge University Press.

Budach, G., S. Roy and M. Heller (2003), 'Community and commodity in French Ontario', *Language in Society*, 32: 603–27.

Button, G. (1987), 'Moving out of closings', in G. Button and J. Lee (eds), *Talk and Social Organisation*, Clevedon: Multilingual Matters, pp. 101–51.

Cairncross, F. (1997), *The Death of Distance: How the Communication Revolution will Change Our Lives*, Boston, MA: Harvard Business Review.

Cameron, D. (2000), *Good to Talk? Living and Working in a Communication Culture*, London: Sage.

—— (2008), 'Talk from the top down', *Language and Communication*, 28: 143–55.

Carranza, I. (1997), *Conversación y Deixis de Discurso*, Córdoba: Universidad Nacional de Córdoba.

Castells, M. (2000), *The Rise of the Network Society*, Oxford and Malden, MA: Blackwell.

Coronel-Molina, S. (1998), 'Openings and closings in telephone conversations between native Spanish speakers', *Working Papers in Educational Linguistics*, 14(1): 49–68.

Coulmas, F. (ed.) (1986), *Direct and Indirect Speech*, Berlin: Mouton de Gruyter.

Curl, T. and P. Drew (2008), 'Contingency and action: a comparison of two forms of requesting', *Research on Language and Social Interaction*, 41(2): 129–53.

Danby, S., C. Baker and M. Emmison (2005), 'Four observations on openings in calls to Kids Help Line', in C. Baker, M. Emmison and A. Firth (eds), *Calling for Help: Language and Social Interaction in Telephone Helplines*, Amsterdam: John Benjamins, pp. 133–51.

Davidson, J. (1978), 'An instance of negotiation in a call closing', *Sociology*, 12: 123–33.

—— (1990), 'Modifications of invitations, offers and rejections', in G. Psathas (ed.), *Interaction Competence*, Washington, DC: University Press of America, pp. 149–80.

Drew, P. and J. Heritage (eds) (1992), *Talk at Work*, Cambridge: Cambridge University Press.

Duchêne, A. (2009), 'Marketing, management and performance: multilingualism as commodity in a tourism call centre', *Language Policy*, 8: 27–50.

Duranti, A. and C. Goodwin (1992), *Rethinking Context: Language as an Interactive Phenomenon*, Cambridge: Cambridge University Press.

Edwards, D. (2007), 'Introduction', *Research on Language and Social Interaction*, 40: 1–7. Special issue, ed. D. Edwards: 'Calling for help'.

Emmison, M. and S. Danby (2007), 'Troubles announcements and reasons for calling: initial actions in opening sequences in calls to a national children's helpline', *Research on Language and Social Interaction*, 40: 63–87.

Escamilla Morales, J., E. Morales Escorcia and L. M. Torres Roncallo (2005), 'La expresión de la cortesía en algunas conversaciones telefónicas de carácter institucional en la ciudad de Cartagena, Colombia: un aporte a los estudios contrastivos', in J. Murillo Medrano (ed.), *Actas II Coloquio Internacional del Programa EDICE*, Suecia and Costa Rica: EDICE, pp. 17–36.

Fairclough, N. (1989), *Language and Power*, London: Longman.

Firth, A. (1995), 'Talking for a change: commodity negotiating by telephone', in A. Firth (ed.), *The Discourse of Negotiation: Studies of Language in the Workplace*, Oxford: Pergamon, pp. 183–222.

Fitch, K. (1991), 'Salsipuedes: attempting leave-taking in Colombia', *Research on Language and Social Interaction*, 24: 209–24.

Forey, G. and J. Lockwood (2007), '"*I'd love to put someone in jail for this*": an initial investigation of English in the business processing outsourcing (BPO) industry', *English for Specific Purposes*, 26: 308–26.

Frankel, R. (1989), '"I wz wondering – uhm could Raid uhm effect the brain permanently d'y know?" Some observations on the intersection of speaking and writing in calls to a Poison Control Centre', *Western Journal of Speech Communication*, 53: 195–226.

Friginal, E. (2009), 'Threats to the sustainability of the outsourced call center industry in the Philippines: implications for language policy', *Language Policy*, 8: 51–68.

Gabbiani, B. (2006), 'La constitución de identidades institucionales en el reclamo telefónico', in V. Orlando (ed.), *Mecanismos Conversacionales en el Español del Uruguay: Análisis de Interacciones Telefónicas de Servicios*, Montevideo: Universidad de la República, pp. 39–59.

Garfinkel, H. (1967), *Studies in Ethnomethodology*, Englewood Cliffs, NJ: Prentice Hall.

Giles, H., J. Coupland and N. Coupland (eds) (1991), *Contexts of Accommodation*, Cambridge: Cambridge University Press.

Goffman, E. (1967), *Interaction Ritual: Essays in Face to Face Behavior*, Garden City, NY: Doubleday.

—— (1974), *Frame Analysis: An Essay on the Organization of Experience*, New York: Harper & Row.

—— (1979), *Gender Advertisements*, Cambridge, MA: Harvard University Press.

Goodwin, C. (2010), 'Building action by combining unlike resources', plenary paper, International Conference on Conversation Analysis 2010, University of Mannheim, Germany.

Greatbatch, D. (1988), 'A turn-taking system for British news interviews', *Language in Society*, 17(3): 401–30.

Gudykunst, W. (1998), *Bridging Difference: Effective Intergroup Communication*, Thousand Oaks, CA: Sage.

Gumperz, J. (1982), *Discourse Strategies*. Cambridge: Cambridge University Press

Gumperz, J. and D. Hymes (1972), *Directions in Sociolinguistics: The Ethnography of Communication*, New York: Holt, Rinehart & Winston.

Halliday, M. A. K. and R. Hasan (1976), *Cohesion in English*, London: Longman.

Heritage, J. (1998), 'Oh-prefaced responses to inquiry', *Language in Society*, 27: 291–334.

—— (2005), 'Conversation analysis and institutional talk', in K. Fitch and R. Sanders (eds), *Handbook of Language and Social Interaction*, Mahwah, NJ: Lawrence Erlbaum, pp. 103–47.

Hofstede, G. (2001), *Culture's Consequences: Comparing Values, Behaviors, Institutions, and Organizations across Nations* (2nd edn), Thousand Oaks, CA: Sage.

Holt, E. (1996), 'Reporting on talk: the use of direct reported speech in conversation', *Research on Language and Social Interaction*, 29(3): 219–45.

Hood, S. and G. Forey (2008), 'The interpretational dynamics of call-centre interactions: co-constructing the rise and fall of emotion', *Discourse and Communication*, 2(4): 389–409.

Hopper, R. (1992), *Telephone Conversation*, Bloomington: Indiana University Press.

Houtkoop-Steenstra, H. (1991), 'Opening sequences in Dutch telephone conversation', in D. Boden and D. H. Zimmerman (eds), *Talk and Social Structure*, Berkeley: University of California Press, pp. 232–50.

Hutchby, I. (2001), *Conversation and Technology: From the Telephone to the Internet*, Cambridge: Polity.

—— (2005), '"Incommensurable" studies of mobile phone conversation: a reply to Ilkka Arminen', *Discourse Studies*, 7(6): 663–70.

Hutchby, I. and S. Barnett (2005), 'Aspects of the sequential organization of mobile phone conversation', *Discourse Studies*, 7(2): 147–71.

Jefferson, G. (1972), 'Side sequences', in D. N. Sudnow (ed.), *Studies in Social Interaction*, New York: Free Press, pp. 294–338.

—— (1973), 'A case of precision timing in ordinary conversation: overlapped tag-positioned address terms in closing sequences', *Semiotica*, 9(1): 47–96.

—— (1983), 'Another failed hypothesis: pitch/loudness as relevant to overlap resolution', *Tilburg Papers in Language and Literature*, 38: 1–24.

Kendon, A. (1986), 'Erving Goffman's approach to the study of face-to-face interaction.' Paper presented to the conference 'Erving Goffman: An Interdisciplinary Appreciation', University of York.

Landqvist, H. (2005), 'Constructing and negotiating advice in calls to a poison information center', in C. Baker, M. Emmison and A. Firth (eds), *Calling for Help: Language and Social Interaction in Telephone Helplines*, Amsterdam: John Benjamins, pp. 207–34.

Licoppe, C. (2001), 'Faire ses courses par téléphone, faire ses courses par internet: médiations technologiques, formes des échanges, de la relation commerciale et de la consommation', *Réseaux*, 106: 75–100.

—— (2006), 'La construction conversationnelle de l'activité commercial: rebondir au téléphone pour placer des services', *Réseaux*, 135–6: 125–60.

Lindström, A. (1994), 'Identification and recognition in Swedish telephone conversation openings', *Language in Society*, 23: 231–52.

Lipski, J. (1994), *Latin American Spanish*, Harlow: Longman.

Lockwood, J., G. Forey and N. Elias (2009), 'Call centre communication: measurement processes in non-English speaking contexts', in D. Belcher (ed.), *English for Specific Purposes in Theory and Practice*, Ann Arbor: University of Michigan Press, pp. 143–65.

McHoul, A. (1978), 'The organization of turns at formal talk in the classroom', *Language in Society*, 7: 183–213.

Mallard, A. (2004), 'From the telephone to the economic exchange: how small businesses use the telephone in their market relations', *Environment and Planning D: Society and Space*, 22(1): 117–34.

Márquez Reiter, R. (2002), 'A contrastive study of indirectness in Spanish: evidence from Peninsular Uruguayan Spanish', *Pragmatics*, 12(2): 135–51.

—— (2005), 'Complaint calls to a caregiver service company: the case of *desahogo*', *Intercultural Pragmatics*, 2(4): 481–514.

—— (2006), 'Interactional closeness in service calls to a Montevidean carer service company', *Research on Language and Social Interaction*, 39(1): 7–39.

—— (2009), 'How to get rid of a telemarketing agent? Face-work strategies in an intercultural service call', in F. Bargiela-Chiappini and M. Haugh (eds), *Face, Communication and Social Interaction*, London: Equinox, pp. 55–77.

—— (2010), '*A ella no le gusta que le digan María y a mí que me traten de tú*: a window into Latin American diversity', *Sociolinguistic Studies*, 4(2): 413–22.

Márquez Reiter, R. and K. K. Luke (2010), 'Telephone conversation openings across languages, cultures and settings', in A. Trosborg (ed.), *Pragmatics across Languages and Cultures*. Berlin and New York: De Gruyter Mouton, pp. 103–37.

Márquez Reiter, R., I. Rainey and G. Fulcher (2005), 'A comparative study of certainty and conventional indirectness: evidence from British English and Peninsular Spanish', *Applied Linguistics*, 26(1): 1–31.

Maynard, D. and N. C. Schaeffer (1997), 'Keeping the gate: declinations to requests to participate in a telephone interview', *Sociological Methods and Research*, 26(1): 34–79.

—— (2002a), 'Opening and closing the gate: the work of optimism in recruiting survey respondents', in D. Maynard, N. Houtkoop-Steenstra, C. Schaeffer and J. van der Zouwen (eds), *Standardization and Tacit Knowledge: Interaction and Practice in the Survey Interview*, New York: Wiley Interscience, pp. 179–204.

—— (2002b), 'Refusal conversion and tailoring', in D. Maynard, N. Houtkoop-Steenstra, C. Schaeffer and J. van der Zouwen (eds), *Standardization and Tacit Knowledge: Interaction and Practice in the Survey Interview*, New York: Wiley Interscience, pp. 219–39.

Mazeland, H. (2004), 'Responding to the double implication of telemarketers' opinion queries', *Discourse Studies*, 6(1): 95–115.

Meehan, A. (1989), 'Assessing the "policewothiness" of citizen complaints to the police', in D. Helm, W. Anderson, A. Meehan and A. Rawls (eds), *The Interactional Order: New Directions in the Study of Social Order*, New York: Irvington, pp. 16–20.

Mondada, L. (2008), 'Using video for a sequential and multimodal analysis of social interaction: videotaping institutional telephone calls', *Forum: Qualitative Social Research*, 9(3): Article 39.

—— (2010), 'Interactional space: the embodied organization of participation and turn-taking', plenary paper, International Conference on Conversation Analysis 2010, University of Mannheim, Germany.

NASSCOM-McKinsey (2005), The NASSCOM-McKinsey Study 2005. Retrieved on 15 July 2007 from www.nasscom.com.

Ohmae, K. (ed.) (1995), *The Evolving Global Economy: Making Sense of the New World Order*, Boston, MA: Harvard Business Review.

Palotti, G. and C. Varcasia (2008), 'Service telephone call openings: a comparative study on five European languages', *Journal of Intercultural Communication*, 17: 1–29.

Placencia, M. E. (1997), 'Opening-up closings the Ecuadorian way', *Text*, 1: 53–81.

Pomerantz, A. (1980), 'Telling my side: "limited access" as a "fishing device"', *Sociological Inquiry*, 50: 186–98.

—— (1984), 'Pursuing a response', in J. M. Atkinson and J. Heritage (eds), *Structures of Social Action*, Cambridge: Cambridge University Press, pp. 152–64.

—— (1986), 'Extreme case formulations: a way of legitimizing claims', *Human Studies*, 9(2–3): 219–30.

Raymond, G. and D. Zimmerman (2007), 'Rights and responsibilities in calls for help: the case of the Mountain Glade fire', *Research on Language and Social Interaction*, 40: 33–61.

Robinson, J. D. (2001), 'Closing medical encounters: two physician practices and their implications for the expression of patients' unstated concerns', *Social Science and Medicine*, 53: 639–56.

Sacks, H. (1992), *Lectures on Conversation. Volumes I and II*, ed. G. Jefferson, intro. E. A. Schegloff, Oxford: Blackwell.

Sacks, H., E. Schegloff and G. Jefferson (1974), 'A simple systematics for the organization of turn-taking for conversation', *Language*, 50: 696–735.

Santamaría García, C. (1996), 'Different verbal routines in telephone call openings', in C. Valero Garcés (ed.), *Culturas sin fronteras: Encuentros frente a la traducción*. Alcalá: Alcalá de Henares, pp. 231–7.

Schegloff, E. A. (1979), 'Identification and recognition in telephone conversation openings', in G. Psathas (ed.), *Everyday Language: Studies in Ethnomethodology*, New York: Irving, pp. 23–78.

—— (1986), 'The routine as achievement', *Human Studies*, 9: 111–51.

—— (1992), 'On talk and its institutional occasions', in P. Drew and J. Heritage (eds), *Talk at Work*, Cambridge: Cambridge University Press, pp. 101–34.

—— (1999), 'Discourse, pragmatics, conversation, analysis', *Discourse Studies*, 1: 405–35.

—— (2007), *Sequence Organization in Interaction: A Primer in Conversation Analysis. Volume 1*, Cambridge: Cambridge University Press.

—— (2009), 'On the organization of sequences as a source of "coherence" in talk-in-interaction', in B. Dorval (ed.), *Conversational Organization and its Development*, Norwood, NJ: Ablex, pp. 51–77.

Schegloff, E. A. and H. Sacks (1973), 'Opening up closings', *Semiotica*, 8: 289–327.

Scollon, R. (1998), *Mediated Discourse as Social Interaction: A Study of News Discourse*, Harlow: Longman.

Scollon, R. and S. Scollon (1981), *Narrative, Literacy and Face in Interethnic Communication*, Norwood, NJ: Ablex

—— (1985), *Intercultural Communication: A Discourse Approach*, Cambridge, MA and Oxford: Blackwell.

Scott, M. and S. Lyman (1968), 'Accounts', *American Sociological Review*, 33: 46–62.

Sidnell, J. (2009), *Conversation Analysis: Comparative Perspectives*. Cambridge: Cambridge University Press.

Sigman, S. J. (1991), 'Handling the discontinuous aspects of continuous social relationships: toward research on the persistence of social forms', *Communication Theory*, 1(2): 106–27.

Stivers, T. (2008), 'Stance, alignment, and affiliation during storytelling: when nodding is a token of affiliation', *Research on Language and Social Interaction*, 41(1): 31–57.

Taylor, P. and P. Bain (2005), '"India calling to the far away towns": the call centre labour process and globalization', *Work, Employment and Society*, 19(2): 261–82.

Tracy, K. (1997), 'Interactional trouble in emergency service requests: a problem of frames', *Research on Language and Social Interaction*, 30: 315–43.

Tracy, K. and R. Agne (2002), '"I just need to ask somebody some questions": sensitivities in domestic dispute calls', in J. Coterill (ed.), *Language in the Legal Process*, Basingstoke: Palgrave Macmillan, pp. 75–89.

Tracy, K. and D. Anderson (1999), 'Relational positioning strategies in police calls: a dilemma', *Discourse Studies*, 1(2): 201–25.

Ventola, E. (1987), *The Structure of Social Interaction: A Systemic Approach to the Semiotics of Service Encounters*, London: Frances Pinter.

Wakin, M. and D. Zimmerman (1999), 'Reduction and specialization in emergency and directory assistance calls', *Research on Language and Social Interaction*, 32: 409–37.

Weizman, E. (1989), 'Requestive hints', in S. Blum-Kulka, J. House and G. Kasper (eds), *Cross-Cultural Pragmatics: Requests and Apologies*, Norwood, NJ: Ablex, pp. 71–95.

Wertsch, J. (1991), *Voices of the Mind: A Sociocultural Approach to Mediated Action*, London: Harvester Wheatsheaf.

Whalen, M. and D. Zimmerman (1987), 'Sequential and institutional contexts in calls for help', *Social Psychology Quarterly*, 50: 172–85.

Whittaker, S. (2003), 'Theories and methods in mediated communication', in A. Graeeser, M. A. Gernsbacher and S. Goldman (eds), *The Handbook of Discourse Processes*, Mahwah, NJ: Lawrence Erlbaum, pp. 243–86.

Zimmerman, D. (1984), 'Talk and its occasion: the case of calling the police', in D. Schiffrin (ed.), *Meaning, Form, Use in Context: Linguistic Applications*, Washington, DC: Georgetown University Press, pp. 210–28.

—— (1992), 'The interactional organization of calls for emergency assistance', in P. Drew and J. Heritage (eds), *Talk at Work: Interaction in Institutional Settings*, Cambridge: Cambridge University Press, pp. 359–469.

Zimmerman, K. and G. de Granda (eds) (2004), 'Sección temática: El español con otras lenguas', *Revista Internacional de Lingüística Iberoamericana*, 2: 9–145.

Zorraquino, M. A. and J. Portolés Lázaro (1999), 'Los marcadores del discurso', in I. Bosque and V. Demonte (eds), *Gramática Descriptiva de la Lengua Española*, 4051–213.

Index

absence (of)
  common ground, 186
  greetings, 17, 50, 55
  offer of assistance, 49
  pause, 45, 159
  tentativeness, 176
  see also presence
account holder, 63, 65, 66, 76, 68,
  73, 134
accountability, 4, 48
accountable action *see* reason for
  the call
activities, specifically-located
  activities *see* closings;
  openings
addressors, 158
adjacency pair, 14, 74, 138
  request-response, 14
agenda, 4, 34, 59, 97, 105, 106,
  108, 113, 117, 122, 171
  holiday, 4
  interactional, 97, 109
  research, 34
  sales, 106
  selling, 122
agreement
  business, 83
  confidentiality, 30
  legally-binding, mutual non-
    disclosure, 27, 30
  non-agreement, 137
  prior, 18
  see also tokens
ambivalent *sí*, 170
analytic perspective, 17, 19, 36–8
apology, 152
appreciations, 13, 138
Argentina, 23, 24, 44, 62, 119,
  124, 134, 169, 171, 177
Argentinean, 36, 43, 62, 63, 64,
  72, 102, 103, 109, 111, 135,
  169, 170, 171–7, 183
arrangements
  arrangement sequence, 132,
    140, 142, 144
  honouring, 126–31
automated mode, 54

background to the research,
  22–4, 30–1

bueno no, 88, 89, 122
bueno bárbaro, 148, 153, 159
bueno listo, 159
business
  convention, 14, 42
  encounter, 144
  environmental business
    conditions, 132, 133, 164
  exchange *see* exchange
  mediated business context, 185
  mediated business
    environment, 168
  mediated business interactions,
    1–2, 38, 166
  relationship, 59, 78, 81, 104,
    125, 133, 165, 175
  transactions, 164

CA (conversational analysis), 31,
  35, 37, 43, 158, 162, 163
call backs *see* calls
call centre
  acculturated, 42
  manager, 31, 32
  operations, 35, 138
call centres
  centralisation, 42
  home-based, 42
  and intercultural
    communication, 5–7
  migration, 3, 6, 7
  national, 20
  offshore, 186
  onshore, 5, 6, 185, 186
call cessation, 160
caller
  caller's query, 48
  caller's request, 14
calls
  backlog of, 24
  call backs, 59, 63, 73, 104, 106,
    109, 110, 111
  complaint, 32, 57, 84, 96
  emergency, 9, 13, 15, 16, 185,
    194
  first-attempt, 59, 104, 110–25
  follow-up, 36, 59, 63, 73, 82,
    104, 106, 110, 118, 126–40
  goal-oriented nature of, 148,
    161, 162

inbound, 39–57
institutional, 13–21, 25, 26, 73,
  77, 158, 159, 164
institutional character of, 16,
  47, 48, 49
intercultural, 37, 44, 83, 135,
  143, 158, 167
intra-cultural, 37, 143, 167
landline, 65
mediated service, 2
non-emergency nature of, 47
non-emergency service, 57
non-mundane, 64
non-mundane nature of, 48, 78
ordinary character of, 47
outbound, 58–76, 104–25
second-attempt, 106
service, 2, 13, 16, 81
structural account of, 15, 39
structural account of
  emergency, 15
telephone marketing, 104, 106,
  125
telesales, 59, 80, 81
third-attempt, 174
volume of, 46, 68, 109, 185
see also closings: Spanish
  service calls
categories, 162
  national, 173
  national stereotypes, 177
  supranational, 172
Chile, 21, 23, 24, 160
Chilean, 62, 64, 163
client
  client information, 4
  client-oriented, 97, 111, 114
    177
  client pool, 23
  client's history, 4, 25, 104
  client-tailored, 110, 111
clientele, 22, 24, 35, 36, 38, 72,
  110, 134, 144, 172, 173, 177,
  187
closing
  elements, 159, 165
  implicative elements, 143
  interpersonally oriented
    (closing), 161
  routine, 12, 153, 155